7/16/03

Happy
"Dolphin Day"!
Love,
"Bear"

THE
CHARGED
BORDER

JIM NOLLMAN

A John Macrae Book

Henry Holt and Company   New York

THE CHARGED BORDER

Where Whales and Humans Meet

Henry Holt and Company, Inc.
Publishers since 1866
115 West 18th Street
New York, New York 10011

Henry Holt® is a registered trademark of
Henry Holt and Company, Inc.

Published in Canada by Fitzhenry & Whiteside Ltd.,
195 Allstate Parkway, Markham, Ontario L3R 4T8.

Library of Congress Cataloging-in-Publication Data
Nollman, Jim.
The charged border : where whales and humans meet /
Jim Nollman.—1st ed.
p.   cm.
"A John Macrae book."
Includes index.
ISBN 0-8050-5523-1 (hc. : alk. paper)
1. Cetacea—Behavior.   2. Human-animal relationships.
I. Title.
QL737.C4N56 1999   98-39470
599.5'15—dc21

Henry Holt books are available for special promotions
and premiums. For details contact: Director, Special Markets.

First Edition 1999

Designed by Michelle McMillian

Printed in the United States of America
All first editions are printed on acid-free paper.∞

10   9   8   7   6   5   4   3   2   1

For Isun, that he may come around

Each time I go to leave
My shoes hide in your dreams
—CREE SAYING

CONTENTS

ACKNOWLEDGMENTS

Most of the experiences that inform this book occurred over many years; all involved collaborators. First and foremost is my wife Katy, who, for over a decade, has collaborated on much of my work with cetaceans. Her formidable skills at truth telling have clearly made me a better writer. My daughters Claire and Sasha keep me humble and smiling. Others include web weaver and cosmic collaborator Gigi Coyle, my children's godmother Sandra Wilson, longtime cohorts Jonathan Churcher and Kirk Fuhrmeister, my Japanese coworkers, Takako Iwatani and Masahiro Mori; Alan Slifka, Brad Stanback, Elisabeth Jones, Christine Stevens, newly winged angel Kit Tremaine, enduring fellow artists Richard Schönherz, Christian Swenson, Mickey Remann, Wayne Doba, and Daniel Dancer. Without the enduring support—communal, aesthetic, financial, emotional—of each of you, I would never have been able to continue this work for so many years.

Other collaborators deserve special mention for helping on specific projects or fomenting key ideas: Iki warriors, Shojiro Suzuki, filmmaker Hardy Jones, and deepest diver Dexter Cate; Chip Lord and Doug Michels of The Ant Farm; John Lilly, Toni Lilly, Georgia Tanner, and Barbara Clarke-Lilly of the Human/Dolphin foundation; Martina Geisler and

Crack from the Kairos who introduced me to the pilot whales of Tenerife as well as to an extended family dedicated to meeting the whales. Thanks to marine biologists Fred Sharpe and Vicki Beaver of the Alaska Whale Foundation for supporting an idea I hold, that together art and science make a whole, and that cultivating the rational and the irrational together make a person more complete. Dolphin biologist Kathleen Dudzinski read over the chapter about dolphin swims, and offered many key insights. I see smiling faces from years past: China Galland who hired me to conduct a funeral-at-sea with gray whales; Charles Amirkhanian of KPFA radio who handed me my first commission to compose music with turkeys; Cindy Lowry of Greenpeace who got me involved in the gray whale rescue on the sea ice off Barrow, Alaska.

This writing would be far less vital without the input of several planetary dreamers who bolster my own premonitions about the cetacean myth. These include Peter Shenstone, Joan Ocean, Kamala Hope-Campbell, Horace Dobbs, Heathcote Williams, Jean-Luc Bozzoli, Robbins Barstow, Jacques Mayol, Paul Forrestal, Patrice van Eersel, Patricia Sims, Ben White, Rauno Lauhakangas, Claude Traks, Richard Heinberg, Credo Mutwa, Linda Tellington-Jones, Victor Perera, and Bill Rossiter. I thank acoustic engineers Steve Gagne, Mike Sofen, and Rich Ferraro. Without the addition of their underwater acoustic gear none of my musical whale dream could have ever happened. Special thanks to guitar maker Phil Cacopardo for one day calling me up to say he'd built me what has turned out to be a monster whale guitar. Thanks to Hartley Peavey for donating a pint-size traveling man's dolphin guitar that has been played in far stranger venues than he could have imagined.

The orca project, on which the last chapter focuses, included over a hundred participants. But it never would have happened without the help of Neal Westbrook, Edie Howland, Gene Groeschel, Joan Halifax, Tai Situ Rinpoche, Lama Tsenjur, Jim Hickman, Jim O'Donnell, Paul Spong, Kim Spencer, Linda Campbell. Thanks to a select group of magazine editors, Sy Safransky (*The Sun*), Aina Niemela (*Orion*), Kevin Kelly (*Whole Earth Review*), Jon Adolph (*NewAge*), for cultivating my writing about cetaceans over several years, and Jas Obrecht (*Guitar Player*) who reviewed my recordings of interspecies music with various creatures as if they were bulleted for the top of the hit parade.

Thanks to my agent Felicia Eth, for patience, cheerfulness, and friendship. Thanks to my publisher, Jack Macrae, for drawing this book out of me when I wasn't quite looking. And to my editor, Rachel Klauber-Speiden, for turning the rough manuscript as smooth as a dolphin's skin.

Any book on the subject of interspecies relations should honor the species. Let us all honor the whales and the dolphins, that they may long continue to throw their flowers at evil. May my words be worthy of the trees whose bodies hold this writing.

Parts of the book appeared, in different forms, in *The Sun, Orion, Utne Reader, NewAge, CoEvolution Quarterly, Whole Earth Review, The San Francisco Examiner, The Interspecies Newsletter, Guitar Player,* the anthologies *Coming Home* (Beacon Press) and *The Soul Unearthed* (Tarcher/Putnam), and lastly, my own books, *Dolphin Dreamtime* and *Spiritual Ecology* (Bantam).

One last note of contextual importance. Although everything described herein actually occurred and has been told to the best of my abilities, sometimes the events occurred over a few years' time and with two or more people. To both strengthen and simplify the flow of the text, I have thus taken the step of creating composite characters to tell the story. These composites include the humpback biologist, Steve Templor; the dolphin swim leader, Carolyn Pettit; the Japanese fisherman, Yamaguchi; and the orca researcher, JS. In the sincere hope of protecting the whales, I have also taken the liberty of changing a few of the place names.

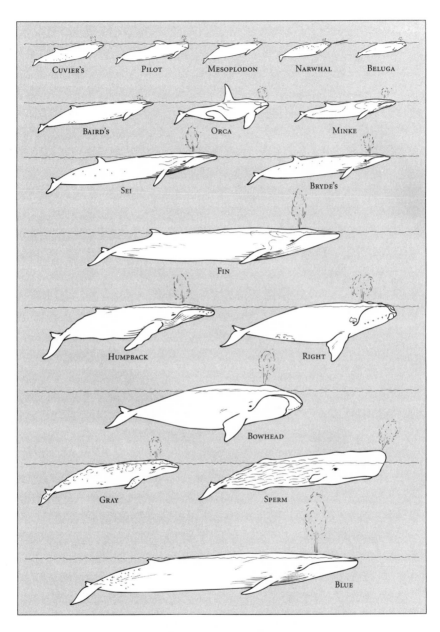

Relative sizes of whales and dolphins

THE
CHARGED
BORDER

1   THE BLACK DAISY

The way of the samurai is found in death. When it comes to either/or, there is only the quick choice of death. It is not particularly difficult. Be determined and advance. To say that dying without reaching one's aim is to die a dog's death is the frivolous way of sophisticates. When pressed with the choice of life or death, it is not necessary to gain one's aim.[1]

—YAMAMOTO TSUNETOMO, *THE BOOK OF THE SAMURAI*

Ocean meeting sky on a seamless horizon. Fluffy snowflakes strike the glassy surface of the water with a gentle *tss tss* shuffle repeated a million times until the sound fills the air like faraway radio static spreading a cold mantra over the face of the waters. It is just after noon on a February day in the Sea of Japan. The snow stops falling after sundown.

A pod of ten pseudorcas migrates south along the main Japanese island of Honshu. These very large dolphins will continue swimming south for the next several weeks along the coast of Kyushu, through the swift currents that lie between Iki and Tsushima, into the labyrinth of the Gotō Archipelago, past Koshiki-jima-Rettō, around the horn of Sata Misaki, onward to the semitropical waters that surround the Ryukyus. One pseudorca echolocates a school of mackerel swimming twenty feet below. The pod stops, animals circle back and forth on the surface. The eldest female whistles her signature by forcing air through her pinched blowhole; the sound informs her extended family that it's time to start the hunt. She whistles again. Three short bursts. Ten dolphins dive together, their black bodies easing up against the mackerel school from ten different directions, churning the fish inward, slapping and waving flukes along the school's shimmery edge, corralling and massing the fish into a tight ball. Task accomplished, the elder emits two short whistles to direct each member of the pod to emit sharp bursts of clicks. The sounds disorient the mackerel, effectively paralyzing the fish on the outer edge of the massed school.

While nine dolphins hold two thousand fish focused into a tight ball, the youngest member of the pod backs up five yards and darts headlong into the pulsating mass. He closes his jaws around one tiger-striped fish, and then another, quickly swallowing them whole. The youngster returns to his position, permitting the next youngest to feed. This one zooms forward right into the dark heart of the school. She too eats her fill. In such a manner the entire pod eats its fill within ten minutes.

A school of yellowtail appears abruptly out of the deep. Although this gray and gold relative of the tuna would ordinarily provide a tasty meal, the pseudorcas are no longer hungry. The yellowtail sense the disinterest and waste no time to strike into the center of the concentrated mass of mackerel. Unlike the cool, orchestrated hunt of the pseudorcas, the yellowtail slash violently. The mackerel ball explodes, silvery bodies scattering before the onslaught like leaves in an autumn gale. A yellowtail grabs hold of a squirming mackerel and shakes it violently from side to side. Without pausing to swallow its catch, the fish slashes at another mackerel that darts past its snout. The first bloody mackerel drops in the process to be picked up by a lone six-foot shark that has joined the feast. The pseudorcas watch the frenzy of yellowtail, sharks, and mackerel for a brief moment, then move on. Heading south again.

The youngest pseudorca pushes to the surface to take a breath of air. The rest follow. *Pooh, pooh, pooh,* muffled explosions punctuate the cold sky as three dolphins breathe in the life-giving air. Then *pooh, pooh, pooh,* three more dolphins blow twenty yards southward. To the north, three more puffs of steam shoot straight up into the still air as three more backs roll across the surface in unison. Altogether, ten animals permute their breathing cycle so that there are always three on the surface, seven down; three up, seven down, never more, never less; dolphins performing a rolling circular dance to an invisible drummer punching out 3/10 time over their local area network. After an hour, they stop to rest upon the dark surface of the sea. Several hours pass.

When they set off again in a rush southward, the pseudorcas swim without pause for half a day and a night. Approaching the Shichiriga Sone bank located obliquely between Iki Island and Tsushima, about midway between Kyushu and Korea, the pod hears the faraway rumble of a hundred diesel engines disturbing the calm of the ocean. So many boats gathered together during a new moon indicates a feast of squid. The large snub-nosed dolphins change direction and swim to reach the source of the commotion forty miles distant. They arrive on the fishing bank at three-thirty A.M. It starts snowing again.

Boats rock back and forth in a crooked line along the northern lip of the Shichiriga Sone. Each sleek white craft is trimmed out in the traditional turquoise and contains two or, at most, three fishermen who, for one reason or another, have chosen to laugh at the February weather. Working through the night in a mutable community of four hundred and forty grizzled souls on two hundred boats, they tend their longlines beneath the dazzling halo of thousands of watts of incandescent bulbs strung above the deck like so many Christmas lights. The fishermen learned long ago that all this light attracts squid to a boat like moths to a candle. On a clear spring night, so many boats may utilize the same glaring array that surveillance satellites revolving high above the Earth's atmosphere show the Shichiriga Sone more brightly lit up than Paris, Tokyo, or Las Vegas.

To reach the undersea mount of the sone, these fishermen have motored an hour across eighteen miles of ocean from the village of Katsumoto on the northern tip of Iki Island. The men stride across the oily wooden decks in midthigh rubber boots, the top inch tucked underneath itself. Each man dresses in a similar red or blue or black polyester jogging suit, matching tops and bottoms, with a white double-line of piping running up the arms and down the legs. The look is of an athlete in training— fit, neat, and agile. If they seem underdressed for the weather, each fisherman is kept warm by one or two pairs of woolen long johns worn underneath the light suit. Few wear hats, although a thick wool scarf is de rigueur. Some favor felt-lined waterproof gloves, although most of them seem satisfied to clench and unclench their fingers all night long while whispering damnations at the icy water that numbs their fingers to the bone. They have all been out on the water for eight hours this night, smoking cigarettes, downing cup after cup of strong coffee, munching on sushi roll *bentō* packed by their wives.

On each boat it's much the same. One man stands starboard, the other port, winding and unwinding the multihooked hand rigs in an attempt to occasionally snag into a few of the foot-long, moon-eyed, iridescent squid that climb up the flanks of the undersea mountain to feed at night this time of the year. The fishermen check each plastic lure to make sure none of the barbless hooks has snarled the line. They spool out two hundred meters of monofilament from a large hand-powered reel bolted onto the boat's gunwales, allowing the line to dangle off the stern for intervals of fifteen minutes or more. During this time they stretch out the arms, splay the legs, start a frenetic arm-over-arm motion that looks like some crazy teenage dance craze from the 1960s, jerking the line in toward the center of the body with one hand, deftly transferring it to the other hand, then pulling that hand away from the body, and dropping the line onto the deck in a neat figure-eight pattern. As a squid comes aboard, the fisherman grabs hold of it and drops it onto the deck far from the pile of line. When the dance is done correctly, the line falls onto the deck ready for the next set. And if it does tangle? If the tangle is severe, it's cost-effective to weight the whole mess and heave it overboard. Between sets, a fisherman might pick a squid off the deck, gut it with a jackknife, cut the iridescent body into long strips, and walk to the other side of the boat to hand a few shimmery pieces of the choice sashimi to his partner. The two men share a cup of coffee and bite into the strips of sweet living flesh. They mutter something about the weather, alternately laugh and condemn themselves for fishing.

The pseudorcas entering the sone are wary of boats but seem keen to fill their bellies. Two years ago, the matriarch of this pod swam too close to a squid boat. A fisherman leaned over the side and shot her in the back with a skin-diving spear. The spear fell out after an hour, but the injury festered for two months before healing. The stiffness seems to return whenever she jerks her head sharply upward from vertical. The incident probably taught her to keep her family beyond the spread of the arc lights. Now, approaching the first boat in their path, she dives, accompanied by her eldest son, to echolocate the squid caught on the hooks hanging at regular intervals along the longline. Locating the first one, she zooms in to twist the mollusk off the lure so deftly that the fishermen on the boat never even register her presence. The male does the same to the second line hanging starboard. Two more pseudorcas rush in to take their place. When each of the four pseudorcas has eaten one squid apiece off that boat, they move to the next one. And then the next.

One pseudorca, a large male approaching twenty feet in length, deftly unhooks two squid. He doesn't gulp them down but carries them to the edge of the fishing bank to present the meal to a pod mate pushing a strange bundle in front of her. More than a week ago, the female gave birth to a stillborn fetus, and, even now, she is unwilling to relinquish the rotting lump of black flesh to the deep waters of the ocean. So she has tucked it under her pectoral fin or bounced it along with her snout across four hundred miles of open ocean. This behavior is recorded frequently not only among certain dolphin species but with land mammals, especially elephants.

A half hour before dawn. The sky lightens. The squid flee the water's surface to start their long descent down the steep slopes of the seamount. Longlines are reeled up for the last time. A few fishermen within the two-hundred-boat fleet curse when they notice remnant stray pieces of squid flesh caught on the snag lures. Such a precision heist could only be the work of pseudorcas. The silence of the predawn ocean is ripped apart by the distorted amplification of men radioing back and forth to one another: "Hey, am I overreacting, or are we losing *ika* to the gangsters?"

"Yup, it's dolphins all right."

Another fisherman reports hearing the unmistakable popping sound of blows. Another man glimpses the shine of large bodies reflected in his lights. "Must be the *oki gondo iruka*."[2]

"Is it worth the effort to call in the boats of the antidolphin committee to start a formal roundup?"

"No need to. Two hundred more boats are already halfway out to the banks to start the morning set for yellowtail and mackerel. That should be more than enough to round up the gangster dolphins."

Pseudorcas, sometimes called false killer whales, are powerful, jet-black, snub-nosed dolphins reaching twenty feet in length. Despite the name, they bear only a passing physical resemblance to the much heavier black and white orcas. Like orcas (and all other species of large dolphins) they have no natural enemies. The pod operates like a wolf pack, relying on teamwork and bursts of speed to hunt prey. Each adult pseudorca consumes about a hundred pounds of squid per day, and, as might be expected, the species is exceedingly capable of catching as many squid and fish as they need. For this reason, snatching squid off a longline is difficult to explain as a matter of simple opportunism. Fishermen report that dolphins grab just a few squid from each longline when they could just as easily take them all. Sometimes, they prey on longlines while ignoring large schools of free-swimming squid half-dazed by the lights.

While fishermen the world over regard pilfering by pseudorcas as theft, behavioralists retort that it might just as easily be a test of skill. An intelligent animal's attempt to steal the bait without encountering the bite of the hook—a game. Cetacean mythologists who rely on the pick of intuition and the shovel of conjecture to corroborate, commend, and even extol dolphin intelligence have recast pseudorca predation as a gesture of communication from a socially advanced dolphin eager to make contact with human beings. The game is being played not for food or even as a display of chutzpah, but to tell the fishermen much the same thing that Humphrey Bogart told his gendarme friend at the end of *Casablanca*: "Louis, this could be the start of a beautiful friendship."

In his seminal work to promote coexistence with cetaceans in Japan, Dexter Cate asserted that the pseudorcas of the Shichiriga Sone were "humans of the sea" and environmental educators trying every communicative tool at their disposal to caution the fishermen against overfishing. With a piercing gaze, high-minded ideals, long hair, a beard, and sandals, Cate appeared as a biblical prophet arrived on the Japanese pulpit to preach a theodicy that equated each dolphin behavior with goodness (by virtue of being natural and intellectually pure), no matter how detrimental it seemed to the fishermen affected by it. Though his rhetoric was sometimes derided as anthropomorphic, Japanese politicians could find no data or logic to counter his basic claim that the dolphin slaughters at Iki follow a historical pattern of human resource abuse that leads to catastrophe. The symptoms feed off one another: Imminent signs of a crash of the target species turn resource managers headstrong and jingoistic rather than cautious. Instead of instilling strict rules to conserve and replenish the stock, the lawmakers attempt to control who catches the last of the fish.

Examples abound. Even as some salmon species approach extinction in the Pacific Northwest, Canadian and American politicians devise policies focusing on tactics that grant an incremental advantage to their own beleaguered fishermen and a disadvantage to the other nation's fishermen. In eastern Canada, fishermen and their political allies first blamed the crash of the cod and haddock fisheries on harp seals, not on overfishing, which led to a government-sponsored slaughter of seals, even after it was demonstrated that harp seals don't actually prey on those species. There was clearly a secondary motive. The European market for baby seal furs had been destroyed by animal rights/environmental groups. Fishing lobbyists hoped that by recasting the seals as assassins of the offshore banks a finicky public would be persuaded to put aside its ethics and start buying fur coats "to save the fishery." It didn't work. Now the fishery is closed. The story varies from place to place, but the symptoms remain the same. On this snowy night in the Sea of Japan, about fifty squid stolen off the longlines will now prompt the fishermen to mount a dolphin roundup costing them more than two weeks' worth of squid caught by the entire fishing cooperative. Ironically, the pseudorcas' predation of squid is as unrelated to the dolphins' own survival as the roundup is unrelated to the survival of Iki fishermen.

What Dexter Cate deemed to be the pseudorcas' message was, in fact, an accurate assessment of the situation, although it was clearly not interpreted by Iki fishermen in the spirit of constructive criticism. Between 1975 and 1985, fishermen rounded up and killed upward of fifteen thousand dolphins, including several thousand pseudorcas. What began as a local and immediate retribution against pilfering was justified and then subsidized by the government as a long-term strategy for eliminating competition for dwindling fish resources. The townspeople buried the carcasses. Katsumoto stank for weeks afterward. When environmentalists started protesting the roundups in earnest, the fishermen naïvely believed they could stifle criticism by exploiting all that wasted organic material. A dolphin fishery was promoted as a vital new industry for the legion of newly unemployed fishermen living in a community that had known prosperity for generations. With assistance from the federal and prefectural governments, the local cooperative purchased specialized machinery to grind up whole carcasses into fertilizer and pig feed. But the fishermen's clever new industry was doomed from its inception. Dolphins do not reproduce as quickly as mackerel and yellowtail. As the roundups succeeded, dolphin stocks crashed. Nonetheless, the roundup process rolled on and on until it seemed a fitting interspecies reflection of Hitler's decision to siphon his troops away from the front to kill Jews while the war was being lost and Germany was being destroyed. The objective at Iki Island was nothing less than a Final Solution for dolphins unlucky enough to travel through that sector of the Pacific Ocean.

An old female pseudorca calls her family together with a distinct, pulsed whistle, notifying each animal that a large mackerel school is swimming southward off the bank. Time to gather together. Time to move south again. As she whistles, two adults are busy at play, nudging and poking each other, and then swimming just fast enough so that the other can catch up and repeat the nudge. Two others, swimming back and forth just below the surface, are engaged in one of a hundred acoustic games that entertain their species—improvising whistles and rhythms back and forth. Two other pod mates teach a deep-diving breathing cycle to two juveniles. Breathe in, breathe out, five times. They all plunge down together, following the edge of the sone cliff, traveling beyond the light into an occluded realm where residents possess huge eyes, ungainly teeth set in lantern-hinged jaws, and spots and dabs of bioluminescence to attract whatever sparse prey may be available. Three more dolphins, including the young female with her fetus, rest on the surface. They look asleep, perhaps nodding off by halves in the peculiar manner attributed to their kind by marine biologists, who postulate that one half of their brain dozes while the other half remains alert, never relinquishing conscious control over the muscles that orient them toward the precious store of oxygen above the surface of the sea. When the sleeping half awakes refreshed, the other half naps.

It stops snowing.

As the family assembles, the female hears a new sound, the faraway pulse of diesel engines throbbing their way toward the sone. Is that what it is? She peers upward a moment to witness one of the world's great wonders, the quicksilver sheen of the ocean surface undulating away in every direction. At this moment, the kinetic surface looks particularly radiant, shimmering with color from a red sun breaking through a cloud on the horizon. The feeling is irresistible. Up she goes, pushing her entire body through the gleam and into the air, hanging a moment, then falling back heavily into the sea with a monumental splash. Then up again, this time spyhopping, pushing herself halfway out of the water to get a different perspective on the situation. She listens south, then north, then east, and, finally, west. Through the air, a fishing boat can be heard from a distance no greater than a few miles. She hears nothing save the squawking of the opportunistic seagulls that follow the pod in anticipation of a wounded fish thrown up by a feeding frenzy. She allows her body to sink below the surface again. Below the surface she hears the engines clearer than before.

Underwater, sound is greatly amplified, traveling at a speed and clarity nearly five times more intense. Even to a human being swimming underwater, the midrange throb of a faraway diesel acquires a disorienting larger-than-life urgency because the sound seems to come from every direction at once. This perception of omnidirectionality occurs because the human ears evolved to hear sound in air and is incapable of perceiving the much shorter lapse in time that underwater sound waves take to travel from one ear to the other. A dolphin's ears, which are spaced farther apart to help them determine the direction of a sound, are further aided by sound receptors located in the lower jaw. Pseudorcas' ears are as highly tuned to sound processing as a bloodhound's nose is sensitized to smell. Now, the entire pod hears the distant thunder of fishing boats rumbling toward them at top speed, even though the boats are ten miles away.

For reasons beyond human logic, the female decides *not* to exit the sone, but to wait for the boats to arrive. One might wonder if she is simply unaware that the boats rumbling toward her pod are no longer a fishing fleet but an armada moving into battle formation. Such an interpretation must be balanced by the fact that roundups have occurred on the sone every winter for the past ten years. Or perhaps she regards the apparent danger as a source of more fun and frolic—an abstract challenge—a gamble? Perhaps, although the risk seems far more apparent than the game's pleasure. The boats will arrive on the sone in twenty-five minutes. The dolphins whistle the current state of affairs back and forth among themselves. Then, for reasons that may forever remain unknown to us, they calmly return to the business of deep diving, teaching, singing their melodies, even sleeping.

Ninety minutes pass. Four hundred boats assemble into a vast horseshoe formation around the pseudorcas to begin a coordinated sweep across the sone. And what's this? At the precise moment the roundup is to commence, a herd of six hundred Pacific bottlenose dolphins (*Tursiops gilli*) enters the fishing bank just to the east of the legion of boats. The radios scream out the bulletin. "It's good luck for us! I tell you, we're going to catch ourselves some dolphins today!" On each boat, two men grasp hold of a *tsukimbo,* a section of galvanized pipe with a pronounced trumpet's flare on one end. They lean over the gunwale and hold the *tsukimbo* firmly against the outside hull of the boat so the bell is immersed a meter below the water's surface. On a radio signal, the loud clanging starts: the excruciating white noise of ball-peen hammers striking eight hundred pipes. The sound slices through the sone to neutralize the dolphins' supersensitive acoustic sensing organs. In a sea with visibility no greater than twenty feet, this sudden inability to hear anything whatsoever has the effect of rendering each animal a "blind" cripple. They cannot echolocate or discern each other's signature whistles; for the first time in their lives each is on its own, disconnected from family, swimming in a hostile environment without the crucial bond of "podness" to guide the decision-making process. The tursiops herd immediately maneuvers toward the open end of the horseshoe. The horseshoe adjusts to keep the dolphins enclosed.

The ten pseudorcas form a dense ball of bodies writhing and rolling around one another. The matriarch tries to signal the pod's potential escape routes. Do they swim full speed to the northeast, directly at the acoustic din of the *tsukimbos,* then duck underneath it heading toward the outer edge of the sone? This choice would be easy to accomplish. Pseudorcas are capable of extended bursts of up to twenty-five miles per hour, faster than the top speed of these fishing boats. Or they could swim eight hundred feet straight down the face of the underwater seamount that forms the bank and remain there for twenty minutes. They would hear some residual sound, but with a thermocline between themselves and the noise, the sound would not be loud enough to upset even the youngest. Down deep, they could swim leisurely off the sone, and not come up for air until they were far from the *tsukimbos*. But the female pushing her bloated fetus in front of her could never keep pace, and the pod will never abandon her.

The pseudorcas roll across one another's sinuous coal black bodies, touching, licking, whistling, gyrating their way to accord. It is this communal caress, and the taste of one another's skin that provides a barometer of each individual's current mood. The youngest animal shivers, expressing disorientation from the din. Quickly now, animals push away from the circle one by one. A strange calm settles over the pod. Dying is in the air, a risk and a ritual to be played out along the tenuous borderline where life meets death.

As always, the inability to sense their mothers sends the youngest dolphins of both species into shock. Because breathing is a voluntary function among the dolphin races, shock leads to drowning. For that reason, four young tursiops become the first casualties of the *tsukimbos'* eruption. The tiny bodies spiral down through the shallow thermocline and into a colder layer of water along the bottom beyond which the noise does not so easily penetrate. It is there, in the world of eternal darkness, that nearly a hundred tursiops congregate to nudge the tiny bodies back toward the precious oxygen. By the time the dead calves have been buoyed to the surface, the boats have passed overhead. The martyrdom of four babies assures that a significant number of tursiops are spared the roundup.

"I don't know how, but we just lost a bunch of them," blares a voice on the radio. Yamaguchi-san, head of the Iki antidolphin committee, who started out this day motoring leisurely to the banks to spend his day jigging for yellowtail, listens to the report while standing beside his skipper in the warm comfort of the heated wheelhouse drinking a cup of coffee. He puts on a jacket and rushes outside, scans the ocean for ten minutes.

When he finally returns, he is shivering. His driver is looking at him, but doesn't dare say a word. "I don't know how they got away," muses Yamaguchi. "Maybe they'll reappear. Let's keep moving, we'll lose the rest of them if we break formation now." He picks up the radio and pushes the button. "Let's make the turn back to town. . . . Over." The boats keep to the horseshoe as they commence a wide sweep, smoothly making a right-hand turn, chugging and clanging, banging and throbbing their way back toward Iki Island. Like most everybody else in the horseshoe, Yamaguchi is feeling annoyed that he has to give up his fishing to direct this dolphin roundup. It starts snowing again. Ninety minutes later it stops. The wind comes up.

Of all cetacean species, the pseudorca and its close cousin, the pilot whale, are most often seen stranding. In the British Isles alone, eighteen mass strandings by pseudorcas have been recorded since 1913. In Fort Pierce, Florida, 150 pseudorcas beached themselves in 1970. The record occurred along the shores of the Mar del Plata, Argentina, in 1946, when 835 shiny black, snub-nosed bodies pushed themselves high up on a beach during a declining tide. How do they die? The larger animals may expire from the weight of their own bodies pressing against the sand and eventually bursting internal organs. Most die, however, when their black absorptive skin becomes exposed to the air and the sun, forcing the temperature of the body core to climb higher and higher like a car engine void of its cooling water envelope. The animals literally cook from the inside out within a few hours' time.

Opinions run the gamut as to why such intelligent creatures seem so determined to rush forward to death while safety is attainable. Indian tribes along the Atlantic coast thought whales stranded in anticipation of a tidal wave or other disaster and heeded the omen by carrying their belongings inland to higher ground.[3] Other tribes believed stranded whales had come under the spell of an evil demon who persuaded them they would be happier living on land. Biologists look for physiological causes and find them. One prognosis emphasizes worm infestations in the animal's middle ear, an ailment that can cause a severe loss of balance. Because it is also posited that cetaceans may fear drowning above all else, an epidemic of worms causes the sick animal to seek out the only real alternative to drowning, which is dying on a beach. Pod bonds insist that the healthy follow the stranded ashore. Whether the safe ones are trying to save their stuck comrades, or actually join them on the beach, is a question that has long been debated and never answered. Some Darwinists reject the interpretation—there is simply no evolutionary advantage to a healthy community dying in support of a single sick individual. Dexter Cate proffered an explanation uncommon among behavioralists. He both cherished and promoted the mystery of it.

No matter how human beings choose to explain it, the pseudorcas' predilection to mass stranding seems debonair in the face of the ne plus ultra mystery we wedge between ourselves and our own impending mortality. What do the pseudorcas know about death that we do not? What have they seen that we cannot? Dolphin mythologists declare that stranding is an act reserved for brains larger than our own. The rush to death is a function of a wisdom beyond what the smaller human neocortex is able to grasp, or to bear.

Every stranding theory has its detractors. For instance, worm infestations plague all cetacean species, while only a few related species of toothed whales strand in groups. All these are among the species whose pod bonds are strongest, yet many other pod-bonding species rarely strand. Some behavioralists contend that pseudorcas are deep-ocean creatures whose echolocation becomes garbled by inshore landmarks like beaches and shoals. Animals touch bottom for the first time in their lives. The novel sensation of gravity exerting an influence upon all that fleshy mass causes a severe disorientation—analogous to the feelings described by astronauts floating in space for the first time. Because young and inexperienced animals are naturally the most curious, they tend to be the first to get themselves stuck on shore. They call for help, summoning mother to the rescue. Mother strands. She calls father, who calls uncles, aunts, cousins, so on. If the tide happens to be in retreat, the pod eventually lies strung out like onyx beads upon the smooth neck of the beach.

In most parts of the industrialized world, the sight of so many ungainly dolphin or whale bodies thrashing, slapping their flukes to raise a huge spray, panting, and farting mobilizes many well-meaning people to attempt a rescue. In Australia, an official whale-saving brigade is subsidized by the federal government. Whenever cetaceans beach themselves anywhere along that country's coastline, the brigade flies in to direct local bulldozer and backhoe operators in the fine art of coercing animals into the water without harming them in the process.[4] Sometimes, the animals swim away. But other times, no matter how much the humans persevere to refloat them, they persist in restranding. New Zealand stranding authority Frank Robson has written that when a single animal from a greater off-shore pod chooses to strand, its calls for help almost guarantee that the entire pod will follow suit.[5] Robson recommends that if the creatures are too large to be pushed back into the sea, as is the case with sperm whales, then the only thing left to do is silence the calling animals with a well-placed bullet. Significantly, Robson's method has achieved a modicum of success.

But not always. Cetaceans sometimes react to their presumed rescue as if it were harassment. In July 1976, twenty-nine pseudorcas stranded high on the white sands of Captiva Island off the west coast of Florida. People arrived to intercede. Over the next several hours, they pushed twenty-four animals back into deeper water. Only one animal died on the beach. Four more were captured by oceanariums. Three days later, thirty more pseudorcas stranded on a beach in the Dry Tortugas, two hundred miles southwest of Captiva. An observer commented that "although many of the whales bore minor scars and a few had open lesions, only one, a large male who eventually died, showed evidence of serious wounds. He lay on his side, with his blowhole occasionally submerged, bleeding from the right ear." One woman wrote of the experience: "I entered the water to snorkel close to the group of pseudorcas. The outermost individual broke from the group and headed directly for me. Without any motion that could be unequivocally construed as an attack, other than moving in my direction, the whale lowered its head and slid underneath me. Its body rose slowly, lifting me almost completely out of the water and carrying me towards the beach. It then slowly submerged."[6] She noticed the pod members taking turns buoying up a very large male as he lay in the shallows. But he succumbed to his wound, later diagnosed as an infestation of worms, within the next forty-eight hours. The woman concluded, "notably, his death served to signal the other animals to propel themselves out of the shallows and back into deep water again." But that was not the end of it. Over the next month's time, twenty more pseudorcas stranded and died within the same general vicinity.

Was this event a mass suicide, caused by an especially bad year for worm infestations, or even by some localized human pollution? Or was it, as a few on-site observers posited, a rite of passage, a kind of cetacean ceremony, in which members of a community assembled to ease the death of a dying family member. When the first stranding was stymied by well-meaning humans trying to "save" the animals, did the pseudorcas search out another beach to complete their ceremony? And after the ceremony? Were the strandings that followed somehow related to the death of a "patriarch"? Of course, any interpretation that implies a ceremony for a nonhuman species must inevitably struggle with accusations of anthropomorphism.

Actually, a death ceremony may occur among corvids (crows, ravens, jays, magpies), which, overall, seem to possess as many instances of intelligent behavior as cetaceans. If a magpie loses a partner during the breeding season, the event is marked within twenty-four hours by a noisy gathering of visitors. Scientific interpretations vary. Some ornithologists refer to the gathering as a ceremony of bereavement. Others describe the putative "well-wishers" as opportunists in the market for vacant territory.[7]

If some whale strandings are a ceremony, the question still remains as to why any community of sentient individuals—whether man or beast— would choose suicide as a behavioral option. Intriguingly, the question itself displays an underlying cultural bias. The Aztecs and the ancient Egyptians had a far more sympathetic relation with death than modern Western culture. Traditional Inuit encouraged their elders, their own mothers and fathers, to walk off into the winter cold during food scarcities. Tibetan religious accession is founded so firmly in the circular logic of reincarnation that after a priest dies, lamas wait a few years, and then conduct a formal search to locate the toddler incarnation of their departed master. Reincarnation also grants a conciliatory ease to the otherwise chilling "rush to death" touted by the Japanese samurai code quoted at the opening to this chapter. Notably, many Iki fishermen insisted that the dolphins died like samurai, and that every dolphin they put to death would eventually be reborn as a Japanese fisherman. Or perhaps Pliny the Elder explained strandings best, if not obliquely, in his description of the death ceremony of the inhabitants of a fictional country. Sorrow was unknown in Hyperborea. The people chose the time of their death carefully, and then celebrated it by feasting and rejoicing. Soon thereafter, they put an end to their lives by plunging into the sea from atop the "leaping rock."[8]

Pseudorcas are found in every temperate and tropical ocean. Populations that never interact could conceivably develop group behaviors as distinct as the social traits of human cultures. A pod of pseudorcas in Argentina might strand under a completely different set of circumstances than a pod in the Dry Tortugas. Other species might strand for unrelated reasons. Fifty sperm whales utilize a different genetic code, behavioral prerogative, and life experience to come ashore in Oregon than a pod of pilot whales employs to strand on a beach in Cape Cod Bay. The reasons may include worms, bad navigation, disorientation, logic, aesthetics, illness, religion. Illogic. But let us be clear. Strandings remain as nonhuman an event as is living one's life in the sea. For each event that we believe we are assigning a tidy rationale, another one occurs for reasons completely incomprehensible to our species. Dexter Cate may be correct after all. When all the interpretations are recorded, the mystery that shrouds stranding is the only unity we may ever find to explain all instances of the behavior.

On the border of the Shichiriga Sone this morning, ten pseudorcas have begun their own long haul to land. They touch one another continually, torso rolling over torso, genitals, flukes, lips, one gently scraping saber teeth along the length of another's body. The parallel scratches etched into their black skin vaguely resemble *I Ching* graffiti or, perhaps, American Indians applying body paint before a ceremony. The pseudorcas travel before the boats as a unit, all ten animals surfacing to breathe in a single roll. Only the dead fetus seems the slightest bit out of sync, as if one of the members of the pod is kicking a soccer ball in front of her. Two hundred yards directly behind the pseudorcas, the herd of tursiops exhibits a different kind of motion. They appear as they are: corralled wild animals desperately struggling to free themselves. Every so often, a subgroup of the herd breaks from the group and charges to the edges of the horseshoe. In such a manner, nearly half the tursiops attain freedom during the painfully slow roundup process.

At the midway point in the procession, the pseudorcas surge forward in a straight line as if enacting a cetacean's version of a military drill. Their efficient restraint seems to provide the tursiops an example of order as well as a clear direction to follow. Four hundred tursiops coalesce into their own formation, heading straight for the small, deeply incised island of Tatsunoshima that defines the outer harbor at Katsumoto town. As this improbable parade of dolphins and fishing boats finally approaches land, the gradual upthrust of a reef in their path causes another fifty tursiops to turn and swim straight at the boats. The sonic onslaught of the *tsukimbos* rushes in on them, causing them to turn again to confront the echo of rocks. The dolphins register the danger with a heightened sense of urgency. They sprint laterally along the coastline, quickly achieving top speed, then zigzag around the ephemeral prison of the horseshoe.

"They're getting away!" crackles the radio. Yamaguchi is beside himself. He dispatches ten boats to chase after the escaping dolphins, then watches through binoculars as a man on a pursuit boat appears on deck with a rifle in hand. He leans out over the stern, aims, fires once, and then fires a second time. Yamaguchi grimaces. The boat is lurching far too much into the swells for the man's aim to hit its mark. The dolphins dive. The shooter stands, lifts his rifle off the railing to permit a steady aim, and then leans way out over the stern. As a wave hits his boat broadside, he loses his balance and falls into the ocean. His driver keeps motoring forward. "Man overboard! Man overboard!" shouts Yamaguchi into the radio. The boat turns quickly as the driver finally realizes what has happened to his companion. The wind starts gusting. The driver can't see the water in front of him and drives his boat right over the spot where the man was just seen floundering. "You drove right over him!" Yamaguchi screams into the radio. The driver turns the boat hard and throws the engine into idle, rushes out of the wheelhouse, picks up a boat hook, and snags it around the arm of the man who is bobbing in the waves. He is lifted over the side.

Then the report: "Fukuda-san's arm is badly cut; he's losing a lot of blood, but he's alive. We'll take him to shore right now."

The human/dolphin procession approaches the headland of Tatsuno-shima. There, like angels of death leading the doomed to their final rest, the resolute pseudorcas usher the resigned tursiops around a rocky reef that defines the entrance of the great fishing harbor of Katsumoto town. Once inside, the pseudorcas pause a brief moment as they enter shallow water where the sound of the *tsukimbos* is greatly muffled. An instinctual hesitation is followed by a danger signal whistled between several animals. The water here tastes unhealthy, a pungent chemical flavor often perceived near fishing boats, but much more pervasive. Although the animals are incapable of surmising a cause, the nauseating taste is an unhealthy brew of human effluent, petrochemicals, and fertilizers that escape from the many pipes draining into the bay, and flow directly at the dolphins on a depleting tide. Directly to the right of the harbor entrance lies the entrance of a deep-cut cove with uptilted sides. The pseudorcas echolocate the bottom. The unfamiliar landscape of sand and rocks signifies something sublime if not forbidding; it is the closest to shore any of them have swum in their lifetime, a new experience for deep-water creatures who have never witnessed boundaries to their ocean.

The two dolphin species turn to enter the deep hourglass-shaped cove. Watching through binoculars, Yamaguchi orders the vast majority of fishing boats to head back to Katsumoto. A small complement of thirty boats remains to keep the *tsukimbos* pounding, while a contingent of twenty fishermen head to shore in small boats to close off the entrance of the cove by stretching a net between stout poles cemented into either headland. Yamaguchi soon heads home himself, feeling unhappy that so few dolphins have been caught. It has taken over eight hundred men a total of eight hours to round up what looks to be about three hundred dolphins. Nearly half the men, including himself, have been kept from fishing for an entire day. The federal government will pay them about eighty dollars for each animal, which works out to about thirty-five dollars per man. The fuel alone costs more than that.

Inside the outer cove, the tursiops mew and whistle incoherently, projecting an urgency that distracts the otherwise unflappable pseudorcas. As the call of fear surges through the water, the young pseudorca female suddenly leaves the group to push her decomposing fetus toward a nearby seaweed bed. She holds it under her pectoral fin, dives to the bottom to wedge it under a crevice in fifteen feet of water. She resurfaces and swims to rejoin her pod. Only then does her family swim the final two hundred yards until they are stopped by a galvanized hurricane fence that separates the deep outer cove from the shallow inner cove. Staccato bursts of clicks strike the surface of the steel mesh. The resultant echo resonates the large bone of the pseudorcas' lower jaw, stimulates nerve receptors, and is sent to the brain. In such a manner, the pseudorcas perceive an inflexible, opaque mesh that rings back at them as if possessed of its own voice.

It is February 1980. I am sitting alone in a small boat at the opposite side of the cove, watching the pseudorcas and tursiops enter what is known as the Killing Cove. It is my third month here on Iki. The fishermen consider me an expert in cetacean acoustics and hope I'll propose a method to use sound to keep dolphins from preying on individual fishing lines. For this reason, they have granted me an observer's access to the roundup. I find the fishermen to be good-natured, practical men who are always polite to me despite our difference of opinion about cetaceans. They tell me that they started killing dolphins because they thought it might save their fishery. They continue doing it even after it is shown to be untrue, mostly to earn a little extra money selling the ground-up dolphin flesh. The Japanese Fisheries Ministry keeps it going and, in fact, has expanded the operation through subsidies but without any clear objective in mind other than to throw money at voting fishermen.

A few nights ago, I grew bold after a glass of *shochu*, a local brandy distilled from rice, and asked Yamaguchi what a dolphin actually tastes like. He grimaced as he did whenever I strayed beyond the fragile bounds of the business at hand, tried to pull my meaning back to the comfortable utility he insisted could always be found within the horror. "We tried selling the meat. But the big ones taste too metallic. Nobody on Iki would eat it more than once."

When I expected him to change the subject, he lowered his glance and kept on talking, aware that the Japanese consumption of cetacean flesh was considered a taboo in the West. How could he not know? As leader of the Katsumoto antidolphin committee, he was a primary target for all the protests, the letter-writing campaigns, and the threats of boycotts levied against his countrymen's businesses by environmentalists and school-children all over the world. "Myself, I can't understand how anybody can like the taste of dolphin meat, although I hear it is considered a gourmet treat at Izu and Wakayama [two other places in Japan where there are established dolphin fisheries]. I suppose it's fine as part of the mix in *ka-maboko* [a fish sausage, often tinted pink, that is popular throughout Japan]. I know some of the people in Katsumoto have acquired a taste for the suckling animals. They cut it into strips for barbecue and tell me it is quite delicious. But I have never tried it." He pulled out a Lucky Seven cig-arette, tapped it on the tabletop, lit it, inhaled deeply, and smiled, display-ing a mouth full of gold teeth. Then he lowered his gaze again. "I believe they still have a few dolphin steaks stashed away in the freezer at your hotel. If you like, I would be happy to arrange a tasting?" He chuckled once, then lifted his eyes to stare at me deadpan.

Yamaguchi was always interested to hear my theories of why Westerners loved dolphins so dearly. No matter how I answered, he would retort, "We too would love dolphins if they would stop destroying our fishery." Although I had learned the value of not reacting to his antienvironmental one-liners, I also recognized that his observations often hit the mark. He convinced me that the type of staged media event favored at the time by Greenpeace would never stop the killing of dolphins. Certainly, en-vironmentalists were skillful at manipulating the media. And the TV coverage they generated successfully publicized the killing outside Japan. Yamaguchi even acknowledged that the resultant mass protests deeply embarrassed the federal government. But when the Japanese lose face, they respond by digging in their heels. Yamaguchi believed that the Fisheries Ministry actually expanded the Iki slaughter just to spite the foreign protest.

Yamaguchi's astute insights were often tainted by cynicism. Even as he vouched that TV coverage in London, San Francisco, and Sydney would never alter the equation, he assured me it would help environmental groups raise funds so that next winter they could send a new batch of potential heroes to Iki. In Yamaguchi's view, the Iki slaughter provided as much a windfall for environmentalists as it did for the Katsumoto innkeepers who filled their rooms with foreigners in the dead of winter.

Now, out in the Killing Cove, I watch the pseudorcas pause a moment to rub their bodies against the metal as if determining an immediate sensual meaning from the galvanized fence. One at a time, they swim through the ringing portal of the gate into the Killing Cove and swim until they hit the sandy bottom with each thrust of their flukes. When they are all inside the fence, they back up few feet into slightly deeper water, then turn to face one another; ten pseudorca bodies emanating from a common center like the petals of a black daisy. The largest animal raises its head a bit to blare once into the still air. In my experience, it is exceedingly rare for a cetacean to vocalize in air, and this one's trombone call takes me by surprise.

I have no microphone on board, but drop a hydrophone over the edge of the boat, don headphones, and turn on the cassette recorder. Underwater, I hear a new call sounding vaguely like a piccolo sliding up an E-minor scale. This is picked up by several animals who resonate the overtones and accentuate the tonic. I imagine the vibrations shimmering off their acoustically sensitive skin, resonating along the length of each animal's body out to the tips of the flukes where it is retained a moment, and then rolls back toward their heads. Even as the harmony seems to transform the daisy into a living musical instrument, it also evinces the destiny of this pod. Tears come to my eyes.

Sound vibration possesses physical heft underwater, which causes me to wonder, in my own yearning for mythology, if the pulse might massage the tender skin of each animal. If so, then these calls may help prepare the group mind for the task ahead. Massage relaxes the body, helps it respond to a situation that causes physical stress. When muscles and internal organs relax, they better withstand the unfamiliar weight of gravity pressing against them. The large male ceases his call. The chorus stops answering. The pseudorcas break from their circle and slip backward into deeper water. Their breathing seems to intensify. One at a time each animal surges forward until its momentum is finally inhibited by the impenetrable mass of the beach. Motionless now. The deed is done. The pod has stranded.

It is quite a different story for the tursiops. About three hundred of the smaller dolphins (eight to twelve feet long) have followed the pseudorcas' path to the brink of the steel gate. Just like the pseudorcas, they stop to mill about for a few seconds. Fearing the finality presented by the steel barrier, individual animals turn to dart back to the open sea. But it's too late; the fishermen have unfurled a stout net between the two headlands of the outer cove. The tursiops rush back and forth along the length of the net, echolocating, rubbing against the mesh, searching in vain for a safe passage. One of them panics, and barrels into the net at full speed, twisting and biting in an attempt to rip a hole in the fabric. But the net holds. A pectoral fin soon becomes entangled. The animal churns its flukes trying to escape. The monofilament still holds, slicing deeply through the dolphin's silky skin. The dolphin startles, thrashes violently, slapping up against the net until flukes get caught as well. Now held beneath the surface, unable to pull free to draw mortal breath, it ceases thrashing. A dolphin life is transmuted into another statistic of the Killing Cove. A minute later, a smaller tursiops charges the net at full speed. Somehow it rips a substantial hole in the fabric. Ten dolphins follow its lead through the gaping hole and swim away to freedom. Men scream at one another until a boat is dispatched to the spot. The two fishermen lift up the section of net, tie several crisscrossed pieces of monofilament to fill up the gap, and then clip a small piece of netting to patch the hole.

In contrast to the pseudorcas' determination to strand, the tursiops' sense of frenzy tends to affirm their resolve not to swim through that metal gate. Fishermen have told me that it can take a full day for a pod of tursiops to pass through the gate of their own accord. For that reason, once the outer net is secure, most of the fishermen head back to Katsumoto. They have learned from experience that almost no amount of shouting, shooting, coaxing, or spearing is ever going to force the tursiops through the gate and into the shallow Killing Cove unless the animals themselves are ready to do so of their own volition. Until the fishermen learned this basic fact, they forced the issue by drawing the outer net forward in an attempt to push the animals through the metal gate. It caused dolphins to descend into a panic, overturning boats and ripping many holes in the expensive net. Once, a wide tear in the net allowed an entire day's haul of dolphins to escape to the open sea again. Another time a man was nearly disemboweled when a panicked dolphin plowed into his abdomen, beak first. The bottlenose dolphin possesses little history of voluntary group stranding. A coastal species, they possess a familiarity with the shore and its inherent danger. Those bottlenose dolphins who do beach themselves are usually close to death. If they seem to be stranding more often these days, especially along the East Coast of the United States, it's almost certainly due to increased pollution in their shoreline habitat, not from any change in species behavior.

On the beach now, unfamiliar sensations vie for the pseudorcas' attention. The imponderable pull of gravity enacts its burden, jamming innards tightly against the spinal column. The exquisitely sensitive skin immediately starts to harden, shrink, and later, crack under the glare of the late-afternoon sun. Body heat cooks them from within. The ten fishermen who remain along the shore to await the tursiops' entrance into the shallows are already holding spears and knives in anticipation of stabbing and hacking them to death, but now with nothing to do, they leave the pseudorcas alone. No spears are angrily thrust into their sides. No unborn fetuses are cut from the wombs of dying females to be kicked around the shoreline.[9] None of that. These Japanese fishermen seem to comprehend a pseudorca stranding as voluntary, the cetacean equivalent of *seppuku*. So even as the Iki fishermen prepare themselves for a gory process in a frenzy of economic frustration and blood lust, they also seem to grasp the pseudorca stranding as an act worthy of their respect. It is a state of grace to be admired.

Pseudorcas heave their torsos upward for breath, occasionally lift their flukes as if testing a remembrance of locomotion, then drop them like an afterthought, with a splash and a resounding thud that echos off the rock face that looms above the beach. Watching them struggle, I weep openly, deeply discouraged by my observer's role, unable to change anything occurring on this beach. I am more confused that these dolphin killers are men just like any other men. They display no innate evil. Just a few days earlier I had shared a drink with a few of them in a local bar. I laughed until my sides ached to hear one of them sing "ta a yero rib u un" (*Tie a Yellow Ribbon*) into the microphone of a karaoke machine. That singer is now standing on the shore, leaning on his lance like an athlete preparing to heave the javelin. He strolls down the beach to stand over the pseudorcas; they likewise watch him in silence through their dark brown eyes.

A fisherman recently described for me his first experience of a pseudorca stranding. It was wondrous, but discomforting to observe no clear expression of their agony. If not suffering, if not pain and pathos, then what is it that the pseudorcas are experiencing? Their dying seems so smooth, so free of stress. They just drift away. As I watch, a fisherman leaning on a spear kicks a pseudorca whose only crime is forcing him into eye contact. There is something deeply communal about that stare, as if the whale is asking: "Will you, won't you join the dance?" A few other fishermen gather to stare at the pair in curiosity. The pseudorca looks them over as well. It must be unnerving, this gaze of death staring them all in the face.

After years of trying to understand, the fishermen no longer know what it is they are witnessing, or how to behave, or what vocabulary to use to discuss among themselves this troubling act. During the brief moment when eye contact is sealed, the pseudorcas demonstrate their awareness. In that revelation, ordinary men abruptly recognize themselves as murderers. One man confided to me that a pseudorca stranding cannot possibly be a mindless act perpetrated by some dumb animal. It is conscious, willed, a cetacean ceremony that invites death into their oceanic heart, not unlike a fisherman praying to his Shinto gods to guard the safety of the fleet.

A minute passes. The man leaning on his spear sighs, finds a flat stone, throws it in the water, lights up a cigarette, and turns to stare at his friends and neighbors, men just like himself who are waiting to enact a carnage that will transform the beach into a bloodbath. Finally, pilgrimage complete, he nods once at the pseudorcas lying before him, then turns around, walks casually back down the beach to join his fellows, wrenching his mind and his heart away from the sense and civility of his ordinary life, to start the horrific task set before him.

Almost too quickly, just two hours after having come ashore, the two juvenile pseudorcas turn on their sides, mouths agape, eyes glazed over, rocking back and forth in the gentle lap of the waves. Dead.

How did they ever manage to die so quickly? Did their livers hemorrhage from the sheer weight of their bodies? Or was it something else? I learned long ago that cetaceans possess voluntary control over their own breathing. This respiratory trait inspires as much conjecture by dolphin mythologists as the large brain, the altruistic behavior, the stranding. Some conjecture that dolphin breathing must be a form of yoga, a be-here-now meditation that leads to supernatural control over physiological function. The ultimate implication is that when a dolphin inhales, it can will itself not to exhale, and therefore die as it wishes. No need to shove a gun barrel in your mouth or jump off the Golden Gate Bridge. Just stop breathing. Go out consciously.

Lying on either side of the two little carcasses, older pod mates choose to hold steady in the conscious meltdown. Mr. Yamaguchi has recently informed me that, depending on the intensity of the sun, most of the stranded animals take about twelve hours to expire. The fishermen can tell when the end is near. Muscles start to spasm. Breathing becomes short. They relax into a vortex too powerful to resist. Ever so slowly they leave their bodies. Do they also experience the long, illuminated tunnel described by human chroniclers of the near-death experience? Do other long-departed pseudorcas swim about them in greeting? Perhaps they pause a moment to echolocate on their own body lying there on the pure white sand. The body spasms one last time. White light. Delight. It is in such a manner that I imagine the pseudorcas drifting off the sands of Tatsunoshima. Gone.

And this afterthought. So many people ascribe reason and thought to these animals. Yet if so, why is it that throughout the long, deadly afternoon, not a single dolphin has figured out the simple maneuver of leaping over the fence and net to freedom?

A more violent end awaits the tursiops. I am at breakfast the next morning in the empty dining room of a drab but immaculate Katsumoto hotel, stirring a raw egg into a piping hot bowl of miso soup. The egg white congeals. My interpreter, Yuki, sits directly across from me breaking the flat dark green leaves of nori seaweed into his own miso until there is no liquid left in the bowl. A TV glares at us across the far corner of the dining room. Yuki suddenly bolts to attention and waves excitedly at the TV. He pulls me off my chair and over to the set. The commentator is talking about the *iruka mundai*, the dolphin problem, on Iki Island. The cook rushes out of the kitchen with a teenage, mop-haired dishwasher in tow. Two waitresses emerge from the china closet behind the kitchen.

An aerial shot of Tatsunoshima Bay fills the screen. The blood spreads out over three acres of ocean, rendering the usually aqua water a shocking opaque scarlet. Cut to the beach. The white sand is streaked with rivers of blood emptying into the ocean of blood. Four members of the Katsumoto antidolphin committee stand in a line holding spears. As they bow courteously to a TV commentator, the camera pulls back to show them standing in the midst of swirling dolphin bodies. Some animals are snorting hard, clearly trying to breathe. The camera pans to the shore where a group of ten fishermen pull on a thick rope. They heave together and arduously haul a six-hundred-pound tursiops high onto the sand. As the men drop the line, the camera lingers a moment on the face of the dolphin. There's that same discerning eye contact I observed yesterday. The camera cuts to a spear bearer's tense face. He peers at the dolphin, displaying neither satisfaction nor sorrow.

He grimaces, thrusting the spear downward until it sinks into the animal's silky throat. Time seems suspended as tissue separates to receive the lance. I feel adrenaline pulse through my body; my own throat feels hot; I shiver. The fisherman sneers ruefully and thrusts a second time. The camera leaves his face and travels down the length of the spear, where the six-inch-long blade has disappeared into the throat of the dolphin. I am astounded to witness such a sight on TV. Standing next to me, one of the waitresses starts crying and rushes from the dining room. The cook hangs his head in shame.

I turn away from the screen to notice Dexter Cate has walked up behind me. He is in his mid-thirties, tall, thin, sharp-featured, a pageboy haircut drooping to his shoulders, a wispy untrimmed black beard showing hints of red. He is dressed in a new pair of jeans, a fairly nondescript Hawaiian shirt, and a pair of cheap plastic thongs. We met briefly last night when he arrived at the hotel with his wife and baby son. He asked me what I knew about a roundup in Katsumoto. I told him the fishermen were holding a lot of dolphins at the Killing Cove. I asked him why he had come here. He told me he was prepared to take direct action to free the dolphins, although he remained vague about how he planned to do that. As we stare at the TV screen, he turns to me and whispers passionately, "The whole world needs to see this footage."

On the screen, the spear bearer grunts as he pulls the spear out for the last time. The blood spurts two feet into the air. The animal thrashes. The fisherman takes a step backward to avoid the blood, and then shouts directly into the camera for everyone to stand back. But the cameraman decides to linger a moment longer on the dolphin. Who could believe that so much blood could flow from a single animal? The camera lens takes a direct hit; a single drop of dark liquid dribbles right down the screen. The dolphin stops thrashing and quivers. The fountain loses its momentum. I look for the "fierce fire" Aldo Leopold described departing the eye of a wolf he once watched die, but the sad miracle does not reveal itself through the cold filter of television. The camera holds the face of the dolphin for one moment longer, then pans along the length of the red river. The dull streak has already been consumed by the maroon repository of the Killing Cove. The camera draws back one more time and lingers on the face of the fisherman. He thrusts out his chin and nods, places the spear on the ground, and walks to the waterside where his mates are already hauling the next animal up onto the sand.

The camera leaves the shoreline and fades to the face of an upbeat reporter dressed in a blue-and-black plaid madras jacket. He stands just beneath the Tatsunoshima dolphin memorial, erected by the local cooperative to pledge sorrow for the dolphins killed. The reporter sucks air in across his teeth, then smiles to inform us that at least fifty dolphins will be dispatched by the end of the day. Every part of the animals will be utilized, most of it for pig feed. He concludes his story by slowing down his tempo to declare a firm defense for the fishermen "who must kill, as a last resort to protect their livelihood."

The cook lets fly with a long string of expletives and storms back into the kitchen again. Yuki translates the cook's words: "This is very embarrassing! We fell for that line three years ago. We're sick of hearing their bullshit. Who are they trying to kid?"

The stone memorial fades away to a gray blur, to be replaced by the bright colors of a Japanese newsroom. An anchorman raises his index finger aloft to offer more commentary about the necessity of the dolphin kill. I listen closely to Yuki's translation but feel I must be missing something essential. While the anchorman defends the killing, the images he's just shown us present a visceral condemnation of that same killing. He drones on, finally smiles brightly, then drops his head in a half bow. The screen fills with the sight of two cute little girls singing gaily in a bathtub. Their mother steps up beside the tub, brandishing a package of frozen breaded shrimp balls. Together, mother and daughters sing the praises of shrimp balls. Dexter growls once, jumps up to the TV, and turns it off. From the kitchen we all hear the cook embroiled in an impassioned debate with his teenage dishwasher. Yuki turns to me. "He is saying that only in Japan could such bloody disgusting footage arouse sympathy for fishermen. He feels ashamed for his country."

Out at the Killing Cove later that same afternoon, I sit alone in a boat tethered to the fence to watch a mother tursiops struggle to keep her restless baby far from the bloody events transpiring on the shore. She forces him into the deepest part of the cove, right up against the wire mesh of the inner restraining fence. The metal bites into his skin. Every time he tries to move away, she pushes him back again. Over the next hour, several other mothers with suckling babies make their way to this deepest part of the cove.

As mothers are protective, babies are curious. What the mother intuits as peril, her baby perceives as excitement—so much movement, so many two-leggeds, and best of all, the incomparable sensation of a hard bottom to his ocean. Even the nauseating taste of blood spreading its thick tentacles through the waters of the Killing Cove offers a curiosity to be explored. As the sun climbs high in the sky, baby grows ever bolder in his attempt to swim away from the tight confines of the temporary nursery. Mother swims after him, nips him on the dorsal fin to scold him, and pushes him back up against the fence. After several hours of this routine, his little body starts to feel the bruises of the metal. By late afternoon, the flowing blood has turned the water so opaque that the dolphins must rely entirely on their echolocation to maneuver underwater. Rat-a-tat clicks fill the water, distorting off the sand in unpredictable ways. Misshapen echoes conceivably affect the dolphin brain like a hallucination. Objects that echolocate as close by turn out to be twenty or more feet away. The animals bump into the fence and into each other with increasing regularity. A growing fear of collisions offers one more reason to keep the juveniles protected.

It is not difficult to imagine the baby inventing games with its own warped echolocation, listening for the bizarre temporal and dimensional distortions as a human child might play in front of a curved mirror at a carnival funhouse. The baby has likewise transformed the floor of the cove into a toy, pushing his flukes off the sand in a rush to the surface, breaching completely out of the water, but nearly landing on top of his mother. She responds to his accomplishment by nudging him back against the fence.

The mother moves sluggishly after spending the last twenty-four hours without food or sleep. Fortunately, when all the other mothers converged on this section of the enclosure, they began tending to the needs of one another's calves. When one mother loses her milk, another one who has lost a baby moves forward to stick a teat into the baby's mouth. Babies who have lost their mothers are tended by several surrogates. Since I have started observing, none among this clutch of nursing mothers has yet been hauled up on the beach.

The mother detects her own baby contentedly rubbing its gums and teeth against the knobby galvanized steel of the fence. She attempts to steal a moment of rest and spends the next half hour languishing on the surface. She wakes to gather her baby back into the deepest part of the Killing Cove, then sticks her head high above the water's surface to notice the pod of jet black pseudorcas. Only a few of them are still breathing, albeit heavily. Their skin is pitted and cracked. Further down the shore, a large tursiops thrashes in its death agony. A two-legged in a wetsuit stands over it, jabbing a spear deep into the animal's throat. Just behind the two-legged stand other humans. One of them has an eye stuck against a gray box possessed of its own shiny eye.

The hours pass. The Killing Cove becomes slightly more roomy as, one at a time, occupants are dragged up on the beach. Then the relative calm of the dolphins' makeshift nursery disintegrates into chaos as the first nursing female is dragged ashore. First one, and then another baby wanders away from the protection of deep water. Two men repairing a net at the back of the beach point toward the water. They stand, walk to a boat; one holds the bow while the other one climbs inside and searches to find something under a pile of line. He holds up a gaff and jumps to shore. The two men stride down to the water's edge. The man with the gaff bends over a tiny dolphin, not more than a meter in length. He strikes hard under the baby's chin, plucks the baby from the water, then holds his bleeding trophy aloft. The two men laugh as the dolphin flops back and forth like a flag in the breeze. The single newborn animal will easily serve two families for dinner tonight. Like choice veal, it is still feeding on mother's milk and has not yet turned gamey.

More time passes. The tidal action flushes away some of the blood. One large animal in the nursery area lifts her head high above the water's surface, ostensibly searching for her baby. She lunges violently across the shallow waters of the cove, weaving back and forth, ever closer to the dangerous shoreline. She stops abruptly before a small dolphin lying half in, half out of the water, digging a small trench with one of its pectoral fins, simultaneously filling in the trench with its other fin. The mother pushes him bodily back out into deeper water where she turns to raise her head out of the water. The humans have gone. Nothing at all except the bodies of several pseudorcas. Then she turns, stares directly at me sitting in a small boat on the other side of the fence. This observer feels ashamed.

The female nudges her nose gently against her baby's soft belly and races to the opposite end of the enclosure. Sensing her energy, he follows in pursuit. Back and forth they swim, now whistling, now bumping one another. Mother breaches high into the air and lands broadside on her back. Several other dolphins join in the game. I pick the oars up off the floor of the boat, stick them in the oarlock, untie my line, and quietly make my exit back to Katsumoto.

Just after midnight, Dexter Cate slips into the tight black skin of his wet suit. He straps a diving knife onto his thigh, hangs a compass around his neck, then loads a small backpack with one hundred feet of climber's rope, a walkie-talkie, and a large flashlight. With the help of his wife, Suzy, he inflates the seven-foot boat that lies in a heap on the beach patio of his hotel room, which is located on the outskirts of Katsumoto. The boat is brought to pressure. The two of them lift it over a four-foot retaining wall, down onto the beach below. It should be just about slack tide. Dexter stows a paddle and swim fins inside the boat, then drags it across the sand into the water. He sits inside and starts paddling the mile from his hotel to Tatsunoshima. Even if the boat capsizes, it will still float; his buoyant wet suit makes it virtually impossible for him to drown under normal circumstances. But the currents through this channel sometimes run six or seven knots, and even now, at slack tide, it is easy to lose one's balance or one's sense of direction in the dark. A capsizing could very easily separate him from his boat. Depending on how the currents are running, they could deposit him either on the backside of Tatsunoshima Island, or on the quay where, even at this late hour, a few fishermen are working on their boats.

Thirty minutes later, Dexter's boat bumps up against the cork floats of the barrier net enclosing Tatsunoshima Cove. The half-moon reflects off the backs of ten or so dolphins bobbing and blowing around his boat on the surface of the black waters. How did these animals manage to get outside the net, and why do they linger at this horrible place when the open ocean beckons? Dexter concludes they are remnants of the former tursiops herd. They were never caught, and are now trying to get *inside* to join their pod mates. He grabs hold of the net, pulls himself to shore, then drags the boat high above the tide line and sits down on the beach to get his bearings. Dexter accompanied a film crew here earlier today and spent a few moments casually examining the net fastenings. He walks over to the pole set deeply in the sand and unravels the two tangled lines attached to it. After several tedious minutes, he finds the knots and chuckles to realize they are bowlines and therefore easy to untie. He picks up a rope end, pushes it toward the knot while pulling the other end away. As it comes undone, the net sags and pulls inward in response to the incoming tide. When he unties the second line, the net falls sideways into the water. Dexter ties the two net lines to his belt, walks down the beach, pushes his boat into the water, climbs inside, and works with all his strength to paddle the heavy, waterlogged net across to the far shore. Arriving, he climbs out of the boat and folds the net onto itself. The passageway between the outer cove and the open sea is open.

A pod of tursiops that has been following his every action now swims right up alongside the shoreline to inspect this strange human thrust into their midst. He walks in among them. They keep just beyond the reach of his outstretched hand. "Go home," he whispers. With his own swim fins impeding forward motion in the shallows, Dexter turns around and wades backward into the bay until he's chest-deep. He kicks off the sand and swims toward the open sea. Most of the dolphins follow him. Then suddenly he turns toward shore and quickly lands back on the beach again. Comprehending the intent of his gesture, the tursiops continue onward. "Good-bye, my friends," he calls after them. "And take care of yourselves."

Now begins a far more difficult task. Dexter climbs back into his boat and paddles up alongside the metal fence of the Killing Cove. Earlier that day he guessed that the barrier was cemented into the sand. He pulls himself along the length of the fence until he reaches the gate. It is tied shut in three places with short lengths of nylon rope. The first knot, positioned above the high-tide mark, unties gracefully. The other two are swollen with algae and do not respond. He pulls out his knife and slices the short strands of rope girding the gate to the fence. The portal falls inward with the thrust of the tidal surge and sinks to the bottom. Almost immediately, dolphins start swimming through the opening. The process develops in an orderly fashion; if anything, the dolphins seem uncommonly courteous to one another. When several animals arrive at the same moment, half of them back off until there is enough space for them to pass as well. Dexter greets each one of them as they swim past: "Be well. Take care. So long."

He paddles the boat inside the fence. Many of the dolphins who remain inside the Killing Cove are in bad shape. Some bob on the surface as if in deep shock. Others rush away from him every time he tries to draw near. Dexter rows into the center of the cove, stows his paddles, then drops into the water. He swims up to one listless animal and starts to stroke it back to attentiveness. Whispering into the animal's ear, Dexter coaxes it toward the open gate and then outside. "Come on, sweet baby. You can do it. Swim home. Come on, you can do it." In this manner, one more dolphin slowly reawakens to find freedom. Dexter reenters the cove.

A half dozen healthy animals have also reentered the Killing Cove and now appear to be working as a team to push and pull their bewildered comrades out toward the open gate. It seems an extraordinary behavior, although it may be nothing out of the ordinary for creatures long known for altruistic behavior. Dexter shines his flashlight across the length of the cove. One healthy dolphin is rubbing its rostrum against the throat of another animal. The healthy dolphins gather several of the others together to lead them through the gate. Dexter is especially pleased to notice that the majority of the animals are juveniles and nursing babies. One of them spyhops right in front of the light. "Swim away, little one. Follow your mother." As soon as the nursery group passes through the gates they all bolt for freedom at top speed.

The next hours are spent stroking dolphin throats, pulling, pushing, whistling, swallowing water, climbing into the boat to warm up his stiff hands, climbing back into the water. Cooing, whispering, flattering. When one sluggish animal starts to regain consciousness, Dexter gets so carried away by the miracle that he starts shouting out encouragement at the top of his voice. As the night progresses he systematically moves closer to the beach, where the animals he encounters appear more and more battered. Where a rocky cliff rises from the shore, he discovers twenty tursiops caught on the sand. Luckily the tide is coming in.

So begins the most strenuous task of the long night, grabbing hold of several hundred pounds of deadweight and trying to yank it off the gradual shelf of the beach and into deeper water. Utilizing whatever reservoir of strength he has left, he works feverishly to rebalance the animals, walks them into deeper waters, cheers them on with encouragement. He whispers admonishments into the ears of those who fail to snap out of their deep shock. "Oooh, my love. Swim away. Swim away." Triage begins. He kneels beside each animal to determine if his efforts will actually help. Is this one going make it? If so, he slaps its jaw, sings in its ear, shakes it back and forth; trying everything within his power to get some response. In three hours he frees five tursiops. The rest are beyond hope, so he simply kneels down beside each one in turn. He hugs its face close to his own, strokes its cheek, and wishes it well in whatever journey it is now under-taking. It is four A.M. His strength is failing him.

Farther down the beach, off on their own, he now discovers the ten pseudorcas. They all suffer from severe sunburn that disfigures their skin with long, festering cracks that show the blubber underneath. By now, the tide has risen high enough to wash all the way to their pectoral fins, although certainly not high enough for Dexter to budge these two-thousand-pound animals. He walks up to each one in turn, to listen for a sign of breath. Eight are already dead. The other two arrest his attention. They are lying next to one another. He sits down directly in front of them, tries to regain some strength by closing his eyes and dropping his chin onto his chest. As time passes, he realizes the two animals are breathing in synchrony. Who would believe him? Dolphins practicing tantra? He lies down on the sand, lingers in that position a full minute, and tries to breathe with them. But he soon falls asleep.

When he opens his eyes, something crucial has altered. The pseudorcas have stopped breathing. The first glimmer of dawn illuminates the sky to the east. Dexter stands, bone weary, feeling groggy. He studies the bumpy, glistening landscape of black pseudorca bodies lying in a row in the gathering light. They have found their peace. He looks out over the dark waters of the Killing Cove and notices a single small tursiops stuck on the sand. Dexter walks to the animal, leans into the task and heaves the juvenile off the shelf and into deeper water. The animal exits the cove without a backward glance.

It is six A.M. The night has fled, replaced by a monochrome overcast. There's still plenty of time to paddle across the channel, be back in his hotel room in half an hour, call a cab, flee Katsumoto, catch the nine o'clock plane to Fukuoka, from there to Tokyo, and on to Honolulu. But what good does it serve for Dexter to take the bold risk of freeing so many dolphins without also taking responsibility for his action? It has always been his strategy to let the Japanese throw the weight of their legal system against him. If he flees, the fishermen will arrive to discover the carefully folded nets, the untied gate lying on the sea bottom, the Killing Cove itself empty. They'd motor back to Katsumoto to tell the bosses in the cooperative. Who can predict how Yamaguchi would respond? What if he decides to keep the whole affair quiet, just to avoid another snowballing media event? No point to that.

If Dexter's backup crew has done its job, then this act of nonviolent confrontation is about to be made very public. Given the time difference between Japan and New York, the story of his deed should be breaking on yesterday's U.S. evening news programs in about two hours' time. How bizarre that people in America will probably hear about Dexter's escapade before most of the local fishermen do.

At seven-thirty A.M., blue sky peeks through the brilliant red clouds to the east. A boatload of workers pushes off from the Katsumoto pier in a large runabout loaded down with newly sharpened spears, knives, hooks, ropes, blocks and tackle, chains, and wet suits. They churn around the corner of Tatsunoshima Island to find the outer net gone. Turning toward the far shore, they notice the folded net lies above the high-tide line. The gate is also gone. The dolphins have escaped! How could such a thing happen? Then they spot him. Perched on a rock at the center of the beach, wearing a wet suit, alone and shivering through his teeth, sits Dexter Cate.

Dexter would report to the world that he'd freed about three hundred animals. The cooperative would disagree violently with that figure, and especially with his choice of verbs. He hadn't *freed* anything, but had *stolen* precisely six hundred seventy-three animals. Six hundred seventy-three? What can we make of such a precise figure amid the muddle of this day? In fact, it suggests duplicity. A month earlier I had personally counted twenty-three dolphins caught in a roundup. Yet I was later informed that, on that same day, the cooperative applied for compensation for a hundred seventy-one animals.

Dexter was tried in a Japanese court of law for the felony crime of grand larceny. He was found guilty and served six months in a maximum-security prison at Sasebo, Kyushu. He would die ten years later, free diving off the coast of the Big Island of Hawaii.

The media's coverage of the roundup of dolphins at Tatsunoshima Cove in late February 1980, coupled with Dexter Cate's subsequent act, was one of the first worldwide TV events to catapult radical ecology, with its key perception of planetary consciousness, into the hearts and minds of the human species. Something had moved on a global scale. The *Melbourne Sentinel* wrote: "Who owns the oceans, if not dolphins?" A Berlin newspaper editorialized: "How dare they kill dolphins whose offspring may someday swim off the beaches of Perth or Vladivostok or even Hamburg?" All of this trenchant planetary indignation also points out a grave failure of the unfolding event, and the main reason I did not wholly agree with Dexter's strategy. The actual issues at stake were never debated within Japan because everybody was too busy saving face. Through the heated days and weeks that followed, while the rest of the world broiled with hostility toward Japan, the Japanese media proved itself more than equal to the task of tailoring their own reportage to neutralize the indignation. I collected these news stories but never read a single account that levied criticism either *against* the fishermen or *for* dolphin preservation. The story was reported as a world media furor, but not as an issue of fisheries' policy. Just as often stories were slanted sympathetically toward fishermen who were faced with the daunting task of figuring out how to deal with foreign angst. Dexter Cate was depicted as a common thief who stole dolphins and cut fishing nets.

Many Japanese expressed guilt, sorrow, and embarrassment to me over the events unfurling at Iki, but their regret was always personal, the expression of a friend who had unwittingly hurt the feelings of another friend. Other than the clear disgust voiced by the hotel cook, I never again heard a Japanese openly express anger or even discontent over the dolphin extermination at Iki. The futility of the slaughter and the dolphins' right to life were always discussed in evenly modulated tones, as "what foreigners believe." At the time, this remarkable evasion seemed as much a tragedy as the slaughter itself, although perhaps it emphasizes the need for a peace corps–style approach that could help locals solve their own problems.

Dexter Cate's goal was not to condemn any particular group of fishermen, or even fishermen in general, but to turn the *criticism* against the killing into a bigger problem for the Japanese government than the dolphins ever were. He also believed the media event served as a karmic mirror. The usurper has to cope with an unflattering public image of himself caught in the act of desecration. Imagine yourself a rural Japanese fisherman, a family man conservative in lifestyle, ethics, and politics. Suddenly an invading army of foreign journalists descends upon you as you stand up to your knees in blood, stabbing and disemboweling dolphins. Pictures are taken. A microphone is thrust into your face. Your dignity is shattered, your identity frozen out of context. And even though your own media never comes right out and criticizes the killing, their long, slow pans of dolphins violently thrashing in a ketchup-colored sea makes words seem beside the point. What a dishonor for you and for your country. Tomorrow, you must warn other fishermen to avoid the journalists. But what's this? It's too late? The journalists have already left town, flown back to the nineteenth floor of the Tokyo Foreign Press Club to edit their footage.

In many years of watching the Japanese react to world opinion about cetaceans, I conclude that well-constructed media events and the peace corps approach are complementary paths. The xenophobic trait of the Japanese to continue killing whales and dolphins, despite clear evidence of a crashing resource, explains why a dramatic and thought-provoking media event can be a useful tool for inducing change. It unmasks duplicity, tutors the rest of the world in bad local policies, and, most important, keeps the pressure up so bad policies do not spread.

Unfortunately, media events do their magic only when sprung in moderation. Overused, they cultivate a gaming atmosphere of *them* against *us*; *us*, of course, meaning most of the rest of the world. *We* demand *they* stop whaling. In response to the Japanese killing of whales and dolphins, groups like Greenpeace tended to overuse the media, resulting in the opposite effect of the federal government stepping in to protect the local status quo as a way to leverage wounded dignity. By the mid-1970s *they* had started responding to *our* ultimatum with non sequiturs: for instance, that extinction is not a pertinent issue, even though data shows that several species of great whales had dwindled to just a few thousand individuals. *Our* tactics intensified. *They* responded to our media events with obtuse legalities that ultimately pointed out the harsh fact that there was no international law forbidding them from killing as many whales as they damn well pleased. An impasse developed. As Dave Phillips of San Francisco's *Earth Island Institute* put it, "By the early 1980s, the International Whaling Commission's [IWC] annual meeting had degenerated into a slugfest. And every year the whaling fleets left harbor on schedule."[10] Today, many within the save-the-whale movement paint Japan as an enemy to conquer. Likewise, many within Japan conclude that the Western environmental movement is anti-Japanese.

Media events are external devices, and lasting change rarely ever gets forced on any culture from outside. Forced to change, locals resent it, resist it, and resort to the old way of doing things the moment the oppressor turns his back. When change comes from within the minds and hearts of the locals, it takes hold. Today in Japan, prompted by a combination of a thriving nature film industry bonded to a thriving tourist industry, whale watching has started to break out all over. I attended a conference in Tokyo in 1995 that was sponsored by something unheard of fifteen years earlier: a Japanese organization (ICERC, pronounced I-search) with large public support to promote living cetaceans. Millions more experienced this new benign vision about whales and dolphins from magazine stories and TV and radio interviews spun off from the conference. Advertising posters using whale and dolphin images started appearing in every subway station. More Japanese people than ever were given the opportunity to entertain the notion that cetaceans possess ways to nourish humanity beyond their old role as a food resource. In retrospect, it seems woefully shortsighted that Western environmentalists simply presumed the average Japanese was immune to the charged relationship that exists between humans and charismatic cetaceans everywhere else in the world. But the charged border between our species is not a Western phenomenon. It is a human one.

ICERC's grassroots strategy is successful because Japan is overwhelmingly one people, one culture—more like a tribe than most other nations. As Ichiro Ozawa writes in his Japanese bestseller, *Blueprint for a New Japan*, "If even one person opposes a decision, it can't be made. Everyone has to conform. . . . There is no room in this system for the concept of individual responsibility." This tenet also provides an insight why the Japanese people reject the antiwhaling strategy promoted by Western environmentalists. They will not and cannot heed a call that vilifies whalers. In other words, "save the whales" also means "hurt the tribe," and protecting the status quo takes precedence over any logical argument introduced by foreigners. Ironically, the Japanese people do not question the irrational arguments their government invents to thwart the international outcry against whaling.

ICERC is successful because it is not *against* anything, including the whaling industry. It is *for* whales. Its printed matter alludes to *saving* the whales only circuitously, by elevating cetaceans to the status of peers, teachers, and fellow residents of Gaia. Because such a vision transcends nationalism and economics, ICERC has masterminded an end run around the open sore of Japan's whaling policy. The Australian founder of the international ICERC network, Kamala Hope-Campbell, might as well be paraphrasing *Blueprint for a New Japan* when she observes, "After one person in Japan changes, everyone else starts to change a little as well."[11]

Today, within Japan, former whaling boats are being converted to whale-watching cruisers, with folding chairs assembled on top of old harpoon mounts. Off the coast of the northern island of Hokkaido in 1997, a whale-watching skipper proudly informed me that just five years earlier his boat traveled these waters hunting whales. Standing in the wheelhouse, he drew my attention to a wide smudge on his fish finder identified as a hundred-foot-thick band of krill. We traveled through this shrimp soup for five miles before the smudge dwindled and disappeared. "Krill is the humpback whale's favorite food," he said, beaming. "In a few years, this place is going to be a big tourist center." Although I wished him well, we saw no whales that day, only a few dolphins. The humpbacks had all been killed. With no predator to contain them, the krill had overpopulated.

And at Iki Island, the scene of so much blood and protest, today there is a dolphin-watching business that attracts tourists from all over the world.

During a recent presentation tour in Japan, I was driven from the Osaka airport into a city whose striking skyline reminded me of Chicago. The most eye-arresting billboard on the highway displayed the likeness of a huge neon whale announcing that the next exit led to one of Japan's best-known whale restaurants. Sitting beside me in the car, Japanese-American dolphin biologist Satoru Yamamoto was quick to point out that the catchy restaurant billboard was an anomaly. "Sure, the restaurant serves whale meat, but it is one of the very last places in Japan you can get the stuff. If you talk to people in the street you'll find most of them would rather watch whales than eat them." He frowned, then admitted that the sign also offered proof that the Japanese delegation to the IWC remains successful representing the last few whaling corporations.

As the neon sign dwindled in the distance Yamamoto-san got a faraway glint in his eye as he described a temple erected centuries ago in the old Japanese whaling center of Taiji. "In those days, life for a whaler was a very risky business. Too often, the men never returned home from a hunt. But you know, the old-time whalers knew something about conservation. For them it was a spiritual issue. For instance, they had a strict rule against killing pregnant females. But it was very difficult to tell the difference between a fat whale and a pregnant whale. Sometimes they couldn't even tell if the whale was pregnant until they cut it open after it had been killed and dragged up on the shore. If they found that the whale they killed was pregnant, the men responsible for the killing would run home to get their best silk overcoats. They would return and wrap the fetus in their coats. Depending on the species, the carcass might be six feet long, so, as you might imagine, it sometimes took a lot of overcoats. Then they'd bury the whale on the temple grounds after a ceremony of atonement."

As Yamamoto-san concluded the story, he paused. The roar of the rush-hour traffic filtered into consciousness. "I don't know why, but those people at Taiji stopped their overcoat ceremony a long time ago. The temple's still there. They still catch pilot whales and dolphins every winter. In a way I guess you could say it's the story of modern civilization. We've all forgotten how to say we're sorry to Nature. If the whalers were able to do that, maybe then they would be able to stop whaling."

2 WHALE NATURE AND HUMAN NATURE

In one hour I invented 62 different meanings for a whale's vertebra, including one ballet, one movie, one painting, one philosophy, one therapeutic interior decoration, one hallucinogenic and one psychological method, all of which are based on a whale's vertebra being connected with lunatic dreams. —SALVADOR DALI

The subtropical archipelago of Ogasawara lies six hundred miles south of Tokyo, a chain of volcanic islands whose steep slopes are draped with lush greenery from an abundant rainfall. Every spring, the warm sea surrounding the largest island of Chichi-jima (Father Island) resounds with the songs of courting humpback whales. Like Muroran, like Taiji, these waters were prime whaling grounds just a few years ago. But when the humpbacks were declared an endangered species, they were crossed off the short list of species available to the Japanese whale-killing machine. Unlike Muroran, whales still visit these waters. Today, Chichi-jima has blossomed into a whale-watching center, one of the prime spots in this beautiful country where the Japanese people are able to express their growing admiration for cetaceans.

It is April 1995. Fifteen years have passed since I attended the Killing Cove and witnessed the pseudorcas and tursiops confronting their own death. I am on Chichi-jima to speak at a conference designed to promote whale watching as the centerpiece of an ambitious national campaign to transform Japanese relations to all of nature. According to my host,

Takako Iwatani, "Whales and dolphins help humans feel connected to nature better than any other animal." My talk focuses on the charged border, a term I've coined to describe the human encounter with whales and dolphins. Like Takako, I believe that experiencing cetaceans in the wild is a profound experience. I can't say precisely why this is so, or why the whales and dolphins have such a unique power to captivate us, although the growing worldwide popularity of whale watching offers some proof of this border's charged nature.

Because Chichi-jima is too steep for an airport, I arrive on the town wharf after a twenty-hour cruise from Tokyo aboard a steamship with a hundred other whale watchers. After a brief introductory ceremony held beneath an imposing stone whale that leaps from the neatly clipped lawn of a sunny park, I am bundled into a car and driven along a new highway that switchbacks through the lava rock and ends abruptly at the top of a headland that looms a sheer twenty-four hundred feet above the sea. Albatross and frigate birds soar along the face of the cliff. A large wooden deck surrounded by wooden bleachers serves as a viewing platform for the whales that cruise the waters so far below. Walking tentatively up to the fence that rims the precipice, I gaze down at the ocean, which appears as a shifting carpet of black and green divided by lines of white froth made by waves crashing against a jumble of sea stacks. It is a daunting task to distinguish even a mighty whale from such a distance. A humpback helps me out by breaching. The oblong gray shape lifts from the froth, holds itself aloft, then turns sharply to one side to maximize the surface area of re-entry. The sixty-foot-long body belly flops, causing the sea to explode. Twenty-four hundred feet away, the whale appears as a thickset minnow leaping for mosquitoes, although the splash is still grand enough to make me sigh, then smile brightly. I turn away contented to notice a throng of people has joined me on the platform.

Much of what we know for certain about cetaceans is anatomical, hard data gathered by biologists employed by the whaling industry who measure body parts and compare physiologies. We know a few things about their behavior: where most of the species reside, where they migrate to and from, what they eat, the social organization of certain familiar species. Beyond that, most of the rest of our knowledge is extrapolated from sketchy information. Besides the sighting of a spectacular breach or of shiny backs rolling over the surface, perhaps bolstered by hissy underwater songs, there is not much human beings can observe about this family whose members spend 95 percent of their lives underwater.

To be clear, the charged border is not the place whales reside but, rather, the desires and notions that both motivate and certify our encounters with them. Mapping the terrain of the interface is exceedingly difficult because of the unfixed manner in which whales and dolphins swim through our collective imagination. The view here is at once intimate and distant, subjective and objective, behavioral and mythic, hopeful yet tragic. The combination of so many contrary features causes the landscape to glow with a vital but unfocused light that blurs the biological with the cultural. People hold strong opinions about what they think they observe here, often relying on reverie to express even commonplace features of the scenery. Much of what is held up as certainty is actually intuited. What we intuit, we believe earnestly, devising ethics to lay over the natural grid. Some cetacean lovers insist that dreams provide a more cogent picture of this border than scientific data. It is not difficult to understand how this view is validated. With 95 percent of behavior unwitnessed, 95 percent is open to speculation. For all these reasons, a multidisciplinary approach seems the only realistic way to proceed.

As a student of the charged border, I am as fascinated by the spectacle of people relating to whales as by the whales themselves. Now I take a seat in the bleachers and notice that every person but me stands against the fence peering downward. A woman on the far left of the overlook spies what she believes is a whale blowing beyond the near clutter of islets. "*Kujira*," she shouts, "whale." A hundred people rush to the left. Many of them hold binoculars to their eyes. Then disappointment. The splash was caused by a shoal lying just beneath the surface making the waves break in a straight line. A woman on the right shouts, "*Kujira! Kujira!* I saw it breach! Look! There! It breached again! It is breaching." Everyone rushes to the opposite side of the platform.

The thrill of watching whales at Chichi-jima is much the same as the thrill of watching at the Stellwagen Banks off Boston, in Puget Sound, Tenerife, Gibraltar, Maui, La Jolla, Argentina. All it takes for elation to assert itself is the glimpse of a black back rolling across the water's surface. People stand wide-eyed and humbled in the presence of these animals that, more often than not, pay us no mind. The hope remains that a whale will turn, swim a bit closer, perhaps parade its baby in front of us so that we may admire its beauty. Flukes slap the water, and we wonder what the gesture means. While some behavioralists interpret tail slaps as a defensive posture meant to warn intruders to keep their distance, whale watchers generally prefer an alternative hypothesis, one that suggests empathy. The whale is waving at us. This explains why so many whale watchers cup a hand around their mouths, bid the whale hello. When the whale slaps the water in response, we take it as a sign the creature is trying to communicate with us. But that's just the bare bones of the relationship unfolding at the charged border. Swimmers in Hawaii report that spinner dolphins have introduced a game of catch with seaweed. In British Columbia, orcas improvise melodies among their own kind, and occasionally they interact with human musicians who play songs in their midst. In a dozen places worldwide, humpbacks sing a song that is so majestic we compare it to the chanting of angels. Bottlenose dolphins save us from drowning.

On the bulwark of Chichi-jima, a seven-inch-long gray thrush known as *isohiyodori* in Japanese bounces along the deck, picking up cracker bits dropped by the whale watchers. Its mate appears, a gaudy creature of blue and orange. What do these distant whales possess that allows them to take over our imaginations, while the birds right before us turn all but invisible? Is it the whale's size? The large brain? The promise of interactive playfulness? The fact that so many cetacean species survive on the edge of extinction? This book examines such questions in detail, if not always answering them conclusively. How could it be otherwise? Charisma is always hard to measure, and harder to predict. At this particular moment, one thing is certain. Whale watching and bird-watching are not variations on a single theme. Bird-watchers are hobbyists. They accrue lifetime lists from hours of patient observation, and they cherish the fine details of taxonomy, calls, and habitat. Whale watching is bird-watching for the masses, a far less intellectual pursuit, more like sight-seeing than collecting. Whereas only a very few people care to add a coppery trogon to their lifetime list, as many people wish to observe a whale breach as hope to visit Yosemite Valley.

Several people offer running commentary about what everyone plainly sees. "The whale has surfaced." "It's swimming away from shore." "Oh, look, it's diving again." One woman asks me where it will surface, as if my role as an expert means I can predict the movements of a whale I am not watching. When I shrug my shoulders, she turns back to the fence. The majority of sightseers are busy adjusting camera settings, conferring with their watches to predict how many minutes or seconds might pass before the whale's lungs prompt its brain to energize the powerful flukes to propel the animal to the surface again. An observer could be blind, speak not a word of Japanese, and still be certain every time a whale surfaces by the whirring noise generated by fifty motor drives. Yet just as I feel on the verge of cynicism, my view makes a back flip. Barreling back and forth across the platform may look silly, but it offers a glimmer of a cultural change occurring before my eyes. These Japanese whale watchers have spent their entire lives perceiving whales as food products and statistics. Yet with every move they make across the deck, they show themselves shaking loose from a profoundly antiecological worldview.[1]

In other cultures the human devotion to cetaceans is ancient, existing since at least 4000 B.C., when the ancient Finns painted what is probably the earliest known likenesses of whales at several sites along the Arctic coast of the White Sea. These petroglyphs depict shamans communicating with, and in some cases transforming themselves into, beluga whales as a prelude to healing. One petroglyph displays the biography of a hero. He is born; learns to hunt, fashion weapons, kill small game, then moose and bear; finally stops hunting to become an interpreter of animal signs, a rattle maker, and a healer. When he dies, the man travels to the center of a mystic spiral where he meets his god and maker, which is a beluga whale.

For at least as long, Australian Aborigines in the Gulf of Carpentaria were known to celebrate dolphins who brought them fish to eat. The shaman was the tribe's interlocutor, venturing down to the shore carrying two painted, cigar-shaped sticks, which were held underwater and clicked together like claves. The first European observers of this ceremony contended it was the sound, which resembled a dolphin's own clicks, that attracted the animals to shore. The shaman disagreed, pointing out that the clicking served only as a preliminary step that helped him compose his own thoughts. Deep in meditation, he formed mental images, visualizing, from an underwater perspective, dolphins corralling fish to shore. The dolphins complied.

The same respect prompted the Greeks to erect a temple overlooking the sea at Delphi where the Oracle held court, and prophesied the future in consultation with the dolphins who inhabited the ocean just below the site. One variant of the Atlantis myth casts the dolphins as former humans who evolved to live in the sea while their Utopian city-state was being inundated. Another variant describes a government whose legislative chamber included a canal to facilitate attendance by dolphin senators. The concept of a cetacean-based political science is not just the stuff of myth. Jacques Cousteau and John Lilly, among many others, have advocated that all seventy-plus species of cetaceans be granted the political status of a United Nations protectorate. Lilly calls it the cetacean nation.

TAXONOMY

Cetacean biology offers an important reality check to the claims and desires that spring up all along the charged border. Though whales and dolphins live their entire lives in water, they are air-breathing mammals who bear their young alive. Stability and propulsion are provided by flippers as well as by fibrous, horizontally flattened tail flukes. Unlike all other sea mammals, including seals, walrus, manatees, and dugongs, cetaceans possess one or two blowholes on the top of the head to facilitate breathing while swimming.

The earliest-known cetaceans, the archaeocetes, lived fifty million years ago and grew to the size of modern porpoises. The snakelike fossils of another early cetacean called Basilosaurus (king of the reptiles) were originally believed to offer proof of the existence of sea serpents until an astute biologist realized it was a sea mammal and renamed it Zeuglodon (yoke-shaped teeth).[2] Up to seventy feet in length, the creature possessed a distinct beak, a mouth full of pointed teeth, and the body of a very stretched-out dolphin. Eliminate the teeth, foreshorten the body, and Zeuglodon resembles the contemporary but relict cetacean genus *Meso-plodon.*

Scientists recognize two suborders of living cetaceans. The mysticetes, or whalebone whales, have one or two blowholes and possess up to eight hundred plates of baleen rooted in the gums of the upper jaw. The humpbacks that excite the whale watchers at Chichi-jima are mysticetes, as are right whales, bowheads, fin whales, and minkes. A species scarce enough that any documented observation of a free-swimming individual would represent a significant contribution to the scanty knowledge of its behavior, the pygmy right whale is the smallest mysticete at twenty-one feet.[3]

The blue whale is the largest, a creature so rare and yet so enormous that it nearly achieves the mythic status of a dinosaur. Its vulnerability and great size hint of a fate akin to the Tower of Babel, where overreaching architecture and human ambition led to disaster. But key aspects of the biblical metaphor are reversed. Mankind creates Babel; God destroys it. God creates the whale; mankind destroys it. This reverse symmetry is troubling. If the blue whale's current plight were somehow appended onto the allegory of Babel, one might imagine rabbis and preachers explaining the revised tale as mankind's revenge against the God of Abraham for the affronts of Genesis.

To say the blue whale attains great size does not tell the half of it. It's almost twice the length of the nineteenth-century whale ships that sailed to the Pacific from Nantucket. A common image writers use to grant the largest cetaceans a context describes a child crawling unimpeded through the arteries that lead from Leviathan's heart. Even at the flukes, sixty or seventy feet from this six-ton pump, the arteries are still four inches wide. The largest blue whale on record was a female harpooned in the Antarctic in 1928, measuring a hundred and six feet. Her weight was later estimated to be a hundred and sixty-five tons, about equal to twenty-five hundred average-sized women. As a baby, this whale consumed five hundred gallons a day of a fishy-smelling milk richer in fat than cow's cream, resulting in an astonishing weight gain of two hundred and fifty pounds per day during the first few weeks of life. Biologist Roger Payne has noted that because this female was the most prodigious individual of the most prodigious species ever to inhabit the Earth, she was also the biggest living organism for which we have evidence anywhere in the universe.[4]

By all biological and historical measures a remarkable individual, the female succumbed to a fate common to the great whales during the twentieth century. Harpooned, her innards burst from an explosive charge, she probably bled to death. Her gut was inflated with compressed air to keep the carcass afloat. Winched onto a platform, she was measured, flensed, her blubber dumped into a cooker to be boiled for oil. Flesh, entrails, and sinew were separated into separate mounds for processing. The remains, including both that unimaginable skeleton and inscrutable brain, were cast back into the ocean within a few hours of her first sighting by a Norwegian catcher boat. As most everyone now knows, these benign creatures have been systematically slaughtered by humankind until, today, all the largest species of baleen whales reside at the brink of extinction.

The suborder of odontocetes, or toothed whales, includes orcas, dolphins, porpoises, belugas, and sperm whales. As the name foretells, all have teeth, although the number varies dramatically from species to species. The narwhal has only one tooth, evolved into a fantastic spiraling tusk growing to eight feet in length. Some dolphin species have up to two hundred teeth. They all possess a single blowhole located above and behind the eyes, although in the sperm whale it is placed distinctly left of center. Odontocete brains approach—and in a number of cases surpass—the size of the human brain.

Odontocetes are behaviorally quite different from mysticetes. While baleen whales are grazers, their behavior sometimes compared to deer and elk, the toothed whales are hunters, quick-witted social animals whose behavior more closely resembles that of wolves. Most species band together in highly organized groups called pods.

Toothed whales of the genus *Mesoplodon,* or beaked whales, are so rare that some species have never been observed alive, identified only from a few rotting carcasses cast upon remote beaches. The various *Mesoplodon* species range between nine and twenty-four feet in length. They all have beaks like bottlenose dolphins, although none of them possesses the outsize forehead "melon." These seldom-seen whales possess two outsize tusks jutting from their lower jaw, granting them the visage of whales depicted on old sea charts. Biologists postulate that the tusks evolved to keep slippery squid from sliding out of their mouths and as weapons in courtship battles. The triangular tusks of the dense-beaked whale erupt midway down the length the jaw, causing them to protrude above the eye. Those of the strap-toothed whale attain a length of twelve inches, curving over the upper jaw until they form an arch.

Mesoplodon demographics are sketchy. For years, the scamperdown whale was known only from a few strandings in New Zealand waters. Then a single animal washed ashore halfway around the world in the Netherlands. Strandings of another species, the dense-beaked whale, have occurred in New Jersey, Madeira, South Africa, Taiwan, Seychelles, Midway Island, and Queensland, Australia. Despite this far-flung distribution, cetologist D. W. Rice speaks for the vast majority of biologists when he writes: "In the course of whale research cruises in the eastern North Pacific totalling some five hundred days at sea during the past twenty years, I have never identified a mesoplodon."[5]

Even pronunciation of the genus name is uncertain, alternately pronounced mes-a-PLO-don or mes-AWE-plo-don. The species are divided between those with descriptive common names—scamperdown whale, gulfstream whale, deep-crested whale, strap-toothed whale, dense-beaked whale—and those receiving the name of the marine biologist who first identified them (and incidentally providing a roll call of the luminaries of historical cetology): Hubbs whale, Sowerby's whale, Stejneger's whale, True's whale, Hector's whale. Until a stranding in 1980, this last species was known only from skeletal evidence.

The most discouraging story I know of human beings interacting with cetaceans involves a *Mesoplodon*. On a September afternoon in 1957, a cetacean was sighted by boys playing baseball at Osio beach near Tokyo. The whale swam in the shallow, muddy water, appearing as if it was trying to decide to strand. When it finally hit bottom, the boys quit their game and walked down to the water to take a closer look. One might imagine the boys chattering among themselves as they scrutinized the outsize flukes and the flagon-shaped head with its small, pig eyes. Two fan-shaped tusks erupted upward from either side of the mouth, giving the creature the look—not of a *real* whale—but of a mythical sea creature illustrating an antique map. The boys might have stood there a while, in awe and humility over this fifteen-foot-long creature cast up before their feet. Perhaps one boy finally gathered up enough courage to step alongside the creature to run a hand along the silky gray-black skin.

As it was, the boys did none of these things. They ran back to the baseball field, grabbed baseball bats, and bludgeoned the whale to death. Japan's preeminent marine biologist, M. Nishiwaki, was on the scene the next morning. He was astounded to realize that the flattened tusks of the bloody carcass did not agree with those of any known *Mesoplodon*. He later wrote, "I ventured to settle a new species for this specimen," he concluded, "and nominated it as *Mesoplodon ginkgodens*, after the way the fan-shaped teeth—which proved to be the only two that the animal possessed—so closely resembled the leaf of a gingko tree." In the years since that bludgeoning and Nishiwaki's subsequent christening, ten other gingko-toothed whales have been identified by human beings. All were found decomposing on beaches along the Pacific rim.

The smallest toothed whales, the dolphins and porpoises, are grouped together as delphinids. The distinction between the two (and between them and the whales as well) is more a mystery of language than anatomy, which is why explaining it sounds so much like an Abbott and Costello comedy routine. The smaller, blunter-nosed delphinids are usually referred to as porpoises. Their smiling, beak-nosed cousins are dolphins. Some people, including some eminent marine biologists, refer to both groups as porpoises. Others refer to both groups as dolphins. Pilot whales and killer whales are dolphins, and, if accuracy of nomenclature actually mattered, we would probably refer to them as pilot dolphins and killer dolphins. The beluga whale looks and acts as much like a delphinid as any killer whale, but marine biologists do not consider it a delphinid. Size often distinguishes whales from dolphins. The bottlenose *whale* is thirty-five feet long and resembles the bottlenose *dolphin* in all respects but size. Yet the sperm whale also has a miniature cousin, the eight-foot-long *Kogia simus.* But this species is commonly known as the dwarf sperm whale, and never as the sperm dolphin. Physiologically, the sperm whale itself has far more in common with dolphins than it does with any of the other great whales.

Altogether there are forty-three species of delphinids, which are further divided into five subgroups based on shape, habitat, and size. The first subgroup includes the largest dolphins—pseudorcas, orcas, pilot whales, pygmy killer whales, melon-headed dolphins, and grampus. Beakless, they all attain ten feet or more in length. The second subgroup includes the true porpoises. None of them grow longer than eight feet. The smallest, at five feet, is the vaquita, a shy creature that resides only in the upper reaches of the Sea of Cortez, and is fast approaching extinction as an incidental catch of a net fishery targeting sharks and sea bass. The third subgroup includes all the species that are *called* dolphins but that resemble porpoises. None have beaks. The northern right whale dolphin has no dorsal fin. Its flukes are no wider than its body, granting the animal a vague resemblance to an eel (or a miniature Basilosaurus). As might be expected, there is also a southern right whale dolphin.

The next subgroup, the river dolphins, live their entire lives in fresh water. They all have long beaks, outsize forehead melons, tiny eye cavities, and fan-shaped pectorals. Despite the clear family resemblance, their distribution is both exceedingly localized and yet far-flung. The Amazon River dolphin, called *boutu*, is bright pink. Although it is threatened, its body parts are sold in local markets as talismans. Both the Indus River dolphin, *susu*, and the Ganges River dolphin (with no cute nickname) are splendidly adapted to life in muddy water. They are completely blind and are the only cetaceans known to echolocate in two separate beams. The former is on the verge of extinction as a result of habitat loss. The Chinese River dolphin, or *baiji*, once lived in China's largest lake, which fed the Yangtze River. The animal survived the pressure of human population growth for centuries because locals believed the animal descended from a princess who flung herself into the lake long ago. When the river was dammed and the lake silted up, the *baiji* escaped into the Yangtze where it came in contact with people not predisposed to treat it as a princess. Now a valiant international effort is under way to protect it. The so-called Irawaddy River dolphin is not a river dolphin at all, but an oceanic porpoise favoring that river's delta.

The last subgroup contains all the species most people think of when they hear the word *dolphin*. These true dolphins are distinguished by beaks, smiles, low-slung melons, and sharp dorsal fins. Their range is restricted to tropical and temperate waters. The bottlenose dolphin is the largest; the species caught at Iki Island sometimes attained fourteen feet in length. The common dolphin possesses the group's most beautiful markings, with golden hourglasses running along each side. The spotted dolphin is dappled. The striped dolphin has four sumptuous pinstripes that flow from its eyes to its genital slit. To add to the chaos of nomenclature, a popular game fish (mahi mahi) is also called dolphin.

A bottlenose dolphin was clocked swimming fifteen miles per hour, and there are many reports of the species bow riding motorboats at a much faster pace. The Dall porpoise, a small white-and-black look-alike of the orca, with whom it shares Northwest coast waters, is considered the fastest cetacean, capable of bursts of thirty-five miles per hour. Until recently, scientists believed it was physically impossible for delphinids to swim that fast, given the immense resistance of water. The basic hydrodynamic principle of laminar flow explains it. Laminar flow occurs when water moving past a streamlined object is held by the surface of that object; therefore water is flowing against water, not against a solid. It is calculated that a dolphin attaining fifteen knots develops a quarter horsepower to overcome the resistance of water, or about the same power needed by a human being to climb uphill at five miles per hour. Without laminar flow, the same dolphin would need to work four times as hard to attain the same speed.

As the blue whale, the pygmy right whale, the *boutu*, the *susu*, and the vaquita all suggest, many cetacean species are rare and/or endangered. There is also a good chance that species swim in the ocean today that have never been seen by, or at least identified by, human beings. In November 1978, cetologists working the whale grounds off Chile made eight separate sightings of small whales they could not identify. The animals were odontocetes, beakless, twenty feet long, with light-colored heads and dark bodies, traveling in a pod of approximately fifteen animals. The observers noted that the animals resembled *Grampus griseus*, also called Risso's dolphins, although they were at least eight feet longer than any grampus yet identified. Intriguingly, the sketchy details we have of sightings closely match similar unidentified animals observed farther south by a cetologist in 1905.

The sperm whale is the largest odontocete. Whale encyclopedist Richard Ellis notes that this species "comes to mind when the word *whale* is mentioned."[6] The size of this whale's heart is no match for the mighty blue's, nor does its blunt, sausage-shaped face offer much competition against the dolphin's beatific grin. But the species possesses its own remarkable organ, a seventeen-pound brain, five times as large as, and with a far more convoluted neocortex than, the human brain. It is, by far, the largest brain of any creature that has ever inhabited the Earth.

Studies of the dinosaur's sparrow-sized brain cavity suggest that a large brain is not needed to control a large body, and that brain size correlates far more closely with intellect and sensory apparatus. Given that promise, the terms of the sperm whale's intellect remain largely unknown. How do we begin to probe this whale's intellect? The species resides in the deep ocean, rarely drawing close to shore. All we discern of its behavior must be gleaned from what it deigns to show us during the 5 percent of its lifetime when it comes to the surface to take a breath. It was whalers who first observed that females with young and the much larger breeding males make up two distinct social groups. These sexually delineated pods come together only for mating and spend the rest of the year otherwise separated by the distance of oceans.

Some lay whale aficionados speculate with science-fiction abandon that five times the brain indicates five times the mind. If so, our capacity to test the claim may be forever thwarted by a barrier more formidable than this species's pelagic habitat. One corollary of Gödel's theorem stipulates that a smaller processor cannot map the capabilities of a larger processor. In other words, if the sperm whale does possess a fivefold intellect, then the human mind is too puny an instrument to confirm it. Ironically, nothing within the sperm whale's repertoire of behavior can ever verify that the premise is false.

Even if brain size is not a reliable indicator of intelligence, the extent of our own ignorance can be amply demonstrated by the fact that until recently humans related to this potential wisdom keeper as only a repository of oil. A unique oily/waxy substance found in the "case" located in the species's forehead is, more special still, the finest grade of machine oil known to man. Called "spermaceti," "the seed of the cetacean," this fluid was erroneously purported to be the whale's seminal fluid. During the nineteenth century, the hunt for spermaceti subsided only after there were too few whales left to finance more hunts. The "seed of the cetacean" was actually the seed of the Industrial Revolution. Engineers employed it to lubricate many of the new machines that defined that age. The less-exalted whale oil was used in lamps to illuminate the darkness. Today, we find an adequate replacement for spermaceti in a common desert plant known as jojoba.

Prior to feeding, the sperm whale rolls across the surface several times to take a succession of deep breaths, arches its body, lift its flukes high into the air, and starts a steep descent. How deep do they dive? A whale was once caught whose stomach was filled with several freshly consumed, bottom-dwelling sharks at a site with a known depth of 10,476 feet. There are fourteen instances of sperm whale carcasses found wrapped up in transatlantic cables, at depths up to 7,200 feet. To move about in total darkness, toothed whales have developed an echolocation or sonar system based on clicks. In fact, the spermaceti-filled "case" located in the sperm whale's forehead is Nature's most exquisitely sensitive acoustic lens, which is used to focus bursts of echolocation clicks. Spermaceti has been shown to be twice as effective a conductor of sound as the oil from another known echolocator, the bottlenose dolphin.

How does echolocation work? Toothed whales concentrate a series of sound waves (clicks) into a beam that echoes off objects in its path. The distance a click must travel before echoing, as well as the clarity of the echo itself, varies depending on the density of the object: whether it's composed of soft body tissue or air sacs. As in an X ray, bones are opaque. The echo returns to the cetacean where it is received not only by ears, but also by receptors strung out along the lower jaw. The whale's brain is exquisitely adapted to interpret the echoed object, perceiving skeletal structure, three-dimensional shape, internal organs, and movement as easily as you or I see shape. The analogy is fitting because echolocation is to a toothed whale what vision is to a human: the primary source of perception. Tests conducted on captive bottlenose dolphins have determined that animals are able to distinguish the difference between hollow metal marbles and solid metal marbles at a distance of a hundred feet. When clicks strike a fleshy object such as a fish, the sound penetrates directly into the animal. The resultant echo displays a three-dimensional image of fishy shape and density.

Like so much else about cetaceans, echolocation has emerged as a fertile ground for speculation. Claims have been made that orcas can distinguish red objects from green ones, although no one can theorize just how they might achieve this. More plausibly, they can distinguish various metals, which suggests they might be trained to hunt buried treasure. Echolocation is actually four-dimensional; distance and shape are perceived as functions of the time it takes clicks to reach an object, bounce off it, and return. Speculation arises that odontocetes naturally perceive an Einsteinian world that human beings can visit only through a monumental act of intellect fostered by counterintuitive probes with advanced mathematics.

The bulk of sperm whales' diet consists of squid and fish under three feet long. One animal caught off Madeira had four thousand squid mandibles in its stomach. Sperm whales also prey on giant squid, a fact described by whalers who observed their surface battles. In his classic of late-nineteenth-century whaling, *The Cruise of the Cachalot*, Frank Bullen writes:

> A violent commotion in the sea right where the moon's rays were concentrated . . . a very large sperm whale was locked in deadly conflict with a cuttle-fish, or squid almost as large himself, whose interminable tentacles seemed to enlace the whole of his great body. The head of the whale especially seemed a perfect network of writhing arms—naturally, I suppose, for it appeared as if the whale had the tail part of the mollusc in his jaws and, in a business-like methodical way, was sawing through.[7]

Hunting in the eternal darkness of the abyss, the sperm whale echolocates its prey and then zooms in for the kill. What happens next is a matter of some dispute among students of whale behavior. Old-time whalers believed the animals stayed very still, opening their mouths until the lower jaw hung perpendicular to the body, and wiggling their tongue as a lure. According to T. Beale:

> The white roof of its mouth, the tongue and especially the teeth being of a bright glistening white color, must of course present a remarkable appearance, and which seems to be the incitement by which his prey are attracted.[8]

Sensory zoologist John Downer describes sperm whales with such badly disfigured jaws that they could never catch a live prey in this manner, although they are otherwise healthy and well fed. Some biologists explain the discrepancy in terms of stereotypical altruistic behavior observed among many odontocete species. In other words, pod mates are feeding their crippled relation. Downer speculates that muscles lining the spermaceti case are capable of producing massive air pressure, which could conceivably be concentrated into a sonic beam with an intensity approaching 256 decibels. Fish and squid have been killed in minutes by volumes far less potent than this. Downer believes sperm whales aim their sonic weapons and then fire off a few whale-sized cracks and booms. A hunter, even one with a mangled jaw, simply scoops up the dying prey and feeds at its leisure.[9]

Sperm whales may be unique among toothed whales for clicking back and forth to one another, as well as at objects. This practice has sparked a speculation that the species uses echolocation in a social, signaling context, transmitting kinetic images back and forth to one another much as we do with movie cameras, although the three-dimensional signals more closely resemble holograms (actually holosonics) than flat pictures. If true, it implies a spoken language nearly beyond our ability to conceive. Imagine two whales recollecting recent events by transmitting fully fleshed-out scenes to one another through a medium vaguely analogous to the three-dimensional environments found on the holodeck lounge in the *Star Trek* TV series. As anyone familiar with digital audio can attest, acoustic information is a processor- and storage-intensive task. Some bioacousticians hypothesize that the sperm whale's large brain was developed specifically to exploit these sophisticated bioacoustic applications.

CONTACT

One aspect of sperm whale intelligence is certain. The ferocious brute of *Moby Dick* never existed beyond the bloody arena where whalers explode harpoons into the guts of whales as a prelude to rendering body parts into household products. Off Sri Lanka and the Galápagos Islands, female pods have been photographed swimming in subgroups of three and four animals spiraling vertically about a common center, never losing physical contact with one another for hours at a time. The few lucky observers who have witnessed the behavior describe it as a vast gray rose with individual whales as the unfolding petals. At Mexico's Socorro Islands, off the Azores, and near Ogata, Japan, humans are beginning to enter the water to commune one-on-one with sperm whales. These first explorers to the realm of this mysterious being report that Earth's largest predator responds to human beings with gentle affability.

Unlike almost every other species of animal on Earth, the sperm whales—and their toothed-whale kin the orcas, dolphins, pilot whales, and belugas—do not flee our advance. What do they know about us that other species do not know? What do they recognize about us that we do not recognize about ourselves? Could they be aware of the recent change of heart that put them off-limits to the so-called "harvest"? Do they speculate about developing contact with us? Dolphin devotees, especially, insist that delphinids are eager to communicate with human beings, but only in the wild. Underwater recording systems have been built into boats in Tenerife, Vancouver Island, and Bequia, and then used to interact musically with pilot whales, orcas, and bottlenose dolphins. Swimmers also interact with dolphins on a regular basis in many sites around the world, entering the water with a snorkel, a mask, and fins, and then maneuvering into a position that encourages dolphins to approach. Some do it with, and some without, an overarching strategy, although the majority of swimmers insist their pursuit is neither entertainment nor a simple manifestation of intellectual curiosity. Many insist they have established a deep spiritual connection with cetaceans, reporting with sincerity that the nonverbal communication has utterly transformed their lives. In Kealakekua Bay, Hawaii; in the Bahamas; in the Sea of Cortez; and off Mikura Island, southeast of Tokyo, these initiates combine their swims with weeklong workshops led by spiritual leaders who teach them how best to communicate telepathically with dolphins and whales in the sea. Joan Ocean, one of the best known of these guides, describes her teaching this way: "As we communicate with these beings and neighboring realities, we see clearly our role in the unfolding enlightenment of our universe."[10]

Although no one can say for certain why any cetacean species would go out of its way to interact with people, many swimmers speculate that dolphins are evolved beings who know full well the havoc we wreak upon the oceans. Interpreting our enthusiasm to swim with cetaceans as a plea for direction, dolphin devotees portray the charged border as a frontier where the natural and the cultural interpenetrate to uphold the supernatural. This explains another breed of workshop leaders who promise one-on-one communion with whales and dolphins without their clients ever getting their feet wet. In Berlin, Sedona, and Los Angeles, spiritual centers lead group meditations to foster communication with blue whales, orcas, and dolphins via telepathy. Timothy Wyllie sums up the dolphins' motivation this way:

> I had the impression the dolphins were starting to come to terms with the nature of man. They were having to make some very basic adaptations in order to understand us. I saw how they had broadened the base of their capacity to perceive negative "emotional wavefronts" in order to make contact with us.[11]

In *The Call of the Dolphins*, Lana Miller goes a step further, reporting a conversation with a channeled entity who explains the dolphin's role as interplanetary:

> Extraterrestrials had to leave [the Earth] because of fear. The dolphins are perceived as lower life forms—now acting as emissaries. We are non-threatening and when we invite people to come and play and share and open to love, they are more ready to accept that there is intelligence beyond self, love beyond self.[12]

It's not only mystics who grant special powers to dolphins. Swimming with dolphins is claimed to heal the sick, especially people experiencing psychological trauma. In Florida, occupational therapist Patricia St. John has implemented a program whereby autistic children are given the opportunity to swim with captive dolphins. While mainstream observers of the medical phenomenon assert that a proximity to dolphins works its magic by simply distracting patients from their suffering, St. John disagrees, insisting that dolphins possess a genuine power that accelerates a child's vocal and physical development. Not understanding precisely how they achieve this objective, she sometimes relies on the universal term *dolphin healing energy*. David Cole of the AquaThought Foundation believes this energy is so robust that therapists do not necessarily need to use real dolphins to reap its benefits. Insisting that the clinical practice of employing captive animals for healing purposes is anachronistic and cruel—and clearly understanding the benefits of the placebo effect—Cole substitutes flesh-and-blood animals with a *virtual* dolphin swim. The patient enters a flotation tank containing water heated to body temperature and made neutrally buoyant by the addition of Epsom salts. Special goggles show videos of dolphins and whales swimming in the ocean. Headphones play their vocalizations. Cole claims this computer-generated therapy demonstrates a measurable effect on the immune system, specifically balancing the two lobes of the brain through the production of alpha waves. Similar results have been attained in Japan, where patients simply listen to cetacean calls and echolocation through headphones. An unusual incidence of alpha waves is the result, even when the sounds are raucous and dissonant.

The best known healing program is in England where filmmaker Horace Dobbs has created Project Sunflower. For fifteen years, Dobbs has bundled up severely depressed patients into dry suits and then dropped them bodily into the Irish Sea to swim with wild dolphins. He reports that the will to live is strengthened almost immediately. Withdrawn depressives suddenly start to talk again, to smile, to enjoy life. Dobbs concludes: "We may not know yet how to measure whatever it is that dolphins radiate, but the evidence for its existence is becoming insurmountable."[13]

Whatever it is these so-called "small, toothed whales" radiate, the other cetaceans seem to possess it, more or less, as well. We admire them all, not only for their playful behavior and intellectual potential, and not only for the vast proportions of certain species and the auric energies reputed to emanate from others, but for the empowering gifts they seem to bequeath to just about everyone who experiences them. Cetaceans swim through our cumulative field of vision as mysterious familiars, untamed wisdom givers who encompass the human yearning to behold the sacred in the wild. Individually, we relate to them not only as species and animals, but as beings, individuals, healers, shamans, teachers. Cumulatively, we regard them as a tribe, a race, a nation, a dream. Many fans conclude that cetaceans are as close as we may ever get to experiencing relations with an alien intelligence.

In so many ways the charged border emerges as a luminous crack between worldviews—a place where mystics, biologists, environmentalists, filmmakers, retailers, historians, musicians, shamans, tourists, fishermen, mythologists, and children gaze upon the same animal with the same basic set of human eyes, and yet take away entirely different meanings from the experience. This also explains the lush diversity of literature on the subject. Cetaceans are the focus of innumerable texts of natural history, ID, and biology; books of art; coffee-table books of photographs; epic poems; stories of whale watching; books of mysticism and songs; histories of whaling and antiwhaling, intelligence, acoustics, and interspecies communication. There are books about individual cetaceans like Flipper in Hollywood and Opo in New Zealand. And, of course, there's *Moby Dick.*

That not one book recognizes a common center to all this fervid activity may bespeak a failure in human relations. In my experience, few whale professionals show much interest in working alongside members of other disciplines, let alone in promoting them. Scientists work with scientists and *occasionally* with environmentalists. But they disavow mystics for promoting intuitive views. Mystics likewise wince to consider whalers, who battle environmentalists, who fight oceanarium trainers, who roll their eyes at musicians seeking a wild middle ground of communication. This book takes the view that every conviction adds to our understanding of why whales have such a hold on us. By illuminating the context of our beliefs, I hope to set the relationship between cetaceans and people on its right course. I suspect that focusing on the border is the only way to answer the question of whether the cetaceans achieve their hold on us through conscious action, in effect manipulating our dreams about them. Or do we simply grant them powers they neither seek nor comprehend?

A fresh understanding will lead to better ways to close the gap that lies between admiration and protection of cetaceans. Whalers in Japan and Norway still head out to sea every year. Several Indian tribes in the Pacific Northwest insist upon resurrecting hundred-year-old treaties that give them the right to hunt whales. Fishing fleets entangle and lacerate endangered humpbacks, fins, and right whales in several places in the Northern Hemisphere. Once common beluga whales in eastern Canada are on the verge of extinction from the effects of chemical run-off in tributaries of the Saint Lawrence River. Tuna fishermen in the tropical eastern Pacific have "incidentally" drowned *millions* of spinner dolphins in their nets as a matter of methodology, rationalizing the slaughter as the price of doing business. The oceanarium industry in a dozen countries trumpets the intellectual talents of dolphins but treats them as caged clowns. In Hawaii, the U.S. military bounces injurious levels of sound off breeding humpbacks to test submarine tracking capabilities.

Roger Payne has suggested that the songs of humpback whales are a form of epic poetry. Beluga scientist Becky Kjare has written that the melodic vocalizations of beluga whales may be the most complex example we have of a nonhuman language. But such testimony, while inspiring, remains anomalous within mainstream science. By habit, if not always by logic, the majority of biologists still reject signs of cetacean awareness as anthropomorphic, insinuating that *only* humans can truly be self-aware. This construct of human preeminence is a false and dangerous god. Certainly, we are an ingenious species. We build complex machines, engage in abstract discussions. But we utilize only 10 percent of our brain capacity. Perhaps the other 90 percent is awaiting our resolve to step beyond the false perception of our own importance.

This is not to infer, as some in the New Age movement do, that cetaceans are waiting patiently to provide us with answers to our most vexing problems. The world is a complex place. Any single factor proposed to explain either the problems we face or the future we hope for is usually simplistic and always risky. Nonetheless, mystics hold as key a piece of information about the charged border as do scientists, environmentalists, artists, and all the other people who have ever interacted with cetaceans. Aboriginal hunters and Japanese whalers also hold a piece. By granting each of them a voice, this book hopes to illuminate the relationship we have with cetaceans, with emphasis placed on the chasm separating admiration from protection.

Like the whale watchers at Chichi-jima, I have traveled my own switch-backing road to the charged border. I am a musician trained in theater and dance, and I spent much of my twenties immersed in the avant-garde "new music" scene that blossomed in the San Francisco Bay area during the 1970s. One winter I headed south to Mexico, and ended up studying native songs in San Cristóbal de las Casas near the Guatemalan border. Every morning I played a native flute for an hour in my backyard. Whenever I hit a certain high note, the tom turkey next door let out a resounding gobble. I ventured over to meet him. There he stood near the back door, fat and brown, red wattles drooped over his nose, a multicolored tail spread as wide as a Spanish fan. When I played my song, he shook his wings before dropping them right into the dirt, raising a small cloud of dust, advancing on me like a flamenco dancer, four steps forward followed by four steps back. Every so often, the red wattles turned deep blue, then back to red again. And every single time I hit a high note, the turkey let out a solitary gobble.

Over the next month, I spent an hour a day inventing strange songs with that turkey, and deciphering the mechanical relationship between loud volume, high pitch, and the turkey's instinct to gobble. It was fun and easy to program his response into any song by accentuating certain notes: ta, ta, ta, TA (gobble, gobble, gobble). The turkey's gobble is one part of a general alarm system evolved over eons to protect a brood from predation. Only the toms gobble, suggesting that the sound warns other males not to intrude on territory. When thunder rumbled, or when a truck backfired, the turkey gobbled no less emphatically than he did in response to my own stimulus. If I accented too many notes in succession, hoping for a crescendo of gobbles, the turkey reached his breaking point and ran.

Our jam session may have been interspecies music, but it was not precisely interspecies communication. Music involves a sharing of tones, harmonies, and rhythms during a set duration of time. Synchrony is the key ingredient, which I was able to coax from the turkey by prodding his instinct to gobble. Communication insists that each party understand the other's drift. It pleads for dialogue, a mutual give and take of shared meaning. Was I communicating with my plump friend? I was skeptical. There was, however, a level of creative interaction I could not so logically explain away. The bird started sitting beside the fence waiting for me to arrive. I got down in the dirt to look him in the eye and eventually developed a sensitivity to his moods; shared feelings about the weather; a dislike of quick movement, dissonance, and abrupt change. I learned how to operate on turkey time, how to distinguish between domination and equanimity, control and harmony. By these tools I was transformed. The turkey and I became friends.

John Cage once wrote that music is "anything you can get away with." On that advice I journeyed back to San Francisco to successfully lobby the Pacifica Radio Network to sponsor a two-hour piece of radio music for Thanksgiving day entitled: "Music to Eat Thanksgiving Dinner By." The session was held at a farm where I experienced the breathtaking phenomenon of three hundred tom turkeys answering a trigger note in unison. The show was a hit. Commissions for music with other species arrived at my door. Over the next three years I recorded myself playing harmonica with bobwhites along the Cuyahoga River in northern Ohio. I spent a week thumping a drum with kangaroo rats in Death Valley and another week blowing a Japanese *shakuhachi* (bamboo flute) with a wolf pack at a caged-in refuge near Pyramid Lake in eastern California. In 1975, I spent a month playing music with spinner dolphins off a beach in Hawaii. As the projects grew in scope, I founded a nonprofit organization, Interspecies Communication, Inc., to provide funding and expand the circle of participants. A growing expertise with underwater acoustics and media events led directly to my two years' involvement at Iki Island. The Killing Cove taught me firsthand that Nature is dying.

Because a critical mass of people do not yet comprehend the urgency of the catastrophe, I have pledged my work to help transform human perceptions toward life on Earth. How does an artist do that? Transforming cultural perceptions about the largest issues in our lives—God, the individual, war, women, technology, nature—has always been a fundamental purpose of art. Someone once said that the environmental crisis is a crisis in human perception. If it's true, then artists play a key role in persuading the collective human sensibility to honor nature. Certainly, saving the world is a greater challenge than any individual, interest group, or country can hope to accomplish alone. But if change is to occur, we all, each in our own small way, need to make the commitment to it and to start somewhere.

Over the past twenty-five years I have played music with cetacean species on four oceans. My own unique brand of interspecies communication is not science but a conceptual art project. Science thrives on the careful replication of data. It seeks absolute answers, best expressed through the language of mathematics. Its tools are objectivity, observation, rigor, skepticism. By contrast, my music with whales honors the axiom that there can be no absolute meaning in a work of art because everyone who experiences it gets to discover their own meaning. The process thrives on subjectivity, participation, and improvisation.

That rare bird known as the interspecies musician learns to dig deep into the elements of musical grammar—melody, harmony, timing, rhythm, call, and response—to attain a real-time flow in which both the musicians and the listeners are mutually immersed. We meet the animal halfway, two species willing to play in the same band, if but for a moment. The symbolism of this mutable bond is at least as powerful as the music produced. Interspecies music flirts with myth, perception, environmental activism, cognitive science, shamanism, underwater acoustics, and the edges of art as much as it flirts with whales. It frolics with our basic conception of what it means to be both human and/or animal.

I am neither the Pied Piper nor Rachmaninoff. Whatever success I attain is neither a function of purported supernatural skill nor musical virtuosity. It's more like naive enthusiasm mixed with a generous measure of perseverance. Although many people tell me that interspecies music seems *possible*, I remain one of the few people in the world who practices it regularly. If something memorable occurs, a tape recorder or a video camera may get turned on to document the event. If a whale draws near, that's terrific. If it chooses to retreat, the performance remains worthwhile. I have been known, upon occasion, to play any of several musical instruments that float or sink and generate their sounds directly into the water. Unfortunately, the human ear is not constructed to hear sound underwater so swimming among cetaceans has never been my preferred means of interaction. The few acoustic instruments at one's disposal are almost exclusively percussive.

Since most delphinid species vocalize in a range far above the high limit of human hearing, I favor playing with the larger cetaceans like orcas and humpbacks whose vocalizations are accessible to the human ear. Today, I often rely on a one-of-a-kind underwater sound system to transmit sounds beneath the surface and receive the response back from the whales. The electric guitar has long been my instrument of choice. Over the years I have produced musical communication projects with fin whales, humpbacks, gray whales, belugas, orcas, pseudorcas, pilot whales, blue whales, as well as several different dolphin species.

3   THE LURE OF THE
MEGAFAUNA

Humanists are the shamans of the intellectual tribe, wise men who interpret knowledge and transmit the folklore, rituals, and sacred texts. Scientists are the scouts and hunters. No one rewards a scientist for what he knows. Nobel Prizes and other trophies are bestowed for the new facts and theories he brings home to the tribe.[1]
                                                        —EDWARD O. WILSON

So many whales. Twenty within a quarter mile of the *Lamarck.* They exhale with the force of mortar fire, a sound so convincing I imagine Vietnam vets breaking out in a cold sweat. About half are feeding; they surface only to breathe, propelling themselves through the water in a succession of slow, sliding rolls. After every fourth or fifth roll, these feeders lift their flukes vertically in preparation for a dive beneath the still waters of Alaska's Claiborne Reach. The underside of each whale's flukes displays a striking black-and-white Rorschach pattern as unique as a human fingerprint and cataloged by researchers to identify individual whales. The designs are mostly symmetrical, although some vary extravagantly from side to side. They incorporate dots, jagged borders, starbursts, rings, spirals. Slashes ambling across a field of wobbly lines remind me of musical notation.

Whale biologists have known about the distinctiveness of humpback fluke markings at least since the 1920s, although using the imprints to catalog both individuals and migratory behavior was not exploited until the cessation of humpback whaling in the 1970s. Before then, marine biologists gathered information about humpbacks by booking passage on a whaling ship. They shot numbered tags into a living whale's flesh, which were eventually retrieved by other whalers. No one can say how many tags were shot, although two thousand of them were recovered from torn-up animals during the years that preceded the general acceptance of identification by fluke pattern. Today, biologists also identify orcas by a similar technique that focuses on the shape of their white saddle patches and nicks in their dorsal fins.

A split second before each whale disappears beneath the surface of the reach, it tenses a moment, gracefully tucking its fifteen-foot-wide flukes inward and back, as if waving to all of us aboard the *Lamarck*. What does the motion express? In fact, I am full of theories today, and imagine the tuck as the outward sign of a slow-motion orgasm humpback whales attain when they surrender to the sensuous underwater realm. If there's any truth to it, how easy it is to comprehend why the whale's ancestors fled the land sixty million years ago. The behavioral scientist standing next to me, Steve Templor, watches intently as I wave my wrist and hand like a Balinese dancer in imperfect emulation of the tuck. He takes off his gray knit cap to display white-blond hair curling wildly down his neck before it disappears below the collar of his flannel jacket. He strokes a pink bald spot on top. "It's a neat gesture, isn't it?"

"It seems orgasmic."

He rolls his eyes, blows air over his lips. "When it gets really windy out here, I've seen whales hold their flukes aloft and actually sail down the reach." He pauses a moment to let the image settle in, but I am too involved watching the whales. "It has nothing to do with an orgasm," he adds. "When a whale tucks, laminar flow alters accordingly. Speed and efficiency of movement are the rewards, offering a clear evolutionary advantage." I smile at Steve and recall how little sleep I got last night lying in a clammy sleeping bag on a lumpy bunk in a windowless cabin cluttered with greasy ropes and stinky tarps. I wouldn't think there'd be any evolutionary advantage to that, except here I am; it's morning, and I'm on deck again, looking at whales and feeling very much alive.

Evolutionary advantage is Steve's most beloved term, meant to explain the best, if not the only, reason an animal is wont to achieve anything in this world. Any organism, whether a paramecium or a whale, that turns nonadvantageous in its deportment stands a good chance of getting cut from the team of nature. That's why animals don't indulge in whimsy, why they don't often fall on self-destructive behavior. Steve's rap is confident, so it's hard to disagree with his point of view, although it makes me worry that so many artists, my own saints and mentors, are mostly second-rate losers in the grand Darwinian scheme. Jackson Pollack, Jack Kerouac, Edgar Allan Poe, Jimi Hendrix, they all self-destructed by pushing too hard against the edges of beauty. I am willing to concede Steve's point that *most* animal species do not possess the imagination to try out new behaviors on a whim. But individuals within a few species can be creative and eccentric, expressing aesthetic and even moral prerogatives. It is recorded that, at the turn of the century in Montana, a lone wolf collected all the leg-hold traps off a trail and laid them into a neat pile, which he promptly marked with his feces. His act mostly saved the other predators—coyotes, lynx, bear—who also used the trail.[2] What advantage, besides a purist's appreciation of Kantian ethics, or perhaps an intellectual foreboding about the politics of extinction, could a wolf be demonstrating by saving other predator species inhabiting his realm?

Organisms are not merely survival mechanisms. Evolution cannot precisely establish why elephants weep over the body of a dead mate. No advantageous reason explains why certain female dolphins push their stillborns in front of them for days and weeks until the fetus rots. And others never do that. Steve nods, then tells me of an experiment in which researchers exposed fruit fly embryos to X rays and found that some of the flies wound up with four wings instead of two. But these so-called genetic mutations were just as commonly replicated by exposing embryos to an environmental stress like heat. My vague stare indicates to Steve that I have no idea what he is talking about. "I'm simply agreeing with your point that genes aren't the only arbiter of evolutionary change." I smile brightly. Just when I've pegged Steve as an old-school reductionist, he shows me his hard line has soft edges.

Calling on the logic of Occam's Razor, Steve assures me that, all other things being equal, the simplest explanation usually suffices. Consider, for example, the question of why humpback whales leap clear out of the water in the act we call *breaching*. Whales breach primarily to rid themselves of parasites. Barnacles and whale lice irritate the whale's skin. Breaching dislodges a few. Satisfied with this explanation, Steve has a hard time entertaining my layman's hunch that they may breach for something as loaded down with psychological implication as "no special reason." Enjoyment? No, he answers, munching through a stack of crackers. Enjoyment is too nondescript, nearly anthropomorphic in its implications. Trying to catch him at his game, I offer the opinion that they breach for the same reason young men stay after school to don shorts and leap over bars in an activity called track and field. It's athletic, fun. "Ah," Steve counters. "Caught ya! The very best leapers later do shoe endorsements. A definite evolutionary advantage."

"What about right whales who are sometimes seen draping seaweed over their blowholes during mating season? It almost looks like a fashion statement."

He raises a finger to his nostril, then grins like the Cheshire cat. "The skin around a whale's blowhole is richly endowed with nerves.[3] I believe seaweed draping occurs primarily at mating time. Put it together. It's foreplay. I can think of several analogies with human behavior. Remember that presidential consultant who got caught sucking his girlfriend's toes?" We return to watching the humpbacks. I note the ten-foot-wide upwellings of water spaced twenty feet apart trailing away from our starboard side, and made by a humpback surging its flukes up and down twenty feet below the surface. Steve is still thinking about right whales. "Seaweed draping is a tactile experience, not unlike getting a massage. Massage reduces stress, which we know causes cancer in humans. Did you know that no whale species has ever been documented with cancer? That includes thousands of specimens examined by the whaling industry."

Steve's inquisitive eyes dart about my face as if some squint or twitch might help him discern my next attempt at finding an exception to his rule. I give it one more try, bring up a subject that stymies every whale scientist I know. "I once saw a pod of pilot whales follow a sick, disoriented family member onto a beach. Why do the healthy animals do that when the result is death for all of them? Is stranding simply a mistake? Bad navigating? Or could it be some kind of a conscious act, maybe a ceremony or a sacrifice to the god of pilot whales?"

Steve chooses his words carefully, demonstrating the creative scientist's inclination to consider every possibility. "I'm willing to entertain your hypothesis that some strandings exhibit a ritual element. The species that strand most—sperm whales, pilot whales, pseudorcas—do have the largest brains. These are highly evolved social beings whose behavior reflects their sentience. We also need to acknowledge that large-brained toothed whales often manifest altruistic behavior. For the most part, this altruism serves them exceedingly well. Sick animals who have trouble breathing get buoyed up before they drown. It's the only way they'd have a chance to heal. But once in a while, as in a stranding, altruism defeats them. It does good, then it does bad. It's like war among humans, which you can logically argue reduces population stress by killing off all the breeding males. The benefits of altruism probably outweigh the strandings, although the former occurs out on the ocean so we never get to see it. The latter happens on beaches so we always see it."

Our whale dreams may be different, but Steve and I thoroughly enjoy exploring our disagreements about the behavior of both the cetaceans and the human beings who gravitate to them. I do not agree with him that observing whales through binoculars and recording the results in a statistical database is the most perceptive way to study cetaceans. Compressing one's observations into neat blueprints of behavior could just as easily produce a description of the Earth that exists, not so much in nature as in the twentieth-century human mind. A whale abruptly breaks the surface right beside the boat, blows twenty feet in the air. The mist hangs there, then slowly disperses. Five seconds later traces of it patter lightly against my cheeks. I close my eyes to receive the whale's breath, inhaling deeply to take the vapors into my own lungs, but I'm nearly bowled over by the heavy smell of rotten fish permeating the air. "I thought I told you guys to start using mouthwash!" Steve yells dryly toward the water.

Steve regards my Gaian view—Nature as a network of conscious, communicating beings—as carrying too much cultural baggage for him to swallow whole. He agrees with the basic premise of the Gaia hypothesis as formulated by chemist James Lovelock: that there is some organic mechanism that has regulated the chemical composition of the Earth's atmosphere for eons. But the common lay interpretation of the Gaia hypothesis, which describes Nature as a mindful overseer who has wired all life forms into an organic version of AT&T, he rejects as a naive fallacy. Granted, it makes a nice metaphor. But nature is neither a body politic, nor a cauldron where emotions, languages, and aspirations bubble and coalesce.

Steve sometimes takes a hard stance only to shake me out of my flabby thought patterns. When I ask him about the meaning of play, he answers that baby animals do not play to express joy. Play is overwhelmingly utilitarian. When I insist that play includes delight, he shrugs his shoulders. "Whether you call it play or delight or joy, it still helps a baby animal strengthen muscles and sharpen agility." I ask him to imagine a Gaian interpretation of evolution. He answers that an ecosystem may be considered a kind of network. But evolution, per se, is not a network, it is not even much *like* a network. It is a deterministic progression, an ongoing series of corrections, formative accidents, a hierarchy. I ask him about humpback creativity. He answers that the fluke tuck only *seems* artful because the observer of the phenomenon, namely me, possesses a concept of aesthetics that includes grace. Evolutionary advantage knows nothing of artfulness, which means that whales know nothing of artfulness either. Certainly, they are more self-aware than classic biology warrants, but they are still puppets to Charles Darwin's holy writ.

Half the humpback whales strewn across the still waters are feeding. The other half are napping. These animals bob on the surface like Brobdingnagian shoes; the warts and bumps that rise along their snouts are lug soles, reflecting the light of the occluded sun. Biologists theorize that cetaceans sleep by halves. Part of the brain dozes while the other part stays semialert. Sleeping in this manner is deemed a necessity for any creature that breathes consciously. It explains why whales don't slip beneath some terminal wave every time they nod off, playing out a classic line from the old blues tune:

> *If the river was whisky and I was a diving duck,*
> *I'd dive to the bottom and never come up.*

I believe sleeping by halves is only a favored theory, an extrapolation at best, and hardly the truth of the matter. I nag Steve to acknowledge that the theory is actually just a guess. How could it be anything else but a guess? We don't even know how humans sleep. If whales sleep by halves, the literature demonstrates over and over again that the awake half does not do a very good job at alerting the animal to imminent threats. There are many documented accounts of ships hitting and killing prostrate sperm whales who showed no evasive response to the noise of a diesel engine bearing down on them. What biologists actually observe is whales lying horizontally on the surface with their eyes closed, generally immobile, but constantly twitching their pectoral fins to keep their blowholes upright. Humans don't sleep by halves, although we do sleep horizontally with our eyes closed, constantly twitching our muscles to keep the blood flowing in our extremities. But E. O. Wilson got it right when he wrote that biologists are the scouts and hunters who bring back knowledge to the tribe. The result is that children all over the world are taught the knowledge that whales sleep by halves. Steve listens intently to my argument, stares at me with his piercing light blue eyes, nods when I finish, then savagely deflates my enthusiasm by agreeing with me. "You're absolutely right. It's only a guess."

My own guess about cetacean sleep seems just as plausible, no more uncertain. A whale prepares for sleep by constricting the blood flow to its skin and blubber, permitting the cold of the water to seep into its body core by degrees. This process slows down the animal's metabolism in stages. Sleep is not an either/or proposition—conscious or unconscious— but a series of precisely controlled intermediary states between deep sleep and wide awake. One favored stage allows the animal to rest horizontally with its eyes closed while remaining attentive to breathing. Ladybugs attain a deeper variant of the same stasis when gardeners place them in a refrigerator, sometimes for months, to keep them immobile until aphid season. The opposite metabolic effect could conceivably occur whenever whales breach. Being enveloped by warm air for even a few seconds might provide a humpback with a literal pick-me-up. Breaching many times in succession could bring on a kind of amphetamine high. A whale who breaches too often might even get addicted.

When I uncork my latest theory for Steve, he answers curtly, "You've stuck in too many *coulds* and *mights*. If you want to play science, you've got to work harder to eliminate the subjunctive tense. When you nail it down, let me know."

I am annoyed by his answer and counter that I am not trying to play science, but merely suggesting an alternate hypothesis for a behavior everyone agrees is inscrutable. He nods once, then ends the conversation by placing the binoculars tight against his eyes. I am left feeling that scientists treat their own guesses as hypotheses, and the guesses of everybody else as so much blather. Amplify this bias by an entire culture that treats the scientific method as the only road to truth, and one understands why so much traditional knowledge has been lost, why so many indigenous cultures have been marginalized. Albert Einstein defends the bias when he writes that "theory allows us [us, meaning physicists] to see the facts." I prefer playwrights Alfred Jarry and Eugene Ionescu, who declared that the laws of science are not laws but exceptions that occur more frequently than others, and should be no more revered than the laws of art or language. Of course, some laws are more plausible than others.

Steve is a biologist, but also a natural philosopher who perceives animals and ecosystems as other nations, deserving of all the considerations and conduct we humans reserve for one another. He is willing to entertain the idea that the scientific quest is a construction, in historian George Johnson's words, "a man-made edifice that is historical, not timeless, not about truth with a capital T—just one of many alternative ways to carve up the world."[4] Physicists construct their subatomic world as a house of cards composed of neutrons, quarks, strong and weak forces that no one has ever seen, and that exist only in a mathematics invented by human beings for the specific purpose of perceiving what is imperceptible. As the theory of sleeping by halves demonstrates, the same house of cards is alive and well in cetacean science.

We both scan the water. All twenty whales are in the process of diving. Although most of them lift their flukes high to give us another demonstration of the tuck, a few simply vanish when we blink, dropping beneath the dark waters of Claiborne Reach without a sound. Steve drops the binoculars, turns to me, whispers, "They're on the move." When I spot them again they're a quarter mile off the bow, traveling away from the boat. More from habit than need, he places the binoculars back to his eyes, then just as quickly takes them away, looks right at them, frowns, and hangs them on a hook beside the wheel. His love/hate relationship with the binoculars reminds me of a man who wishes to quit smoking but keeps lighting up cigarettes unconsciously.

"It looks like a family of whales, wouldn't you say?"

"No, I don't think so; there's no cohesiveness or loyalty to this group. Today, these twenty animals are content to spend time together. Tomorrow we'll see some of them with different whales. Others might swim a hundred miles before they stop again."

Steve turns his gaze onto the white-blue haze of a distant glacier, then offers his own example of the house of cards. It spotlights John Lilly, a researcher who has long been the whipping boy of orthodox whale scientists. Lilly spent many years trying to devise a way to communicate with bottlenose dolphins, who vocalize most of their whistles in frequencies inaudible to the human ear. As a prelude to the far more daunting task of talking to them, Lilly first needed to figure out a way simply to hear them. To do so, he relied on computer gear that essentially transposed the inaudible whistles into frequencies accessible to the human ear. But what was the point, Steve asks, of relying upon a machine to provide an imprecise translation of dolphin whistles when the interface was already so inscrutable? Did Lilly end up communicating to dolphins or to Apple computers?

Do whales sleep by halves? Is breaching a drug?

I propose to Steve that, as breaching is a whale drug, so science is a human drug, an antidepressant that helps our species alleviate some of the fear we all feel about living in a world of cruel mystery. Like any other mood attenuator, science constantly plays havoc with our perceptions, presenting hunches as facts, maps as territories, while decreasing our ability to honor the presence of mystery. If the physicists are correct, if there are parallel universes to our own, worlds where we go about our day just as we do now but in skewed circumstances—where an hour is only half an hour and the substance of dreams and waking are somehow reversed—perhaps a parallel science exists in one of those worlds that cherishes and encourages mystery in direct opposition to the standard Earth model that confronts mystery only as a puzzle demanding solution. Seeking a solution for every mystery, some researchers end up perceiving nature as the mother lode of data, which they collect and edit for publication in what amounts to a great almanac that informs our current perception about life on Earth. So much for Wilson's romance of scouts and hunters.

Steve laughs to hear me so high on my soapbox. "Okay, okay," he says, pumping his palms like Rodney Dangerfield. "I have two things to say in response. First, as far as I'm concerned, you can bash scientists all you like. Too many of them are aimless for the same reason there are too many aimless lawyers. Both jobs are stimulating. Both carry prestige. Both pay well. Both uphold an arcane system of knowledge created for service, although practitioners too often interpret it as a base of power. Since corrupting the law will land you in jail while corrupting truth just turns you arrogant, power seduces scientists even easier than it corrupts lawyers. Most biologists I know don't seem to care that information pollutes. They treat their data as if it were a synonym for goodness." Steve pauses, shakes two fingers in my direction. "Second, I insist you show more respect for biology. It's the best tool human beings have ever devised for understanding the workings of the natural world."

The whales vanish into a fog that drapes over the sheer basalt cliffs of a group of islets that loom in the middle of the reach. A dull yellow sun pierces the haze, turning the air the color of custard and reflecting a shard of light off the shiny back of one straggling animal. I hear the blows in pairs, "*pfoo, pfoo,*" the first one from a whale, the second one an echo glancing off a steep cliff of one of the islets. Finally, that, too, disappears, replaced by a silence so absolute the whine of my own nerves rings in my ears. Then I hear one more blow, although the rich sonorities are reduced to a thud from a half-recalled dream. Fifteen minutes later, still standing beside Steve at the wheel, I hear another blow. "Sometimes, the sound doesn't go away for days and days at a time," he comments wistfully.

I climb down to the main deck and locate a stout drop line to try my hand at fishing. In these waters, catching dinner is as predictable as a trip to a supermarket. A few minutes later, helping me haul a twenty-pound halibut over the stern, Steve turns to me with an impish grin. "You know, whale charisma *is* quantifiable. We measure it as the ratio between the number of biologists studying whales over the number of biologists studying flatfish. It remains steady at about a hundred to one."

Steve's research foundation owns the fifty-foot motor yacht the

Lamarck, named after Jean-Baptiste Lamarck, one of the foremost natu-ralists of the late eighteenth century. Lamarck is best known today for a pre-Darwinian theory of evolution, upheld during his own lifetime, based on the idea that acquired characteristics can be inherited. When a plant with robust leaves and large seed heads is grown in poor soil it is apt to put out smaller leaves and just a few seeds. This alteration is called an acquired characteristic. If, over a few generations, the plant starts to encode these small leaves and few seeds into its genetics, this is called Lamarckian inheritance. Today, most biologists dismiss Lamarck's theory. Yet despite Lamarck's quaintness, some evolutionary issues make better sense explained in his terms than in Darwin's. One well-known example focuses on the case of the camel's knees. The camel has evolved calluses where the skin is ordinarily subject to abrasion when the animal kneels. Neo-Darwinists assert that the calluses are a genetic mutation that just hap-pened to produce calluses in the right place; the mutant gene "for" knee pads was favored by natural selection because of the advantage it gave camels born with pads.[5] Steve is among the small minority of free-thinking biologists who aren't so sure. Common sense suggests that the calluses are acquired characteristics that eventually got coded into the genes. Steve chafes to hear his colleagues rant that Lamarck has to be wrong because Saint Darwin is always right. He named his boat after this evolutionary heretic to remind himself and his peers of the humbling incongruities of their chosen path.

Steve was recently granted a federal research permit by the U.S. Marine Mammal Protection Agency granting him unique authority to harass whales. This he does occasionally, but not enough to make me wish I was sailing some other ocean watching somebody else's whales. I might feel different if I had been aboard the *Lamarck* three weeks ago when he used a crossbow to shoot quarter-inch-wide cookie-cutter darts into the flesh of the humpbacks. "It was an experiment; although, granted, it was nasty work," Steve assures me. "But I seriously doubt the whales feel more than a pinprick, if even that. It's not much more than a burr that gets evicted from the skin after a single moment's irritation." This description causes me to lift a single eyebrow and wonder why biologists, who otherwise pride themselves in not making unsubstantiated statements about animal behavior, so often treat their own aggressive tactics as a nonissue when it serves their research. Granted, there's a lot at stake. Darting is *the* happening field within whale biology. It has its specialists, an entire line of radio collars that get stuck to whale flesh for days or weeks at a time, and sophisticated machinery costing tens of thousands of dollars that analyze the samples.

I am discouraged that Steve treats my own view—that a dart "probably pisses the shit out of a whale"—as the rant of a sentimentalist who insists that the dignity of whales overrides any information we gather about them. In my view, the darting of whales displays science at its most arrogant. Our difference of opinion does not go away. A day after Steve's pinprick pronouncement, I find myself bringing up the subject again. A toothy grin peaks through a droopy blond mustache that conceals his upper lip. He confesses that the particular whale he shot spent the rest of the afternoon at the back of the pack, as far from the boat as physically possible. "That whale never once flung its flukes high into the air before diving."

"So what do you conclude? Was the whale unhappy about being a target?"

"Pro-o-obably," he answers, drawing out the syllables. "But that's just a hypothesis."

"Forget your hypothesis. Did you feel the dart bothered the whale or didn't you?" By pleading for emotion, I realize I may have given him a professional out.

"Pro-o-obably," he answers, a hint of glumness infecting his tone. "But it has to be balanced by the fact that genetic sampling is a valuable procedure."

"Valuable?"

Steve laughs tentatively, shakes his head to recognize I am on the verge of catching him. "Well, yeah. Genetic samples can show us how these humpbacks are related to one another. Or if it's an environmental reason you want, skin samples tell us what toxins lurk in the flesh."

During my stint on the *Lamarck,* Steve will bring up the subject of darting several more times. His comments run the gamut. Sometimes he renounces the practice as an abomination. Vows never to do it again.

Other times, he restates his belief in the ultimate value of the procedure. I conclude that my probing dart may not be so easily evicted from his own flesh as the one he shot into the hide of an agitated humpback. The next morning it is raining hard; the two of us sit on the bridge dressed in Gore-Tex, munching through our bowls of soggy Kellogg's Special K, and cruising through a choppy black sea littered with kelp fronds. Steve asks me if a nonscientist can possibly judge the value of scientific procedures. I turn the question inside out. Are scientists fit to judge the value of scientific procedures? He laughs heartily, making it clear he is not attached to darting. But before he can respond, he jumps off his seat to point off the port side at six Steller's sea lions formed into a perfect hexagon. Each one holds its right flippers high in the air. Steve pushes the throttle into neutral and turns off the engine. He grabs his video camera to document this bizarre formation of fifteen-hundred-pound "sea grizzlies," as he refers to them. We pass a bar of semisweet chocolate between us and soon forget we were ever engaged in a meaningful discussion. "So what do you think?" I ask him. "Are they sailing? Is it synchronized swimming?"

"It's wonderful," he responds, deeply satisfied to witness and videotape such an eccentric behavior. "It's social bonding of some kind. Notice that they're rotating slowly around a center point, but they've kept the same, precise six-sided symmetry for over ten minutes. From straight above, it must look just like a snowflake. And you know what? With this ten-knot wind, they really could be sailing." He puts down his camera, stares at me with a radiant smile, and, without another word, retreats below to turn the engine back on.

An hour later, we are in the middle of the channel surrounded by twelve humpbacks. One animal at the back of the pack starts a maneuver called "spyhopping," heaving its head and pleated throat twenty feet clear of the water to survey the air world. The whale is still spyhopping half an hour later. It has moved to within two hundred feet of the *Lamarck*, and peers intently at Steve and I, who stand at eye level on the bridge. When it falls back into the water, its loose throat sags, showing off the inside of the pleats, which are as pink as a Louise Odier rose. These pleats expand with seawater when the whale opens its mouth to feed, and categorize the humpback as a *rorqual*, a designation that places it among the blue whales, the fins, the seis, Bryde's whales, and minkes; and distinct from the baleen whales without pleats—the grays, rights, and bowheads. While all the other rorquals reside in the genus *Balaenoptera*, and possess the same basic body shape except for size and shading, the humpback is the lone member of its own genus, *Megaptera* (Latin for big wing), named in honor of its extra-long pectoral fins. Whereas the flippers of a normal ninety-foot-long blue whale have been measured at twelve feet, the flippers of a fifty-foot humpback are about sixteen feet long. They may look like wings, but they are used more for maneuverability than locomotion. The humpback is the only great whale documented swimming backward. That it breaches so easily and so frequently may be a function of these flippers.

The humpback eventually stops spyhopping and pulls within a hundred feet of the boat. Now it starts breaching, lifting its forty-foot bulk free of the sea and landing with a splash that hurls water twenty feet into the air. The spray alone defines an area the size of a basketball court. The boat rocks from the turbulence. The animal jumps repeatedly, twisting its body in midleap to land several times on its right side, then on its left. I watch the display with admiration, my mouth wide open, one hand gripping tight to the rail to keep my balance. I am surprised to notice Steve has binoculars pointed not at the whale, but at a brown scum staining the surface of the sea for a hundred yards in every direction around the boat. "I wonder what that plankton bloom's about," he mumbles, handing me the binoculars and reaching for his notebook. When he finishes writing, he sighs, looks at me. A long silence intercedes. The whale has stopped breaching. Steve continues to stare perplexed at the gray, flat, sea-blotched muddy brown. I sit down on a plastic cushion, close my eyes to listen to a hundred sea lions roaring their throaty raga from a fogged-in rookery off to the southeast. A light drizzle massages my face. The fog closes in. Steve pushes a button, starts the engine, pushes the throttle forward, heads us toward an anchorage in the midst of the same islets we spied yesterday. He is wearing a one-piece red foul-weather suit. No hat. His feet are bare.

"I've been thinking about your charged border," he says, chomping on a carrot. "People love big mammals. The bigger the mammal, the bigger the love. I call it the lure of the megafauna." He disappears down the hatch for a moment, then reappears with a bag of crackers. "I don't think whales possess psychic powers to control the way human beings perceive them. When I hear that stuff, it always makes me think there are two kinds of whales: the ones who live out here in the water, and the ones who live inside the heads of people who don't study them."

His answer reminds me of the story of two Makah fishermen out on the ocean in a longboat when they spy a strange orca with two dorsal fins. One of the fishermen picks up a ballast stone and hurls it at the orca, drawing blood near the blowhole. The orca lurches, then swims through the shore break to strand itself on a beach. The fishermen paddle into a nearby cove and then jog around the point to observe the creature more closely. But instead of finding the orca, they encounter a stranger repairing a hole in his boat. He is nearly finished with the job, and he asks the fishermen to help him lift the boat into the water again. This they do. As the stranger jumps aboard and starts paddling through the breakers, he turns to smile as his boat suddenly dips below a cresting wave. When the wave collapses, the Makah are startled to notice that the boat has vanished. In its place, they once again observe the orca with two dorsal fins. The whale blows, then dives.

The concept of duality is common to Native American mythology. Animals live two lives simultaneously. In one life they are spirits and shapeshifters who possess powers to control the way human beings perceive them. When they're in this form, we are able to communicate with them. In the other life, they are the animals we observe in nature that end up in front of our arrows, guns, darts, binoculars. In the Makah myth, the orca as whale is depicted as vulnerable. It metamorphoses into a man with a damaged boat because that is a savvy disguise for a spirit who seeks aid from whalers.

Myth reflects life. Cetaceans do respond to human behavior. In Johnstone Strait, British Columbia, a study has demonstrated that orcas will not vocalize as often or as intensely in the presence of noisy motorboats.[6] Yet until recently, most studies of orca vocalizations were directed by scientists tracking whales in noisy motorboats. In all likelihood, the act of collecting data biased the behavior of the whales and, therefore, tainted the data. While the biologists who cruise in motorboats recording whale calls still insist they are holding up a one-way mirror to the whales, a more appropriate metaphor may be a roomful of mirrors reflecting observer and observed in an infinite progression of interactive behaviors. Physicist Max Planck tried to explain the inherent inflexibility of his scientific colleagues by pointing out that truth does not triumph by making its opponents see the light; truth triumphs because the opponents eventually die, and a new generation grows up learning the new paradigm. Such is the case here. A growing number of young biologists now conclude that invasive studies are valid mostly for measuring the effects of invasiveness on behavior. Seen in a historical light, the unmasking of an incongruity of research has always been a key function of science. New truth prevails over old truth, at least until an even newer truth arrives on the scene. So evolves the scientific process.

The shtick we bring to whales can also affect perceptions. The scientist's whale is a data hostage, a cool medium, a marine mammal, a Darwinian puppet, and a target for darts. The environmentalist's whale is a casualty of biodiversity statistics, vulnerable far beyond what its vast size may suggest, and the planet's preeminent symbol for all that is wrong with human resource management. The mystic's whale is a blithe spirit, an artist, a hot medium, an ambassador to angels, never a specimen and always a being, a Gaian diplomat that communicates mind to mind with any human willing to cultivate a relationship. I peer into a fog so thick the air seems to drip into itself. The coastline has vanished. I sigh deeply, turn to Steve. "I wonder how whales would look if we met them without our various shticks in place."

"Do you think it's possible to watch whales anywhere else besides the charged border?" he asks quietly.

Standing on the bridge, our two faces tipped upward to receive the cool touch of the mist, I whisper a firm no to his difficult question by describing the work of a woman, Carolyn Pettit, who runs a dolphin swim program on a remote island in Baja, California. Carolyn believes that whales and dolphins commonly communicate with people mind to mind. As much as cetaceans live in water, they also reside in the spirit realm. The spinner and bottlenose dolphins who visit the bay fronting her campsite are ambassadors for extraterrestrials and various channeled entities.

When I finish, Steve remains silent a while longer, then answers, "You know, I can respect the sincerity of her view. But it's hard for the biologist in me to respond with anything but 'gibberish.' So, no comment."

Steve is far more willing to comment on the way the media grants power to whale scientists. This summer his boat has hosted two film crews representing French and American nature programs. After a few weeks observing the way various scientists in the vicinity were depicted by the film director as comic book heroes and earth healers, he became distinctly uncomfortable. "Before this summer, I would never have imagined that the humble act of data collection could possibly be made to look sexy and heroic. I mean, there are only so many Jane Goodalls and Aldo Leopolds in this world. What the rest of us do is mostly tedium masquerading as . . . how does Cousteau describe it?"—He puffs up his chest and bellows—"'expanding the frontiers of human knowledge.'"

It is not always soul-searching aboard the *Lamarck*. Steve retires to the aft cabin to update his humpback ID database. I climb off the bridge and into the galley to fix a sandwich. Steve's colleague, Milly Mukerjee, sits down beside me to start jotting behavioral information into her notebook. A capable first mate and Steve's research assistant, she spends most of her time on the *Lamarck* sitting in front of the twenty-one-inch screen of an onboard Macintosh, updating an elaborate database that correlates photo IDs of all the whales in the area with feeding behaviors. Milly is an exceedingly cheerful woman, with piercing blue eyes set off by a long, jet black braid, which is bound by a turquoise and silver barrette decorated with a single multicolored snowy owl feather. I ask her how the whales relate to their boat.

"Relate?" she answers. "I've never given it a thought one way or the other. Should I?"

I put down my pen. "Well, sure. I mean, you could." I return to my book, start drawing the outline of a whale with a vacuum cleaner fixture for a mouth. Milly turns to stare out the window. I follow her eyes to watch a single shaft of sunlight plunge through the fog, illuminating a rock outcropping looming off our port side. I can tell she is wary about getting into a conversation with me about any subject concerning whale awareness. I try again. "A lot of people think whales are special beings. I mean, for every two films shot about whales, there may only be one film shot about the entire rest of the ocean. And where's the army of researchers out here studying halibut or northern phalaropes? I'm just curious if these whales let you get closer to them than they do other boats? Or maybe they don't let you get as close. Or maybe it depends if your engine is on or off."

I wish I hadn't sputtered out so many "maybes" at once. Milly puts her pen down again. Her black hair falls over a light gray Polarfleece top. Her sleeves are rolled up, exposing a dirty, white, waffle-patterned cotton jersey. She is wearing badly torn Levi's. She peers at me like an expert witness staring down a slick lawyer who is trying to bait her to uncover inconsistencies. Steve appears by her side. I feel a bit disappointed knowing he is about to come to her rescue. "Who knows what it's all about," he answers pointedly. "I mean, let's take your example of phalaropes. Those birds have a feeding behavior as complex as anything the humpbacks do. Flocks of them spin around on the water's surface all day long, each bird kicking several times per second. A vortex is formed that actually sucks the plankton and brine shrimp up from the depths. And the phalarope's beak is a masterpiece of hydrodynamic design. They don't bite or jab their prey. The act of dipping causes an adhesive flow. The food gets drawn up into the birds' mouths like soda through a straw. Can you imagine? They detect their prey, catch it, and swallow it at a rate as high as a hundred and eighty dips per minute."

Milly breaks in. "Look, I need to get back on the computer, so let me just finish up our conversation by saying that I'm here to do science. I don't know if the whales relate to me or not. Studying that relationship is not my primary interest. If it was, I'm sure I'd have an intelligent answer to offer you." She tips her head sideways and smiles brightly, then disappears into the computer room.

Steve and I spend the next hour debating the heightened lure of the megafauna, in contrast to the much diminished lure of the pint-sized northern phalarope. He uses the phalarope's example to point out that large-brained mammals certainly have no monopoly on highly sophisticated behavior. He also acknowledges that the reductionist approach is limited in its ability to explain such behavior. The whole is usually greater than the sum of its parts. No thinking person today can study complex traits that have evolved in a cohesive manner over a hundred thousand generations without, at least once in a while, acknowledging that there is some element of intellectual culture at play. Animals do have a sense of aesthetics. Some birds clearly *compose* their nests, adding a bit of turquoise yarn here and rejecting the brick red leaf there. As always, I move the conversation toward less firm ground. Juvenile orcas spend time engaged in learning behavior, in the care of various adults who are not their parents. One orca may teach a juvenile how to catch a sea lion, another may teach it hydrodynamics, and a third, the pod's own distinct dialect. Why can't we call that a school? Not like a school of fish, but a school of students. "It's mostly your choice of words," answers Steve. "It implies culture, even civilization. It's anthropomorphic."

I chuckle to be told, once again, I'm in danger of hitting a hard wall. Anthropomorphism is the arch sin of behavioral biology. Any researcher who spends too much time cooking up similarities between human culture and animal behavior stands a good chance of having his credentials burned at the stake. No evolutionary advantage there. But anthropomorphism is also a straw man, often used by biologists to keep human beings separate from animals at a time when we should be doing everything in our power to integrate ourselves into nature. Let's call a school a school and then applaud ourselves for having one more thing in common with the mighty orca.

A seaplane drops out of the sky. Two Dutch filmmakers come aboard the *Lamarck* for four days. Hans is the director, Yves the cameraman. Steve clearly relishes the opportunity to hang out with media professionals. Just as he provides them with access to the whales, they assist him by repairing electronic equipment and providing insight into video techniques. They also help fulfill a permit obligation that Steve takes seriously—disseminating humpback whale information and images to the general public. Hans informs me that the main challenge of his film is figuring out how to capture the outsize image of such huge creatures to fit the format of a twenty-one-inch TV screen. To do so, he must spurn images of whale bodies interacting with other whale bodies upon the vast ocean's domain, and focus on closeups of humpback faces, flailing arms, and rolling backs. Breaches and spyhops are de rigueur.

Within a few hours, Steve, Milly, and I watch from the bridge as Hans commandeers Yves and his camera as close to a group of whales as possible without getting their inflatable boat upended. I realize that a few of the propeller scars Steve occasionally detects slashed across humpback hide could conceivably be caused by filmmakers just slightly more aggressive than Hans. Steve draws my attention to one particular animal who seems the most disturbed by the process, cutting its surface time short to swim directly away from the camera boat. "That's pretty much the same reaction I observed when I darted my whale." He grimaces, then cusses under his breath. As a federal permit holder, one of his jobs is to make certain the animals are kept from harm's way. He drops his voice to murmur, "Those guys don't seem to realize that my research has to drive their film. Not vice versa." He excuses himself, and climbs up to the wheelhouse to radio the two of them back to the *Lamarck*, promising, in an upbeat voice, "Hot tips on how to get the best kind of shots."

"It's my fault," he says, returning to my side. "Hans has shot whales before. I took it for granted that he'd know the rules."

With darts in their backsides, cameras thrust into their faces, whale-watching boats tagging behind them for hours on end, the same question arises: Who among us is objective enough to say what consequence such behavior has on the peace of mind of a whale? Studies of orcas off San Juan Island in Washington, and Alert Bay, in British Columbia, conclude that the animals demonstrate no evasive maneuvers around whale-watching boats. If anything, they seem to draw closer to boats as tourism expands, although pod movements appear more regimented, and vocalizing decreases. Historical ecologist Rich Osborne has studied the growth of Puget Sound whale watching for twenty years and believes the orcas have simply acclimated to the steady increase in boat traffic. "If you took an orca from the Gulf of Alaska and plopped it down in Puget Sound, it would probably go crazy."[7] What about humpbacks? Do they acclimate? Or do they display a sense of being violated by their brave new world of outboards, cameras, action? Do they react at set distances, ten feet, fifty feet? Or is it loudness, say a hundred decibels? Does the violation vary depending on who does it? Steve has traveled with these whales for eight summers. Do they let him draw closer than Hans? And if so, did Steve lose a few chits when he pulled the trigger on the darting crossbow? When I let loose with this barrage of pointed questions, he simply shrugs his shoulders in reply. I watch the humpbacks churn the sea into a froth in a rush to avoid Yves's camera and wonder if humpbacks might conceivably share a belief attributed to tribespeople in the New Guinea highlands: that every photo peels a layer off the subject's soul. If the tenet has any merit, these humpback celebrities of Southeast Alaska have sacrificed as many layers as a movie star.

Some filmmakers indulge in the same nettlesome paradox as some biologists: Harassing whales is acceptable conduct in the cause of educating the public about "the whales." The harassment that would land the rest of us a hefty fine and a guilty conscience seems, in their case, a source of professional legitimacy. I imagine a film archiver, a hundred years in the future, reviewing the vast archive of nature films produced in the late twentieth century. She concludes that because people of that era were getting into the face of animals all the time, even the films they made to educate themselves not to harass the animals had to do so just to get the message across.

The two Dutchmen return to the *Lamarck*. Steve sits them down at the galley table for hot soup and Earl Gray tea. He does not chide them but, instead, outlines the provisions and limitations of his research permit, as well as those of local whale-watching guidelines. In response to Hans's declaration of working under a time constraint, Steve calmly replies, "No film director deserves his perfect shot without first learning what it means to deserve it." Recovering his preferred upbeat mood, he asks Milly to skipper the inflatable for their next foray. "She's the best there is around whales. And all you have to do for payment is give her that box of white chocolate I saw you bring aboard." Everyone laughs. Half an hour later, Steve and I watch from the bridge as Milly deftly zigs and zags the inflatable toward an aggregation of humpbacks preparing to feed. This time, the sortie has the look of an interspecies team effort. Milly keeps her speed minimal and constant, and as a result, the whales learn to trust that her movements hold no surprises. She makes a concerted effort to keep eye contact with her quarry. The whales remain indulgent as long they are able to see her. When the filmmakers finally return to the boat, they are smiling broadly and are elated to have discovered the technique to getting the good shots.

I remain alone on the bridge, lean my head against a ventilation grate to watch the whales, and listen to a recording of guitarist Ali Fakre Toure waft up from below. Four Steller's sea lions appear, tagging along beside one of the humpbacks. They let the whale pull ahead of them, then abruptly speed up to bump right into its flukes, then speed up even more to corkscrew around the flippers, finally breaching to create huge splashes. The whale seems content. If it felt otherwise, it could easily escape by diving or swimming away, or even by swatting a sea lion senseless with one uppercut from its long pectoral fins. At one point, the four sea lions and the whale pull within a few yards of our boat. The combined exhales of five large animals carry the stench of tons of fermenting fish erupting in giant burps and farts.

Milly arrives, asks me if I'd like to visit a rookery. I accept, and, later that day, she and I spend an hour working our way over boulders and through a forest of spindly spruce understoried by the two-foot-wide splayed leaves of devil's clubs that sprout from eight-foot-tall spiny stems. We finally spy the sea lions through the trees. Fifty or more blubbery bodies lay strewn in front of us belching and vomiting, roaring threats to every other animal in sight. The sound of it is revolting when heard up close, although sweet and alluring when experienced as a blended sound from a mile offshore. Sea lions are powerful swimmers and easily lunge from the sea onto the granite shelf in one graceful motion. Once on land, though, they immediately turn ungainly, pulling themselves along the shelf like overstuffed sausages doing push-ups. They locate a perch and stretch. Some roll over on their backs and snort several times as a prelude to baking on the griddle of a rock slab in the cold, wet fog of the central Alaska coast. A few animals watch us climb down the ridge toward them. We are dwarves to them, and they show no concern. We settle into a rocky nook downwind and slightly above the animals to watch in silence. Milly pulls out two thick slabs of her newly won white chocolate and hands one to me. "So what made you decide to work with humpbacks?" I whisper tentatively.

"I got a degree in marine biology and immediately landed a job as an assistant to a dolphin trainer in an oceanarium in southern California. When the opportunity arose to work here with Steve, it seemed like the next logical step in my career."

"What drew you to dolphins?"

"Oh, I suppose the same thing that draws everyone to them. They took my breath away the first time I saw them at an oceanarium. I didn't like the show very much. The water had too much chlorine. I felt the program director worked too hard to make these evolved beings appear cute and cuddly. I felt driven to learn about the animal underneath the gloss. Then I got involved for a while with some people doing therapy with autistic kids swimming in the dolphin pool after hours."

Milly points to a huge male sea lion whose middle is wrapped in yellow packing tape. I notice a pathetic-looking female shrouded by what must be a hundred pounds of monofilament gill net. She seems barely strong enough to keep her head erect. Compiling a list of all the animals suffering from human jetsam is precisely why we're here. Once Milly makes her report, the local Marine Mammal Agency has promised to visit the rookery, immobilize the cripples, and free them from their bondage.

"What was the therapy program like?"

"Worthwhile. Occasionally profound. Disabled kids swam with dolphins for an hour once a week for two months. The therapists would get the kids to stretch their muscles by reaching out to touch the dolphins."

"Anything unexpected happen?"

"Well, you know, dolphins turn people on just by being themselves. We chose two of the older animals we felt were reliable and mellow. They'd swim close. The kids would get a ride by holding on to a dorsal fin. It was amazing how quickly the dolphins determined each kid's ability. A weak kid got a slow ride, a strong kid got a faster ride. All the kids brightened up so much."

We return to the boat. Milly telephones her sea lion report to the wildlife agency. But three days later, passing by the rookery in the *Lamarck*, we spy the same yellow-taped male swimming in front of us and the shrouded female residing on the same high perch. A quick call to the office on our cell phone informs Steve that the agents have run out of operating funds for that particular program. He hangs up, looking more glum than

I've seen him since I joined the boat. "It's about budget cuts in Washington D.C. It means certain death for the female. The male may survive a while longer. But I wouldn't bet on him ever winning another courtship battle."

Much of the intellect and altruistic social behavior that humans attribute to whales actually pertains to toothed whales, the family that includes orcas, dolphins, belugas, and sperm whales. The toothed whales developed echolocation to locate prey and whistles to communicate group tactics for capturing them. Baleen whales don't hunt prey by stealth, so they never developed echolocation. They rely on keen ears and good vision to locate the cubic acreage of krill that composes their primary diet. Instead of teeth, humpbacks have a stiff comblike material, called "baleen," that lines their mouths. When the jaws open, pleats expand to double the size of the throat and mouth cavity, sucking inside tons of salt water full of krill or small fish. The whale closes its mouth. Now the animal's pickup truck–sized tongue goes to work, squeezing the water out and depositing hundreds of pounds of shrimp against the baleen plates. Then it gulps the meal down.

A baleen whale's feeding strategy resembles grazing, which is the reason their behavior is compared to land-based ungulates like deer and cows just as often as it is to their distant cousins the dolphins. Most grazers feed individually. Unlike wolves, lions, and orcas, grass eaters and krill eaters have little impetus to band together to hunt cooperatively. If humpbacks seem to group into herds, it is mostly a function of individuals gathering at the place the krill live. But humpback behavior shows several dramatic differences from that of other baleen whales. As a prelude to mating, the male humpbacks sing complex songs to attract females, a trait that, curiously, closely reflects the courtship bugling of male elk in rut. Much has been written about the complex musical structures employed, the repetition of eighteen-minute-long melodies, the remarkable consistency of the performances from year to year.

Roger Payne and Scott McVay codiscovered humpback mating calls in the waters around Bermuda in the 1960s. Since then, Payne has done more than anyone to elevate these vocalizations from the plebian category of *calls* to the creative category of *song*. Playing the songs as a part of a presentation he performs around the world, he has found that people are physically affected to hear them, and some are moved to tears. Payne believes these strong emotions are aroused by the striking musical affinity between human song and humpback song, "as though something unaccountably ancient was overmastering them." He concludes:

> This commonality of aesthetic suggests to me that the traditions of singing may date back so far they were already present in some ancestor common to whales and us. If this is true it says that the selective advantage of singing and the laws upon which we humans base our musical compositions (laws we fancy to be of our own invention) are so ancient they predate our species by tens of millions of years.[8]

In the early 1980s Payne and his associate, Linda Guinee, discovered that the verses of humpback mating songs actually end in rhymes. Payne postulates that humpbacks employ rhymes as oral poets do, to facilitate the memorization of long verses. Rhyming is an exceedingly specialized use of sound that breaks tones and timbres into blocks to convey information about timing, rhythm, quantity, and abstract meaning. The discovery of humpback rhyming adds momentum to the claim that these whales understand the building blocks of language if not language itself. One thing is certain. Humpback songs are as complex a use of sound as can be found anywhere in nature. The sheer number of identifiable elements at play in any single song communicates far more subtlety than is needed simply to advertise sexual prowess, as a bull elk's song does. A good humpback singer, often but not always male, attracts an audience, usually female. The very concept of *audience* implies a species-specific sense of aesthetics. Aesthetics is art, and art is culture. Roger Payne speculates that humpback songs may be epic poems that communicate rhymed information about the lineage of the singer.

Courtship songs are not the only songs humpbacks sing. Humpbacks vary from other baleen whales, and all other land grazers as well, by joining together in a cooperative strategy called "lunge feeding." One whale senses a herring school and vocalizes a particular song. As few as three or as many as twenty whales will answer the call by swimming closely together. The team of whales dives in tandem directly underneath the herring school, then swims in circles while releasing a curtain of bubbles that rise in the water column. The turbulence caused by this "bubble net" captures the herring as tidily as if they were caught in a purse seine. The humpbacks then rise as a group inside their own net. Just before breaking the surface they open their huge mouths to suck in the silvery herring by the ton.

Milly, Steve, and I are standing on the aft deck watching a hundred-foot-wide ring of bubbles snap and shimmer on the water's calm surface. Milly hollers loudly to Yves and Hans, who are in the aft cabin tidying up their gear. They pick up their camera, lenses, and film canisters and rush outside to join us just as a volcano of six humpbacks rises to the surface in an eruption of open mouths. The sight is riveting, an agglomeration of sharply pleated throats in grays and pinks lifting out of the motionless sea to a height of fifteen feet, causing the cumulative mountain of rubbery flesh to sag when it hits the pull of gravity. Huge spouts of foam, mortar-fire blows, iridescent fountains of herring spray outward, shimmering in the occluded light; bright red whale gums, brown briar patches of baleen, and those soft brown whale eyes occasionally gazing sharply into the eyes of the three of us staring at them with our mouths open.

The whales lunge in ten-minute intervals over the next hour; most of them do so within a few hundred meters of the boat. It's easy to film them. Yves merely focuses his camera on the center of the bubble ring and waits for the explosion of mouths to break the surface. The whales stop lunging, bob on the surface a quarter mile from our starboard side. Yves and Hans go back to tidying up. Milly and Steve fix themselves a lunch of peanut butter sandwiches.

I take an Irish skin drum off the wall of the aft cabin, step back onto the stern, hang the drum over the gunwale, and begin pounding out a simple rhythm. Within a minute, first one and then a second humpback breaks from the pack to propel themselves directly toward the boat. A hundred yards away, they both dive. Vanish. I commence a yodeling chant. For the next quarter hour I continue my yodeling, drumming. No whale ventures within a hundred yards of the drum. The boat is still.

Steve has asked Hans not to document my attempts at music making aboard the *Lamarck*. It is too new for him. He demands some time simply to get used to the music, needs to learn how to discuss it—possibly defend it—among his peers before it shows up documented for the whole world to see on videotape. He has already mentioned the fact that a permitting committee could conceivably construe my music making as breaking the law. When he mentions his concern, I shake my head. "You're overreacting. These are the same people who enthuse over darts! How could they possibly call it harassment for a musician to bang on a skin drum from the deck of a boat?"

"It's dumb, I admit it," he replies in a subdued voice. "But one of these days you're going to dangle your underwater speaker below the surface, pull out an electric guitar, and then start vamping James Brown riffs to the whales. I've got to be able to document that event in a manner that makes sense to the committee." Although he agrees with me that music making at a volume lower than a ten-horsepower outboard doesn't stand a chance in hell of harassing whales, he worries it will harass the sensibilities of permit givers.

Half an hour passes. I get out the drum and start banging again. Yodeling. This time Steve's call for discretion makes me feel ten years old. I've slipped into my father's workshop to hammer nails into boards. It's impossible to do so quietly. I stop hammering the drum and climb onto the bridge. Almost immediately, a humpback rises next to the place on the stern where I was standing just a moment earlier. It brushes the inflatable dinghy with its fifty-foot-long body, raises its head to stare deeply into my eyes, and exhales mightily, spraying me on the second story while soaking Yves, who has stepped onto the transom to wash dishes. Milly walks up beside me with a reverent look in her eyes. The whale blows again, then sinks out of sight. The three of us are smiling. No one on board ventures a guess as to whether there is any connection between my drumming and the whale's close encounter. No one says anything.

Biologists are usually called upon to fulfill the human interest component of whale films. Three times this summer Steve has been lured to play the expert for big-budget nature films, and the experience has been unsettling. He possesses one of the coveted federal whale permits in this cetacean-rich area, and filmmakers depend on his cooperation whether they actually need or care about his research. One of the directors sensed Steve's mounting dismay and went so far as to turn the camera on him as a kind of vanity reward, ostensibly to keep him engaged and happy. Steve shakes his head to confess that he worries about becoming dependent on film crews to pay for the upkeep of his boat. Every few days he quotes Frank Sinatra, who said that "a boat is a hole in the water into which one throws money." Steve has suggested that celebrity biologists who show up in a lot of nature films, including some of his own heroes, cannot possibly have time left over to conduct valid research. He refers to what they do as "sound bite research."

One production company showed up in early July on a 150-foot ship equipped with its own minisubmarine. A French crew appeared in early August with a helicopter and proceeded to spend most of an entire day hovering directly above the whales. When Steve insisted they cease their aggressive tactic, the director looked Steve up and down as if he wasn't grateful for the ample money they were paying him. Early the next morning Steve suggested that the film crew visit a nearby sea lion rookery. He fired up the inflatable and dropped them all off on a rocky, slippery islet, promising to return in an hour. Back on the *Lamarck,* he shut off his radio and unplugged the cell phone, stranding the crew on the rookery for half a day. He laughs heartily when I suggest we capsulize his film experience in the form of a mathematical equation:

$$\text{RESPECT FOR ANIMALS} = 1/\text{CAPITAL INVESTMENT}$$

With so many nature films needed each year to feed the black hole of TV programming around the world, the format has, over time, deteriorated into a stereotyped image of biologists peering through binoculars, turning the dials of arcane hardware, and pointing off into the distance at some animal while whispering so as not to scare the beast away. A famous voice transmits a sense of authority by reading a script that describes the sober facts concerning the particular human/nature cusp being depicted. Yet few nature films bother to present nature in the traditional sense, as a place of spirit or enchantment where animals are aware beings who communicate to one another. Few describe the cusp between humans and nature in the deep ecological sense of being a primary source of communion. Instead, experts do the best they know how to present data in the most entertaining way they know how. But it's still data, and nature is thus treated as a bag full of numbers and facts.

There's a hidden message implied by the ubiquitous presence of so many experts. It is as if there are no children, no artists, no dreamers, no poets, and very few women or elders who have anything to teach the rest of us about the human relationship to nature. Instead, year after year, we watch a continuing parade of field biologists pointing and whispering and ultimately promoting the classic scientific schism between observer and observed. Take, for instance, the simple image of humans peeking through binoculars and whispering. The first part is a voyeuristic cliché that subtly magnifies our separation from nature. Whispering represents a presumption of invisibility. Yet these days humans are invisible nowhere else *but* in nature films. An entire generation of children has grown up believing that the fine art of comprehending nature is primarily a matter of astute observation and unwavering objectivity. In so many ways, the stereotype of the nature film is revealed as the public face of the current biological paradigm.

"You think it's a cliché for a filmmaker to hire a biologist to turn a few dials and jot down a few notes on camera?" Steve blurts out, closing the hatch before joining me at the table. "Maybe so," he continues, "but it's easy for scientists to look like they're doing science, so the filmmaker doesn't have to waste a lot of words justifying his images. People playing music with dolphins come across as a bunch of dilettantes or quacks. Who can verify it? It's music. You know, money for nothing, chicks for free."

I burst out laughing, then reply, "You forgot to add how unpredictable it is. The first time I was filmed playing music with orcas, it took four days before I got a reply. And that occurred at night so it was too dark to film. The crew ended up staying a full week, but they never did get the interaction on film. It only started happening the day after they left."

There is also a legal reason biologists' faces appear in more whale films than musicians playing with orcas or swimmers splashing with dolphins.

With the best of intentions, the U.S. Marine Mammal Protection Act strictly regulates human access to cetaceans. Unfortunately, the American bureaucrats who grant the access permits—who serve essentially as customs agents to the charged border—are all scientists who grant the coveted permits only to other scientists. This careerist approach to access makes it practically illegal for a nonscientist to draw close to cetaceans in American waters. In my case, it makes no difference that I play a guitar at a low volume. Nor do the permit givers care that I always transmit sound at a fair distance from a whale, allowing the animal to draw near if it likes. Ironically, when a whale chooses to stay away, I cannot be cited. But if the whale draws close of its own volition, any whale cop who witnesses it is sure to cite me. Penalties can range as high as ten thousand dollars.

Steve and I sit in silence and listen to a waterfall roaring like a thousand sea lions bellowing the boundaries of their territory. It starts to rain hard outside the *Lamarck*; the water runs in cold sheets off the upper deck and down the windows of the pilothouse. Then the wind explodes to port, pummeling the boat to starboard. The noise is overwhelming. Thankfully, the cove we're moored in is well protected, with a narrow deepwater entrance and steep slopes to dull the brunt of the gale. A violent gust of wind shoves the boat sideways. We grab the table and hold on tight. When the floor regains the horizontal, we hear a new sound: something is rolling around on the top deck. Steve zips up his foul-weather suit, opens the hatch, pulls himself up the ladder. I stare out the window at the wet black, then put on a pot of hot water. How easily one forgets that so much about life out here is tending to the basics of survival. Even on a clear night, we see no sign of humanity besides a random satellite blipping a trail through the Milky Way.

The hatch opens. Steve pulls himself inside the galley, pulls off his suit, sits down beside me, and starts sipping his licorice tea. "I think about all the cheetah films I've seen over the past twenty years. They all show the same five shots. A female licks her kittens. Then she outruns an antelope and makes the kill. The narrator appears walking toward the camera. He tells us that the cat's habitat has been trashed by local ranchers. Next we see some zoo guy dressed in khaki shorts shooting a tranquilizer 'to save it.' Finally, we see the cheetah in a cage about to get shipped five hundred miles to a safer habitat." Steve pauses a moment to let the image sink in. "I mean, there's got to be something else to show about cheetahs. Strange, I can't think of one other thing."

We continue to sip our tea. The rain has stopped for the moment. The wind keeps pummeling the boat. "The medium itself is a lot of the problem," he continues. "Nature films are mostly made for TV, where there's very little depth of field. Maybe it's simply not possible to translate the fractal reality of nature onto a small screen without corrupting nature itself."

The clichéd images suggest to me that the failure is one of imagination. With nature writing emerging as a richly evocative art form, one can only wonder why producers don't borrow from it to devise more thought-provoking scripts. "Someone ought to try the dogged interview style to discuss darting. Talk to the usual gang of expert biologists, animal rights activists, and marine mammal bureaucrats. But don't question them about regulations, utility, or ethics. Ask each one of them to describe how it must feel to be shot by a dart commensurate in size to a whale dart. Also interview an equal number of bright people who don't make their living arguing the issue. Ask the Dalai Lama what he thinks. Ask children to draw how it must feel. Get the opinion of someone who channels whales. Ask a science-fiction writer how people fifty years from now will judge today's darting epidemic."

Steve is clearly excited by the possibilities. "Since these animals have a slower metabolism than humans, speeding up the images might give an audience a better idea how a whale actually perceives its environment. To a whale, the clouds may zoom across the sky. Their own migration between Alaska and Hawaii must feel like a walk in the park. And since engine noise is a significant issue to a whale, the filmmaker could add 'visual noise' to his images to give a more accurate picture of the altered interface that occurs every time he draws near in a motorboat. The tighter the shot, the more aggravating the noise. For the narrator, let's hire a weathered old Tlingit woman whose tribe has been collecting seaweed alongside humpback whales for years."

Wendell Berry once said that television is not a tool for education but for stupefaction. Georges Clemenceau once said that war is too important to leave to the generals. I say nature is too important to leave to a TV formula.

Steve, Milly, and Hans do not willingly cook or wash the dishes. Within a day of the filmmakers' arrival, Yves and I are doing all the food preparation and most of the cleanup. Unfortunately, Steve and Milly seem shy to discuss this lopsided arrangement. When the two Dutchmen finally make their exit back to civilization, Milly is forced to pick up Yves's slack. One afternoon I peek into the aft cabin to watch Steve standing with both palms extended forward, assuring Milly he will do the large stack of dishes that has accumulated in the galley sink. But he doesn't do it. Later that day, Milly erupts at me within Steve's earshot, announcing that she is not going to wash the current stack. I suggest we hold a seminar on the virtues of human cooperative feeding. Washing dishes provides an evolutionary advantage. It's kindergarten stuff, really. Everyone takes turns. Those who cook don't clean up that particular meal. No one is exempt because everyone eats. While research and boat maintenance are part-time activities, community is a full-time occupation for everyone. I suggest a schedule. They both like the idea. But it never happens. Steve's little-boy expression of shame over his lapse coupled with Milly's misplaced feminist vehemence makes me imagine the issue eventually corroding their otherwise splendid working relationship.

How strange is the human power of recall. Amid awesome whale encounters, constantly edifying conversation, and the challenge of making music to elicit a response from another species, the dirty dishes remain my strongest memory of the weeks I spent on Steve and Milly's research platform. I look back on my time aboard the *Lamarck* and witness the orderly scientific lifestyle broken into shards through the lens of a black comedy routine. Two people spend years of their lives dedicated to the careful study of cooperative feeding behavior in humpback whales, yet come to blows because neither of them will do the dishes. Milly is right after all. She does not study how the whales relate to her.

A marked change in the weather quickly dissipates the frenzy of the melodrama. It's sunny after a solid week of rain. The sea is flat as a mirror. Milly hands Steve a sponge and a bottle of soap and then retreats with me to the bridge where the two of us indulge in a slow-motion feeding frenzy of white chocolate. When six whales dive together, she videotapes their black, white, and gray fluke patterns. I study the barnacles adorning the pectoral fins of a seventh whale that lounges a few feet from the boat. More barnacles adorn its snout. Milly informs me that the fluke patterns are partially composed of barnacle scars.

Whale historian Ivan Sanderson produces an unintentional tongue twister when he writes that adult humpbacks are "a parasitologist's paradise, and a happy hunting ground for any conchologist, helminthologist or crustaceologist."[9] Humpbacks are infested with whale lice and several species of barnacles: One species is found exclusively in the pleats; another favors the flukes and the lips; a third, the stalked barnacle, grows only atop another species and never on the whale's skin itself. Many whale scientists regard breaching as a technique adopted specifically for ridding parasites. The unusual sighting of a humpback breaching within the mouth of the Congo River was explained as a savvy exercise in barnacle dislodgement, as the invertebrates cannot survive long in freshwater. I have noticed that the placement of barnacles differs subtly from animal to animal. On certain whales, they almost look applied, and carefully, at that. When Steve joins us, I ask him, "Do the whales play a passive or active role in adorning themselves. I mean, are barnacles more like athlete's foot or tattoos?"

He grabs a square of chocolate, pops it into his mouth, and grows pensive. "There's a rare species of *Mesoplodon* called the dense-beaked whale that has six-inch tusks jutting up above its jawline like a warthog. In one of the only photographs ever taken of the species at sea, the individual had perfectly round clumps of barnacles growing on the tips of each tusk, like two razor-sharp breasts jutting above each eye. When I saw that picture, I distinctly remember thinking that the animal had attached the barnacles to make a fashion statement appreciated only by other dense-beaked whales." Steve stares at a second piece of chocolate, then smiles. "Obviously, barnacles impede laminar flow. There's no benefit to that. In Hawaii, however, male humpbacks have been observed using barnacles in courtship battles with other males. They scrape each other with the leading edge of their pectorals, sometimes deep enough to draw blood and leave scars. I suppose the careful placement of barnacles would provide an evolutionary advantage for any combative male. So we can assume the relationship is symbiotic. But there's only a slim chance the humpbacks actually adorn themselves."

"How would a humpback attract a barnacle to a specific body part?"

"It could abrade its skin by rubbing against a rock. Fluids oozing from the superficial wound might attract the same plankton upon which the barnacles feed."

"Imagine if all those uniquely scarred flukes you photograph are actually adornments used to attract the opposite sex."

"No, we're quite certain they're beer advertisements."

One whale takes our breath away by holding its flukes aloft for Steve and Milly to videotape and for me to admire. Watching whale flukes is like watching clouds; both activities spark us to seek the familiar within the random. This pattern displays a pure white sky emblazoned with six constellations of black dots and charcoal rings composing an alternate zodiac viewed from a perch in a distant galaxy.

"Has anyone ever postulated that the barnacles are in charge of this relationship?" I ask tentatively.

"Well, no, although it's always good science to turn a postulate inside out. E. O. Wilson writes about leaf-cutter ants farming fungus for food. But at the end of the essay, he turns the tables and asks the reader to consider that it was the fungus that captured the ants millions of years ago as a convenient freight service for hauling vegetative matter to their underground chambers. The same case is made about prehistoric humans and dogs. Some anthropologists make a pretty good case that it was the dogs who cultivated the humans and not vice versa. There's a remarkable instance of a microscopic parasite that uses certain species of ants as a secondary host. The parasite enters the ant's brain, injects chemicals that cause the ant to alter its behavior. The drugged ant climbs up on the tallest blade of grass it can find, then starts waving its front legs to the sky with the result that a predatory bird soon has itself an easy meal. Except there's a catch. The parasite is in charge here and its goal all along was to make its way into the stomach of its primary host, which just happens to be an ant-eating bird."

"So it's plausible that the whale rubs itself in key spots to attract barnacles. The barnacle colony drives around the ocean on their whale until they find some nice cozy rock pile to make a suitable home. They start injecting hormones into the whale's bloodstream that work like cocaine, fostering a sense of omnipotence and aggressiveness. It's breeding season, so the whale picks a fight. If it's feeling sufficiently omnipotent, it stands a better chance of winning the battle. The barnacle colony gets rubbed off directly over its new home. It's a win-win situation!"

Steve curls his top lip, nods his head several times, then points out to sea where I observe more spouts heading our way. Milly attempts a head count, informing us there are at least fifty humpbacks within a half mile of the boat. Probably ten or fifteen more when we consider how many whales must be in the middle of a dive during any single count. Steve turns off the engine. He places his tiny digital video camera to his face to record fluke patterns. After a minute he puts the camera down, to whisper in awed tones, "Individual animals we've ID'd in this channel each summer turn up each winter in Puerto Vallarta, Maui, and even Ogasawara, Japan. They all share the same basic song structure, which is quite distinct from the songs of the Atlantic or Antarctic populations. They also alter their songs a bit every year. It's not much, but it's enough to track a distinct pattern of change over several years. Since this is the only place they're together for any length of time, you'd think we'd hear them practicing new variations on old tunes. Strange thing is, they rarely sing here in Alaska. What do you think? Does it make a case for telepathy?"

The presence of so many whales has reduced me to silence. It is a scene perhaps impossible to witness anywhere else on the planet. There are no houses, no roads, possibly no other boats within twenty miles of here. We gaze with some of the same sense of awe that must have guided Samuel de Champlain when he entered the Gulf of Saint Lawrence in 1603 and wrote of seeing thousands of great whales representing six or more species. Captain Cook saw something similar when he sailed into the Lahaina Channel in the late 1700s. The Norwegian whalers certainly saw it again when they explored the Antarctic coast at the turn of the twentieth century.

The whales are everywhere.

Steve grabs the video camera, motions to Milly. The two of them climb down from the bridge and into their small inflatable, heading off toward a group of lungers. Acutely aware that I am alone on the *Lamarck*, I watch the two of them dwindle into the distance. I sigh deeply, drop down to the wheelhouse to start the process of connecting the waterproof box containing my underwater sound system to the ship's battery bank. Then I attach a hydrophone cable to the box, drop the hydrophone over the side, stop at fifteen feet, tie off the cable to the gunwale. Slipping headphones over my ears, I hear several whales singing with a mournful fullness reminiscent of a taut fence wire vibrating in the wind. Throwing the headphones onto the table, I lunge into the hold to find my equipment bag, extricate the twenty-pound flying saucer–shaped underwater speaker, climb the stairs with it cradled in my arms, and connect its cable to the box. For purposes of audio separation, I unwind the cable along the opposite side of the boat from the hydrophone, then carefully take hold of the speaker's attached rope to drop the heavy piece of hardware over the side until it lies fifteen feet under the surface. Then I tie the rope and the cable to a cleat.

I take a half-size guitar out its waterproof carrying case, find an electronic tuner to put it into D modal tuning, then carefully lay it on the seat beside me. I favor the small guitar on certain occasions simply because it is so much easier to travel with than a full-size instrument. The guitar permits me to reach notes an octave above a normal guitar, which is effective when I'm interacting with squeaking dolphins. The humpbacks should be able to hear it just fine. Putting on the headphones again, I close my eyes and concentrate on the sound of the underwater environment. Only a single humpback seems to be singing. The hiss of water current flowing across the hydrophone provides a constant drone. Small waves lick and lap against the hull. When I drop a tin cup on the floor, it registers through my ears as a faraway clink.

I take hold of the electric guitar, settle back in my seat, and initiate an Indian folk raga entitled "*Jinjhoti*," a melody that suggests wide-open spaces. I stop playing every thirty seconds. My thumb keeps pumping out a drone on the low D and A strings, just in case a humpback might get the idea to fill in the gaps. Slowly but surely I accelerate the rhythm over the next half hour; not a single whale seems interested enough to draw closer than a hundred yards from the boat. The one whale continues vocalizing just as it would if I was silent. I stop playing. No interaction today. I sit in silence a while longer, then rise to dissemble and store all the electronic components.

When my two buckaroos return to the boat, Milly winks at me, a clear sign that Steve is quite aware of what I have been up to during their absence. Later, she asks if any whales responded. I shake my head. "Too many herring around this morning," she says. "When these animals are feeding on a herring school as big as the one we just saw, the ocean would have to boil to get them to do anything else. Feeding is why they're here. They eat all day long, all summer long, to put on a thick layer of blubber. When they leave these waters in November, heading south, they may not feed again for several months."

"And when they're not feeding?" I ask.

"They're sleeping. There is only a brief window each day when they turn frisky, playing with one another or with the sea lions."

Milly and I stare out the window at a group of whales lunge feeding near the boat. Steve sits down across from us. "I've concluded that the so-called 'whales' are never going to be respondents to your communication experiment," he says in a tired voice. "To succeed, you need to search out those few individual humpbacks who have the musical skill and the intellectual curiosity to interact with another species. They're just like humans in that respect. Most humpbacks can keep a tune. But only a few of them are artists."

Two whales are resting so close to stern that I can easily imagine starting a triple jump from the bridge to the transom, onto the back of the first whale, and then onto the second whale. From this perspective, they are void of features, two charcoal oblongs resting on the mirror of the sea—pleats, fins, flukes, and even their eyes beneath the surface. The closer animal lets loose with a five-second exhale, which penetrates so deeply into my body that I shiver under its spell. Listening starts at my toes, then rolls up my body like a perfect wave curling onto a beach. The vapors float ten, twenty feet straight up, hang a moment in the air, and then waft my way on the ghost of a breeze. I close my eyes, receive the mist, feel the patter on my cheeks, and breathe the glorious whale stink deep into my lungs.

4 ON THEIR OWN BEHALF

Tell me of deep origins, of eternal things . . .[1]
—THE KALEVALA

No matter how luminous the charged border may appear to us, it is the dark, festering topic of whaling that dominates our historical relationship with cetaceans. Until a mere thirty years ago, human beings were involved in a mass slaughter of whales that left several species at the brink of extinction, a precipice from which several of them have never fully recovered. Today, the clamor to resume whaling remains loud in the halls where resource policies are legislated.

The actual holocaust of the great whales is a historic event that began in the middle of the fifteenth century. Before that time neither the technology nor the will was sufficient to pursue such large animals on the open ocean. Nonetheless, human beings have killed cetaceans for thousands of years, although ancient whalers like the arctic Finns sought their prey only when they ventured close to shore, or were stranded, providing a local windfall. Coastal tribes ate whale meat and burned the oil in their lamps. Northern people used the rib cages as framing material for house construction. The baleen plates in the whale's mouth provided a durable material that was springy and light. Beluga whale skins provided a high grade of white leather, and raw blubber was the primary source for vitamin C in the far North. The Arctic narwhal provided a spiraling ivory tooth up to ten feet long, which upheld the medieval myth of the unicorn.

To understand the rush to industrial whaling, it is essential to recognize that oil derived from petroleum products became generally available only after the middle of the nineteenth century. Before that time, people relied on vegetable oil to light their lamps. Whale oil burned just as well, but it was far more expensive to acquire. This changed in the fourteenth century after the Basque people of northern Spain perfected the design of whale-boats and the method of pursuit. They began their whaling adventure on the Bay of Biscay, pursuing the right whale, which, as a slow swimmer, was the easiest species to harpoon. Unlike most cetacean species that sank when killed, this was the "right" whale for staying afloat.

Whaling played a crucial role in the colonial expansion of Europe. A map drawn in 1413 entitled *Carta Catalán de Mecia de Viladestes* shows a Basque caravel hunting a whale on the sea far northwest of Iceland.[2] Some historians believe the Basques hunted bowhead whales along the east coast of Canada half a century before Columbus landed in the West Indies. In the sixteenth century, the Basque captain Francois Sopite Zaburu hit on the ingenious idea of building a stove right on deck to ren-der whale blubber into oil and store it in barrels for months at a time.[3] This invention completely freed the whalers from their onshore facilities, while the early rumblings of the Industrial Revolution produced an increasing number of new machines that needed lubricating oil. Dutch whalers started exploring the New World. French whalers tapped the seemingly bottomless marine mammal resource in the Gulf of Saint Lawrence, an action that eventually led to the French colonization of Canada. The Basques, more tribe than nation, eventually lagged behind as European industry came to depend upon stable supplies of whale oil.

When the right whale population declined from overhunting off the coast of western Europe, a Dutch businessman learned from a Basque whaling captain that vast herds of bowhead whales congregated around the remote arctic island of Spitsbergen located above the north coast of Norway. In 1625, a wealthy Dutchman built Smeerenburg, or Blubber town,[4] installing a massive platform for dragging whales whole out of the water and dumping the bodies directly into a giant pressure cooker. The process was quick and efficient, producing a half dozen grades of oil, animal feed, and high-grade fertilizer. Between 1675 and 1721, the Dutch recorded a kill of thirty-three thousand whales. The unrelenting pressure of the hunt eventually caused the bowhead population off Spitsbergen to collapse.

Over the next hundred and fifty years, larger boats from several European nations explored distant oceans and different species. Advances in winching technology finally made it possible to pursue species whose bodies sink after death. The British focused on humpbacks in the Hawaiian Islands as well as the thirty-five-foot bottlenose whales that once thrived off the northeast coast of Scotland. On a tip from a Chinese pilot, Joseph Scammon, an American, learned that gray whales congregate in the shallow lagoons of Baja California. Within thirty years, the grays were commercially extinct. The bottlenose whales soon followed. The Hawaiian humpback population was devastated. Unique in the annals of whaling, the gray population actually recovered, was hunted a second time, then crashed again.

It was Nantucketers who figured out an efficient method to hunt the powerfully muscled, deep-diving, and lucrative sperm whale. The sperms quickly became the "right" whale, at least for Americans, by virtue of several superlative products rendered from its body parts. Although the flesh of this creature is considered inedible by humans, the average-size sperm whale yields more oil of a higher grade, by body weight, than any other whale. The peglike teeth protruding from the lower jaw are ivory. Ambergris, a waxy excretion from the whale's large intestine, and composed of the partially digested remains of squid beaks, was a major component of fine perfume.[5] The most valuable product was spermaceti.

The discovery of petroleum in Pennsylvania in 1859 led to a new, inexpensive source of machine oil. The Civil War interceded, causing the sperm whaling industry to lose its workforce and its capital, neither of which it was able to recover after peace was won. Lamp oil, rendered first from the blubber of right whales, then bowheads, and finally sperms, turned night into day, lit factories and homes until Edison destroyed the market forever with his invention and subsequent marketing of the electric lightbulb in the 1870s, incidentally turning the inventor into the greatest whale saver in history. For all these reasons, the sperm whale hunt tapered off just as the species became depleted to the point of commercial extinction. The hunt resumed again just before World War II, now focused primarily on acquiring spermaceti. In the 1957–58 season, a total of 18,853 sperm whales were taken,[6] mostly by Japanese and Norwegians. In the last year they were hunted, 1979–80, whalers took 2,203. Since then sperm whales have been granted a full reprieve, and the species has rebounded to a certain extent.

The mysticetes have not been so fortunate. At the end of the nineteenth century, there were not enough baleen whales anywhere in the known world to support a continuation of the hunt. The fleets of "whalebone whalers" rusted in their moorings. Then, during the first years of the new century, almost too improbably, explorers reported sighting vast, unexploited herds of rorquals—the family of whalebone whales that includes blues and their smaller look-alikes, the fins, the Bryde's, and the seis—swimming off the remote coast of Antarctica. Huge factory ships were built, capable of slicing up a hundred-foot blue whale in just a few hours. Advances in refrigeration technology permitted the meat to be stored for the duration of the voyage, transforming it from a local and seasonal specialty into an item of mass global marketing. New harpoons were introduced equipped with exploding tips and shot from cannons mounted on the decks of catcher boats. Air hoses kept the carcasses afloat.

Antarctica became the whaler's mother lode, the site of a systematic slaughter that outdid every previous hunt by efficiency if not by ferocity. Administered first by Norwegians, and subsidized by British and Greek capital—Aristotle Onassis was a major investor—and later enjoined by the Japanese, the Antarctic "fishery" yielded, at its peak, a whale every twelve minutes. The blues, the most massive and most valuable of the rorquals, were the first to vanish. The industry then targeted the next in size, the fins. They vanished. Next came the seis, which eventually vanished as well. Then the Bryde's. Today Japanese whalers still venture into Antarctic waters to hunt the last healthy population of rorquals, the thirty-foot minke whale, despite an overwhelming vote by the International Whaling Commission to designate Antarctica as a whale preserve. Even as politicians jab and parry over the terms of whale preservation,

illegal "pirate" whalers hunt several protected species to provide meat for
fish markets throughout the Orient.

In his epic poem *Whale Nation*, Heathcote Williams devotes several
pages to an inventory of products produced from whale parts. Because it is
so long, and because so many of the items seem superfluous, the list finally
attains the dimensions of a great tragedy, documenting better than any
historical account the nearsightedness of human commerce.

> *For brushes and brooms;*
> *For linoleum;*
> *For medical trusses;*
> *For oil cloth;*
> *For sausage skins;*
> *For drum skins;*
> *For sword hilts and scabbards;*
> *For laces;*
> *For surgical stitches;*
> *For tennis racket strings;*
> *For riding crops;*
> *For chess-men;*
> *For buttons;*
> *For tanning leather;*
> *For artist's pigments;*
> *For wax crayons;*
> *For engineering coolants;*
> *For golf bags.*[7]

Whale meat is exceedingly oily, fishy-smelling, and the color of clotted
blood. Even when it was readily available in the United States, it was never
regarded as more than a specialty item. Today whale meat is marketed primarily in Japan, and to a lesser extent in Norway, two places it has always
been considered a traditional food. An entrée can fetch $150 in a Tokyo
restaurant. Norwegians primarily target the fin whale, a species otherwise granted full protection under international law. It doesn't seem to
faze them that their outlaw act has provoked an international boycott

paralyzing the Norwegian fishing fleet. Nor does it seem to matter that the resource and the market are so diminished that the relict industry survives only by a steady infusion of government subsidies.

Their industry must also contend with the guerrilla tactics of the Sea Shepherd Society—the world's only paramilitary group fighting for the rights of another species. This whale war is deadly serious and, in recent years, has resulted in the destruction of two Norwegian whaling ships. Yet the otherwise environmentally sophisticated Norwegians remain implacable, if not jingoistic in their insistence that their national identity is at stake here, a disposition apparently so vicious that it can be kept alive only by slaughtering several hundred endangered fin whales a year. Nor does it seem to matter that this whale is a nomad, a roamer of oceans that, in its currently foreshortened lifetime, travels far beyond Norway's territorial boundaries and is therefore the resource and the responsibility of every country through whose waters it passes.

As the brand-new road winding up to the whale-watching platform at Chichi-jima verifies, within Japan living whales now provide a viable commercial alternative to killing whales. Worldwide, whale watching probably earns as much money today as whaling ever did. A 1992 study disclosed that 3.4 million Americans and 4.4 million people worldwide partook that year, spending over $46 million on tickets and $225 million on related travel expenses, excluding food and lodging. While the industry generally promotes preservation, in a few places its actions flagrantly disregard that message. There is a story, perhaps apocryphal, of a Japanese entrepreneur who owns both a whale-watching boat and a whaling boat. If his whale-watching skipper sights pilot whales in the morning, there is a fair chance his whaling skipper will be dispatched in the afternoon.

Where I live, on San Juan Island, in the Pacific Northwest, whale watching has become so frenzied that boaters besiege the local orca pods every weekend, all summer long. On July 4, 1996, a hundred motorboats surrounded sixteen orcas for over an hour. Naturally, these whale watchers buy what touches them. In my town there are orca art galleries selling orca carvings, paintings, coffee cups, cutlery, buttons, glass, mobiles, calendars, clothing, all adorned with the image of the black-and-white totem.

Just as no one on the viewing platform at Chichi-jima paid attention to the little gray bird with the red throat, one may also wonder why, in my town, there is no commensurate harbor seal–watching industry, no fast-selling line of sweatshirts silk-screened with murres, no cups adorned with sea urchins, no keychains showing the threatened yelloweye rockfish, which lives up to a hundred years and bears three million live young at a time. In the same vein, why are there no musicians building studios to play with the exceedingly musical lemurs of Madagascar or the bell birds of Australia, as is done with pilot whales off Tenerife and orcas off Vancouver Island? Alaska has no commensurate billion-dollar marmot-watching industry. Florida has no tourism based on swimming with turtles. No one makes spiritual pilgrimages to sites in western Australia where dugongs cavort in the shallows, though many travel to nearby Monkey Mia where bottlenose dolphins cavort near shore. Even the scientific community is affected by the charged border. Researchers cannot expect the same level of support or attention when they mount elegant language experiments with parrots, although the relationship between a parrot's social behavior and its calls seems as evolved as any dolphin's whistle.

The behavior of all these other creatures is just as worthwhile to observe, and just as important to the general health of the environment, as that of the whale. When sea lions are spotted preying on salmon in Seattle's Ballard Locks, mountains of paperwork are generated to give officials the option to kill these mammals who are otherwise granted full protection by an act of the U.S. Congress. Yet when orcas in the same vicinity are documented losing weight during the same bad salmon run, op-ed pieces are written proposing that commercial and sports fishing be ended until the orcas recover.

In the Arctic, I once had an experience with a raven that walked up so close to me I could reach out and pet him. He started croaking and cooing in a whispery, soothing tone as if trying to tell me something. I later learned that my experience occurs often enough that many people in the Arctic feel quite certain that ravens possess a language. Yet there are no ecotours to raven habitats, no raven appreciation societies, no celebrities who travel the workshop circuit lecturing about the deeper meaning of croaks and caws. I have concluded that what the raven lacks is not friendliness, intelligence, or even a willingness to communicate with us, but charisma. By contrast, a recent conference in Brussels brought together twenty organizations and three thousand participants to discuss not the cetaceans themselves, but the varied ways that humans interact with them.

"If the whales can't save us, nothing can"[8] is a sentiment echoed over and again by environmentalists. But why do we treat this group of animals with such respect? Steve Templor reflects the feelings of many scientists when he asserts that bigger is better, or, in the case of dolphins, that we can't resist those vibrant leaps tied to such a happy face. Are these the only reasons whale watchers scream with delight at a humpback sighting, why the campaign to adopt orcas sometimes accrues the look and feel of the Elvis Presley Fan Club? Whale watchers have been known to swoon in the presence of a leaping humpback like groupies fainting before a movie star who winks in their direction.

Cynics contend that our culture's shallow obsession with celebrity is the primary reason "saving the whales" became the first and perhaps the most prolonged rallying cry of the environmental movement. In other words, the lure of the megafauna is irrational, emotional, and stylish, and, therefore, our admiration is spurious. Some ecologists vouch that global environmental healing can never occur until the concern we feel for the cetaceans transcends celebrity to include less glamorous species. If only people loved spotted owls, grizzly bears, and snail darters the way they now love cetaceans, how might that affection tip the balance for saving all of nature? Then again, what's the point of moaning? Some species of great whales would be extinct today without that tidal wave of human passion.

Being large may help generate charisma, but it is certainly not the only reason we love whales and dolphins. The "save the whale movement" often portrayed the cetaceans as mentors who could teach us how an advanced mind could flourish in harmony with the Earth. This capability of the whales and dolphins to generate hope for our species is nothing new. The Sumerians, the ancient people of the Indus Valley, and, later, the Greeks praised the ability of cetaceans to rejuvenate human culture.[9] According to Homer, Oceanus existed before the gods. Dolphins and whales lived within Oceanus, which is why the Greeks believed cetaceans, and especially dolphins, held the power of the creator. *Delphys* shares a common root with the words for womb, navel, and birth. Homer praised cetacean wisdom because "they always try to be gratefully useful to human beings."

For much the same reason, cetaceans have emerged today as an enduring subject of nature films and magazine articles. Our vision of the intelligent, "gratefully useful" cetacean led directly to *Flipper*, the most popular
wild animal TV series of all time. Another boy-meets-cetacean story line
titled *Free Willy* has become a high-grossing film with several sequels. The
dolphins' Mona Lisa smile and the humpback whales' gravity-defying
leaps compete with pretty female faces as advertising icons on Tokyo subway kiosks, which are used to sell solar panels, computers, and watches.
The message is "think smart, have hope, be free."

Few dispute the fact that the cetaceans have coalesced a new environmental consciousness. Some whale lovers disagree, however, with the
conventional wisdom declaring that cetaceans are mere *passive* recipients
of our attention. They uphold the conclusions of Horace Dobbs, Patricia
St. John, John Lilly, and Lana Miller, who espouse an "energy field" surrounding cetaceans that is so vibrant it transcends symbolism and
metaphor. The whales' role is active, transforming the charged border
into the place we visit to listen to environmental philosophy and, possibly, get our orders. According to believers, cetaceans are benevolent
strategists working within the Gaia-wide network to save us even as we
work to save them.

Those who hold the view assert that from Delphi to Chichi-jima, from
Moby Dick to Keiko, from the Aboriginal dolphin dreamtime to the
Greenpeace Zodiacs, cetaceans have always served humans as friendly
arbiters of perception, exerting a subtle, but nonetheless firm, role in
transforming the way human beings perceive their place within nature.
The symbolism of this interspecies mentor is mythic, communal, and
deeply cultural. Its examples are not always founded in nature, nor are
they necessarily cetacean-specific. "Nuke the whales," an anthem of the
punk movement of the 1980s, was a declaration of protest not against
whales, but against the perceived excesses of environmental bathos.

When pop idioms start to sound like myth, Joseph Campbell's writing
is sure to offer some guidance. Campbell informs us that myths are active,
serving society by highlighting the deepest truths of a culture. This particular myth of the mentor cetacean starts with the shape-shifting kinship
elaborated by traditional shamans, devolves into the horrors of whaling,
sputters as the populations of several species start to collapse, then rises

again like a phoenix as people all over the world become aroused to save their once and future guide from extinction. The mythmakers insist cetaceans are here to teach us compassion, altruism, environmental stewardship, and perhaps to acquaint us with etheric energies. These gifts are given freely, but with the express purpose of instructing us to reinvent our own species, save ourselves, and therefore save the planet. The poet Jeff Poniewaz describes this mentor role, not as professorial or patriarchal, but as childlike and lighthearted.

> *I believe we should*
> *apprentice ourselves*
> *to whales & dolphin*
> *more eagerly than*
> *to any human guru . . .*
> *Yes, the whales*
> *sing & play all day*
> *& don't have to mail*
> *their songs to any*
> *publisher whales*
> *in order to be free*
> *from factories & blow*
> *geysers of ecstasy*
> *all day long . . .*
> *Their only*
> *reason to go mad with anguish & agony are*
> *the lightning bolts*
> *exploding unaccountably*
> *into their brains,*
> *harpoons expertly hurled*
> *by beings made in image*
> *of Jehovah.*[10]

Whether we believe the cetaceans' role is active or passive, aspects of the mentor myth ring true. Before the save-the-whale movement ignited a tidal wave of righteous protest, no animal advocate ever swayed a government body by arguing that a nonhuman species deserved to exist *on its own behalf.* Few conceived a human relationship to nature beyond resource management, with the result that environmental and animal rights prerogatives had to make sense to a culture implicitly committed to the predominance of the human species as well as to the inherent goodness of progress, resource development, and technology. The whale movement presented us with something original. This was not a human-centered movement. Whale activists were engaged not for personal gain, but *for* the whales. Their number started out small, composed of people mostly under thirty who were roused to action by Rachel Carson's *Silent Spring*, edified by John Muir, provoked by Edward Abbey, and mobilized by Joan McIntyre's *Mind in the Waters*. They called themselves Project Jonah and Greenpeace. Dexter Cate was active in the latter. I joined in the second wave and soon found myself on the front line at Iki Island, Japan.

The surge to save the whales gathered steam throughout the 1970s. The people who initiated the struggle waged their campaign with passion and conviction, employing the same media tactics developed earlier by the civil rights and anti-Vietnam protests. Some whale savers put their lives on the line to protect dolphins and whales. The sensational image of a Russian harpoon soaring over a Greenpeace Zodiac and then striking the side of a whale was the breakthrough event that turned the politics of extinction into front-page news. It gave the seminal movement a podium that dramatically expanded its influence. As the number of supporters grew, the commando tactics that initially drove the fray evolved, became less edgy, more philosophical. Proponents became cognizant of a new term, *ecology*, with its essential lesson that nature is a community of inter-dependent members. Every being, every plant and animal, every thing is intrinsically engaged; destroy one member, and the whole falters. The original premise of saving whales for their own behalf acquired the urgent addendum of saving ourselves as well.

Driven by such a compelling holistic argument, the organizations that formed solely to save whales bonded to form greater coalitions, continually adding converts. The objective of preserving drastically depleted whale stocks *and* stopping the whalers now ignited the imagination of scientists, politicians, and just plain folks. Of perhaps greater significance, saving the whales mobilized schoolchildren, who channeled their innate love for animals into an unprecedented letter-writing campaign in support of a transformation in international wildlife policy. This was a new kind of mass engagement: the first international social protest fought entirely for the cause of another species. By 1980, the compounding energy had blossomed full-blown into what we now refer to as the environmental movement. Today, the whale movement is generally regarded as the first major rallying cry of what has become a transformation in human consciousness toward nature.

Before "save the whales," only a few idealists and poets talked about nature as sacred. After "save the whales," many more people came to regard natural balance as an authentic challenge to what was always considered to be a human economic and intellectual birthright. The results were significant if not subtle. By the late 1980s, when the World Wildlife Fund mounted its campaign to save the rain forest by treating its ample resources as an entrepreneurial golden land full of marketable nuts and vital medicines, the aftershock left by the save-the-whale movement had already made that pragmatic proposal seem woefully anthropocentric. When the journal *The Futurist* declared that ecological posterity was primarily an engineering opportunity—building better cars and distilling fossil fuels so our great-grandchildren attained better gas mileage and spewed fewer pollutants—the displayed value system seemed only to promote a future without hope.

When the issue is captivity, agreement about the mentor relationship is far less certain. The oceanarium environment shortens the lives of highly social dolphins and orcas through stress-related diseases provoked by isolation and boredom. How could it be otherwise for vibrant social animals forced to spend their lives swimming in endless circles through chlorinated water? It's an unfair image, shout the oceanarium promoters. This is an educational enterprise. Captive cetaceans serve as ambassadors for wild cetaceans by virtue of their visibility to hundreds of thousands of children. The protesters avow that oceanariums are actually circuses. How can children be educated about the behavior of wild cetaceans when they are shown captive dolphins enacting unnatural behavior such as jumping through hoops? How can children be educated about the degradation of wild stocks by entrepreneurs who degrade wild stocks in the process of capturing dolphins?

Just as great whales have their human militia, so captive cetaceans have their human abolitionists. The best-known freedom fighter is Rick O'Barry, who many times has put his life on the line to defeat ("monkey wrench," in radical environmental jargon) an oceanarium's expensive capture operation. O'Barry was converted to this risky vocation while working as the first trainer of the TV star Flipper. Of his famous student, he concludes,

> Though he seemed as real as life—or more actually, as art is supposed to be—Flipper was an illusion, an elaborate fabrication, the work of hundreds of talented people who came thousands of miles and spent tens of thousands of dollars to create the legend of a fabulous creature combining both actual and imaginary delphoid powers with that of a family pet specially blessed with human intelligence.[11]

Today, whale savers turn their attentions to nonwhaling issues that give them common cause with other environmental activists. Pollution from the offshore dumping of garbage is diagnosed as the cause of a chronic die-off of bottlenose dolphins along the U.S. Atlantic coast. Chemical runoff into Quebec's Saguenay River has devastated the once-large local population of beluga whales, leaving the carcasses so contaminated they are disposed of as toxic waste.

Acoustic pollution places whale savers increasingly at odds with the U.S. Navy. In May 1996, thirteen Cuvier's beaked whales stranded on the coast of Greece just a day after a navy sonar test bombarded the area with dangerous levels of low-frequency sound. A French cetologist called to the scene wrote, "Although pure coincidence cannot be excluded, it seems improbable the two events were independent."[12] He later concluded that the low-frequency-sound tests had injured the whales' inner ears. In a maneuver that violates every principle of public relations, the navy relocated its low-frequency testing to Hawaii's humpback breeding grounds during the height of whale-watching season. During the winter of 1998, the otherwise fully protected whales were consistently targeted with dangerous levels of sound to determine precisely how they would react. As predicted by most lay critics, several whales responded by immediately abandoning the sanctuary.

Jacques Cousteau spent his later years translating complex environmental problems into terms nonexperts, especially children, could readily understand. He wisely predicted that the most urgent environmental problem of the next generation will be dealing with the pervasive human vandalism of this generation.[13] Vandalism is defined as a conscious tampering with the natural order undertaken to satisfy self-interest. Norwegian whalers and Iki fishermen are vandals. Oceanarium owners who snatch juvenile dolphins from their pods are vandals. Chemical company executives who dispose of pollution through pipes open to rivers are vandals. Their act of destruction would be no more unconscionable if they captured every beluga whale in the Saguenay River and inoculated each one with poison.

Vandalism is often a mindless act, perpetrated by people bewitched by intellect, who sincerely believe the alteration they prompt is more important than what already exists. Teenagers who spray paint subway cars argue persuasively that they are misunderstood artists. Puget Sound whale-watching entrepreneurs argue persuasively that they are educating the general public. Steve Templor argues persuasively that the data provided by his cookie-cutter darts is more important than the harm it poses for the humpbacks he loves so well. The scientists who directed the Hawaiian low-frequency-sound tests sincerely believed they were helping whales by measuring the effects of low-frequency sonar that the navy will employ whether the whales are affected or not. Though the biologists considered themselves good guys, and were genuinely embarrassed that so many protesters rallied against them, they did not quit their test when the breeding whales became stressed.

The Cousteau myth of vandalism is repeated every day on the news. The characters change; the scenery alters so often it blends into an unidentifiable Everywhere. Today it's whales off the Kona coast; tomorrow, it's some rain forest on an island no one has ever heard of. Yet if we are conscientious about following the trail of blame, too often we find it leading back to ourselves. As I write these words, I am listening to a radio report of an algae bloom along the Florida coast that has devastated the local marine mammal population. Algae feed on nitrogen and phosphorus. The reporter informs his listeners the farmers won't be blamed. Without legislation, they will assuredly continue spreading the nitrogen and phosphorus fertilizers that keep you and me in winter vegetables, whatever the marine damage.

5 WHEN NATURE IS LARGER THAN LIFE

It is said that he who knows well how to live meets no tigers or wild buffaloes on his road, and comes out from the battleground untouched by weapons of war. For in him, a buffalo would find no butt for his horns, a tiger nothing to lay his claws upon, and a weapon of war no place to admit its point. How is this? Because there is no room for death in him.[1]
                                                                    —LAO TZU

In 1986, the Russell Glacier sealed off the mouth of a fiord southeast of Anchorage, Alaska, trapping seals and porpoises behind an impenetrable ice barrier that cut off the tidal flow. With so many rivers and creeks dispersing their load into the fiord, the level rose, turning the saltwater fiord into a freshwater lake. A rescue was undertaken. The well-financed, well-equipped team of mostly marine mammal rehabilitation professionals from up and down the West Coast agreed that the best hope for success lay in corralling the animals inside a net enclosure, and then freighting them, one by one, by helicopter if need be, over the glacier and back into the open sea. I knew something about capturing small dolphins by making loud grating sounds into the water, having witnessed the technique a few times at Iki Island, Japan. For that reason, the director of the Russell Glacier operation invited me to join his team.

I waffled interminably before deciding against putting my research group's acoustic resources to this task of corralling Alaska sea life. No one in command could tell me whether or not the animals would die if we simply left them alone. Nor could the director convince me that this was a necessary rescue and not just another case of human beings interfering in natural processes. With so little money available for animal rehabilitation, I encouraged him to consider putting the substantial funds raised for this project into a savings account to be sprung loose for a genuine ecological emergency. But this liberator was clearly bewitched by the opportunity handed him to ease a crisis a-brewing at the charged border. What did I know? I was no expert. His crew soon flew north to the Russell Glacier, insisting that sheer altruism must overwhelm any inference of tampering.

The rescuers exhibited a bit too much yearning to turn aside a natural process by exerting maximum human ingenuity and minimal wisdom. And why not? Weren't we humans guilty of massacring marine mammals to the point of extinction? By God, didn't we owe it to those icebound seals and porpoises? That line of reasoning crystallized into a rallying cry as the Russell Glacier mission evolved into a media event of the first magnitude. Journalists from newspapers and broadcast news networks from a half dozen countries descended upon the Russell Glacier like vultures around a poached rhino on the African veldt. Over the next few weeks, the nightly TV news treated its viewers to shots of rescuers in foul-weather gear zooming their inflatable boats through the choppy waters of the fiord straight into groups of marine mammal dorsal fins in an attempt to corral them toward a net. Unfortunately, the tactics of a cattle roundup, which were devised to shepherd animals standing on firm ground, proved futile for directing aquatic animals that are able to maneuver in three directions. When the porpoises dove, they effectively vanished, leaving the rescuers scanning the surface for some slight surface irregularity, often for several minutes at a time. The *tsukimbo* method favored by the Japanese dolphin fishery was also ineffective; to succeed it demands a few hundred boats making noise simultaneously. The Russell Glacier rescuers had a tenth as many boats. The animals proved far too nimble at eluding their captors.

In a typically wry insight, Barbara Tuchman has argued that there can be no history unless there are historians around to write it.[2] If so, then the task of ordering and reordering history is an act of human creation. Historians dream up history as much as they report it. But most news journalists—who are historians of the present moment—disagree with this assertion, viewing it as an assault upon their virtue as objective observers. But whatever journalists choose to believe about their participation in the events they cover, most of the rest of us notice that the media creates the news as much as reports it. In the case of the Russell Glacier rescue, large-scale media attention meant that the saviors did not pack up their bags and go home when they started to suspect that their efforts were hopeless. Not only was the sheer immensity of a cold, damp Alaskan fiord dampening their enthusiasm, the porpoises themselves had perfected their role as ingrates or even dimwits, stubbornly resisting every opportunity to be corralled.

But celebrity engenders its own validity. The applied force of seeing one's image up there on the tube induces euphoria. It invokes the seductive impression that the whole world is offering encouragement and overwhelms any gut feeling that it may be time to throw in the towel. At the Russell Glacier, news reporters and news makers ended up working together with all the teamwork of a Super Bowl champion to stimulate what might just as easily have turned out to be a natural event bound by the laws of entropy. Because the machinery of the mass media clogs when events do not develop at the news' own inherent velocity, the rescuers were coerced into providing more and more newsworthy morsels until even the project's most ardent supporters noted that the rescue was deflating into parody. During its final days, the rescue took on the look and feel of an aging sports hero having an embarrassing last year.

How did it end? In fact, the glacier acted very glacierlike. One day it receded on its own, rescuing sea mammals, rescuers, and journalists in one fell swoop. The trapped seals and porpoises stayed right where they were, displaying no interest in taking advantage of what the humans had interpreted as a positive swing of the icy pendulum. To this day, marine mammals cavort intemperately through the waters of the Russell Fiord, oblivious to the hazards that the rescuers insist swirl all about them. My intent here is not to shame the rescuers for their sincere act of trying. They caused no harm. The rescue was not an act of vandalism, although, ironically, its success could have been interpreted as such.

A handful of well-meaning idealists do not easily leave lasting footprints on a glacier.

October 1988. I am invited to join another Alaska rescue effort. This time, three gray whales are stuck in an ice hole located a few miles outside the town of Barrow on the southwestern coast of the Beaufort Sea. Because of my reputation for coaxing whales to a sound source, it is hoped, once again, that I can transmit some acoustic message to either attract or repel the whales out of their hole and toward the open sea.

The difference between the two rescue events is mostly a matter of scale. In Barrow there are three whales trapped inside a twenty-by-twenty-foot hole in the sea ice located five miles from the open ocean. Chopping a ten-foot-wide channel through the fourteen-inch sea ice demands far less hubris than trying to stop the advance of the Russell Glacier, reckoned to approach the size of Rhode Island. The bond between saviors and saved is also different. Clearly, the gray whales are active participants in this rescue. Without human assistance at keeping the ice hole from freezing over, the whales will drown within a week. If a channel can be chopped through the ice (and everyone agrees it's possible), then my own transmitted sounds might be able to help guide the whales down the channel. Failing that, I can possibly crank up the volume at the hole itself to evict them from it.

For these reasons, I board a charter flight to Alaska within hours of my summoning.

The ambience in Barrow is altruistic and urgent, to which I would add a notable measure of Eskimo bewilderment over how such a common occurrence as marine mammals getting stuck in the local sea ice could have mushroomed into such an improbable media extravaganza. Their perplexity seems only natural. The local Inupiats' yearning for whales originates not in their imaginations, but in their bellies. They hunt, kill, and dismember whales, dine on whale blubber, and regard whale flukes to be a special delicacy. They perceive the charged border as a kind of offshore supermarket; therefore they have no context to explain why this event has generated so much attention. From their gastronomic perspective, news coverage about these whales is conceivably comparable to, if not nearly as absurd as, the ongoing front-page stories generated about George Bush's disdain for broccoli.

Soon after I arrive in Barrow, hosts from the army and Greenpeace whisk me off to the ice hole to meet the whales. I walk up to the edge to stare at three bruised, oblong faces thrust twelve feet out of the jet black water and just a few inches from my own face. The proportions are out of sync with my gaze. To look a whale in the eye at such close quarters demands a peripheral vision more acute than my own. To focus on one eye is to give up the other eye, not to mention cheeks and mouth and brow. The basic ground color of these faces is a shiny charcoal gray. The skin is overlaid with a profusion of gnarly, light gray patches, granting it the texture of a three-dimensional contour map depicting hilly plateaus surrounded by dark shining expanses of water. A few of these plateaus are overlaid a second time by ranges of sharply peaked volcanoes. These ranges are composed of communities of barnacles growing on the whales' flesh like razor-sharp pimples sprouting on a teenager.

When I squint just right, the identities of the three oblong shapes alter dramatically, rousing the same barnacle quandary I discussed with Steve Templor. Most of the time it's whales in charge here. Squint again, and it's barnacles. In this latter mode, the surrealism implicit in the event becomes altogether disorienting. The U.S. Army, Greenpeace, and several oil companies are spending hundreds of thousands of dollars to liberate three barnacle colonies from an ice hole.

Gray whales are predominantly bottom feeders. They dig their lower jaws into the sea floor and thrust forward and up until they've collected a heaping mountain of biomass and mud inside their mouth. They work the mud against their baleen filters with a tongue the size of a compact car; pushing and grating, filtering the mud through the baleen. Clams, crabs, and worms are trapped inside. All those razor-sharp clamshells lacerate the animal's thin skin. Barnacles attach themselves to these vulnerable areas, ultimately functioning as a calcium armor protecting the skin against further scrapes. The barnacles benefit as well. For nourishment they depend on the flow of water to carry plankton to their mouths. Any whale plowing through mud raises a shroud of microscopic organisms, upon which the barnacles feast. Letting my eyes glide across the bumpy panorama of three upthrust slabs, the view alters accordingly as I make the intellectual leap of perceiving barnacles and whales inextricably bonded in a symbiotic relationship. The two vastly different organisms compose a single system.

The gray whale is the most primitive of the great whales, a living fossil possessed of unformed baleen plates and no dorsal fin. In many respects their behavior seems more akin to human behavior than that of any other whale species. They dote on our attention. Many whale watchers have commented that gray whales seem as fascinated by observing us as we are distracted by looking at them. Whale-watching operators along the Pacific coast of North America and in the lagoons of Baja consistently report gray whales venturing up to people to rub a rostrum against the sides of the boats. Grays are the only cetaceans that regularly allow human beings to pet them. Even dolphins, commonly accorded the status of friendliest cetacean, rarely permit humans the gift of touch, despite the fact that in the Bahamas and Hawaii people have been swimming with the same pods for years. In one well-documented petting encounter with grays, an animal became so frisky that it rose underneath the boat, lifting the human occupants into the air like a waiter lifting a platter onto his shoulder. When the balance went awry, everyone on board fell headlong into the water. Tragically, one man died of a heart seizure.

Old-time whalers referred to this friendly, if not overexuberant, creature as "devil fish." Not unlike a human, the species fought violence with violence, the only great whale to consistently attack the longboats when harpooned.

Gray whales once migrated down both coasts of the north Pacific Ocean, although the Asian group eventually fell prey to shore whaling by the Japanese and Koreans. Less well known is the fact that grays were once a common sight on both sides of the Atlantic Ocean. "How long ago was it?" asks Farley Mowat in *Sea of Slaughter*, his landmark account of the mass extinction of Atlantic sea life at the hands of humankind.[3] In the mid-1800s, a few years before the Pacific population of grays was first encountered off the coast of Baja, the bones of an unknown species of baleen whale were dug up in Sweden. Biologists couldn't identify the bones, so they labeled it a *prehistoric* whale. Much later, it was discovered that the Basques had a long history of taking a whale they referred to as the *otta sotta*. Apparently, the population was extinguished from the coast of Europe as late as the mid-1700s. Along the American coast, many Native American tribes described a species that was clearly a gray whale. That so many indigenous people gave this whale a name is a testament to the fact that it traveled close to shore, a behavior typical of gray whales. The Algonquin people called it *powdaree*.

New England whalers called it the scrag whale. During the species' northern migration of 1669, Samuel Mavericke noted that they were so abundant that several could be seen every day in Southampton Harbor on New York's Long Island. But the hunt was unrelenting. By 1725 the powdaree was extinct along the American East Coast. Mowat grants the Atlantic gray the tragic distinction of being "the first major extinction to be perpetrated by Western Man in North America . . . the first of many."[4]

Out here on the ice, all three whales turn their heads to stare directly at me as I take five steps backward to ponder the whole animal rather than its barnacle parts. The smallest one, a female, has been named Bone by reporters because the ice has sliced the tip of her snout down to the bone. Staring into the long face of the yearling, I am startled to notice the severity of the gash and end up feeling offended by the foreboding nature of the name. A name can either be a dividend or a hex, nurturing or interrupting a being's aura by providing a field of reference for every person who understands its meaning. To call a listless, wounded whale after its deep, festering wound seems a thoughtless act, carrying too much weight for a crippled being to bear at such a dangerous moment. I am told the animal was named by an unknown journalist. All the other journalists soon took it up as well.

The Inupiat call the same whale "Kanik," meaning snowflake. I speak her name out loud—"Kanik"—and see the face of a fragile beauty dropped down from heaven. Her six-foot-long cheek is skewed sideways against the edge of the ice, which enables her to look out at all the human beings who likewise crane their necks sideways to gaze upon the meaning of life as expressed in that scanning cetacean eye. Bonnet is called "Putu," or icehole, by the locals. Crossbeak is "Siku," or ice.

I wear a six-inch-thick coat. The whales wear six inches of blubber. Nonetheless, I feel stunned to watch them lift their seemingly naked upper bodies into the subzero atmosphere for minutes at a time. Actually, this ability of theirs to generate body heat goes far beyond appearances. Should these animals be freed from their ice hole, they will eat no food whatsoever as they spend the next three to four months swimming six thousand miles nonstop to the warm Mexican lagoons. I can only conclude that this species of Leviathan is an alchemist that stokes some significant part of its golden inner flame directly from a brutally leaden atmosphere.

The social behavior of the eastern Pacific gray whale has made it especially vulnerable to the excesses of whaling. While most great whale species are relatively difficult to locate because they roam ocean currents far from land, the entire eastern Pacific stock of grays migrates close to shore along the coast of North America, and winters in just a few clement lagoons in Baja California. Twice in the past 150 years this population was brought to the brink of extinction. The first slaughter occurred during the so-called golden age of whaling, when a few ships traveled to Baja, anchored in protected water, set up a tryworks on shore, and methodically killed hundreds of whales within rowing distance of their operation. The whalers turned away from Baja only when the population dwindled to the point of commercial extinction. But this species has proven to be the most robust of the great whale species, recovering its population within a mere fifty years. The slaughter commenced a second time. This latter foray is a recent event; the last gray whaling station was shut down in California in the early 1960s. By then, most biologists considered the gray whale migration gone forever. But the population recovered again. A mere twenty years passed from the time the slaughter ended until gray whale watching developed into a major form of tourism along the Pacific coast of North America.

As their numbers grow, the grays are sighted with increasing regularity in various harbors along the coast including Bodega Bay, Coos Bay, Puget Sound, and Tofino. Whale scientists interpret these inshore sightings to be a form of cetacean house hunting—whales investigating alternatives to their long, yearly Arctic-to-Baja sojourn. Long ago, before whaling diminished the population, the grays were known to frequent the inland waters of San Francisco, San Diego, and Puget Sound. Because humankind does not always clean its own nest, this habitat expansion poses mortal problems for a creature who feeds on worms and shellfish by sifting mud through its baleen. Today, many gray whales entering industrial sumps like Puget Sound end up stranded, ostensibly poisoned by pollution.

Grays face other dangers as well. In 1982 a gray whale stopped to linger in the Bay of Tofino, along the west coast of Vancouver Island. Having learned to interact with affectionate whale watchers in Baja, this whale immediately ran its rostrum against any boat that drew close. Not everyone in Tofino was a whale lover. One man placed his dog on the whale's back. The dog bit the whale; the whale dived. When it surfaced again, the man drove his outboard over the animal, inflicting deep wounds. The whale vanished. One may only hope that the luckless creature survived long enough to alert his migrating community to avoid the greeting that awaits them in Tofino.

Although such sinister encounters are rare, this, too, could change. After the grays were taken off the endangered species list in 1996, the International Whaling Commission (IWC) granted the Makah tribe of Neah Bay, Washington, a coveted "aboriginal dispensation" to mount their own gray whale hunt.[5] Tribal promoters argued that whaling has always been an integral part of Makah culture. They consumed several species, especially humpbacks and grays, although one tribal elder pronounced the minke whale as the tastiest of all. Environmentalists countered that the tribe has not whaled in nearly eighty years; that today the Makah work primarily as loggers and fishermen, and can by no stretch of the imagination be called a subsistence culture. Ironically, a few years ago some tribesmen accidentally caught a gray whale in their fishing nets. They butchered the animal but, by their own reckoning, no one could stomach the foultasting flesh. This jibes well with the verdict of an Inupiat whaler in Barrow who told me that gray whale flesh is inedible because "it smells like shit." Palatability may not be an issue, however, because Makah whaling is not precisely an issue of subsistence but of tribal sovereignty.

The Makah defend their right by arguing that, whether they eat the meat or not, killing four animals a year will not harm the thriving gray whale population. Critics insist that the real issue is not the small number permitted but the precedent it abets. The Makahs' permit has already triggered other tribes along the Pacific coast to announce their own whaling revival. Far more worrisome to environmentalists is that some of the specialized hardware and expertise needed to mount a hunt has been pledged to the Makah by the Japanese whaling industry, which seeks political allies in the IWC. For all these reasons, a few Makah leaders have joined environmentalists to publicly decry the hunt. Tribal elder Alberta Thompson has described the real possibility of a friendly gray whale swimming up to a Makah boat seeking a caress, and being greeted instead by an exploding harpoon in its gut.[6]

It has grown dark out on the Barrow ice. We helicopter back to town. I unpack, then walk to meet my hosts at a local coffee shop packed with reporters. I wonder if the assembled journalists may be forfeiting a monumental opportunity by focusing their reportage on the ethos—the human-interest aspects of the rescue operation—while recording nothing whatsoever about the mythos represented by three whales' struggle simply to continue breathing. Through that evening the majority of journalists I talk to seem acutely sensitive to the mythic proportions of this event where nature is larger than life. But they describe the event as if compiling a box score at a baseball game. Three whales have now spent six days stuck in one ice hole. There are at least eighty-seven rescuers involved. So far, over $400,000 has been spent. Nearly every account concludes by invoking a daily payoff, as if the whole story is best subdivided into segments of a cetacean soap opera. It doesn't seem to matter much that the momentum of the event has, at least so far, avoided even the semblance of a climax. The whales have not budged an inch. Their faces show barnacles but no emotion. None of the people in charge seem to have much of an idea about what to do next. They promise to keep trying.

I ask a receptive reporter about his own objectivity in reporting an event that very likely would not have happened without the active participation of himself and his colleagues. "Yeah, I suppose it's true, none of us can really tell anymore if we're reporting the news or creating it. But it's still the news, and there's lots to tell in a thousand words." He notices my smile, glares back a moment, then chuckles. "Oh, I see. You don't think we tell the real story? Well, I disagree. In this business, writing what people enjoy reading is more important than writing something recondite. What would you prefer? A Zen koan? How about this one: When does the real story never tell the real story?"

"Maybe we find a way to let the whales speak for themselves," pipes in my host from Greenpeace, Cindy Lowry.

"How do we do that?" replies the reporter, still staring at me.

I sigh, then answer. "Some TV network ought to try pointing a camera at the whale hole, and then leave it there, running, for the entire duration of the rescue. No commentary. No sound bites. No 'we'll be back after these messages.' Just three whales breathing, struggling, staring, maybe dying right there in our living rooms."

No one disagrees that this whale rescue sets a unique challenge for the assembly of journalists. Most journalists' cool professionalism melts under the mystifying brown-eyed gaze of the three whales. Everyone who makes it onto the ice pauses every few minutes to gaze in wonderment upon this scene of a frozen ocean and overcast sky illuminated by a lemon yellow sun that hardly ever peaks above the horizon. The mystic Carlos Castaneda has written volumes about perceiving human beings as eggs of heat and light. After a few hours spent outside in this abominable cold, all of us who are bundled up in the prevailing beige parkas do start to look like eggs with the astonishing flame of body heat burning at their center. I cannot stop humming the Beatles tune: "I am the eggman, they are the eggmen, I am the walrus." It makes me wonder if John Lennon was ever aware that his song is an Arctic ode to body heat.

I have worked with gray whales before.

In 1976, Governor Jerry Brown sponsored a weekend event called "California Celebrates the Whale," which included cetacean-influenced music, film, and scientific programs. The celebration was referred to as the first government-sponsored totem program in U.S. history, and it received so much positive publicity that Brown decided to focus some attention on the gray whales, whose coastal migration he described as one of the state's great natural wonders. He hired a group of conceptual artists collectively known as The Ant Farm to produce a program to bring the gray whales into the consciousness of the citizenry. The Ant

Farm responded by building an underwater radio transmitter consisting of a buoy containing hydrophones on the submerged end, an amplifier in the middle and an antenna on the skyward end. People driving down the coast could turn on the radio and tune into whales singing a few miles offshore.

In 1976, most laypeople did not yet distinguish clearly between cetacean species. They were simply *the whales*. When recordings of humpback whales made off Bermuda by bioacoustician Roger Payne became an overnight pop sensation, most people concluded that all whale species must sing the same beautiful songs. For that reason, The Ant Farm's plan possessed a critical flaw. If they had done their homework better, they would have learned that the gray whale is among the least vocal of whales. Biologist Thomas Poulter had recorded over sixty thousand feet of reel-to-reel tape of gray whale sounds and categorized the sparsely produced vocalizations as "clicks, rasps, and the bong of a big Chinese gong."

The Ant Farm needed to get the whales to vocalize. They called me. I had recently written a magazine article about playing music with dolphins from a Hawaiian beach. It was, however, the sum of my cetacean experience. When I explained that to Doug Michels of The Ant Farm, he pointed out that no one since the ancient Greeks had tried playing music with cetaceans, which made me the world's greatest living authority on the subject. I was twenty-nine years old at the time, making a living by building wooden tongue drums that sounded vaguely like a humpback whale. The Ant Farm commissioned a huge, floating drum to play with the grays. I waterproofed it inside and out with marine lacquer, and added outriggers to make the drum seaworthy in the swells. Nine times during the winter of 1976–77 I slipped into a leaky dry suit, jumped off a tiny, tipsy boat into the ocean, got handed my drum and two mallets, draped my arms and legs around the whale singer's outrigger, and started to play.

The drum's top surface was made from an inch-thick slab of a hard tropical wood called purpleheart, into which four tongues were cut. My primary playing technique consisted of rubbing the tongues with a mallet tipped with a dime-store Super Ball. Different-size Super Balls emitted different pitches and textures. The largest was the size of a tangerine and moaned deeply when rubbed against the wood. A medium-size Super Ball sounded like a human with rubber lungs. The smallest Super Ball screeched.

All these sounds evoked whale songs heard on record, in the ocean, and especially in the human imagination.

If the drum tipped too much to either side, water flowed in through the tongue slits. Ten seconds' worth of tipping could swamp the craft. Because I was drifting in fifteen-foot swells, allotting even 50 percent of my attention to the task of making music was risky business. One might suppose that the wave crests would be most difficult to handle. The valleys concerned me far more because I lost sight of both land and The Ant Farm boat. There I floated, a mile offshore west of the rugged Point Reyes Headland, working up a musical sweat, making whale-type sounds with all my body and soul. To keep warm, I experimented with fire breathing, a Tibetan technique of forcefully scooping air into the lungs, relaxing completely while holding the breath, then exhaling forcefully. It is said that lamas sit naked on a frozen lake, inhaling and exhaling for hours to generate enough body heat to melt the ice. If done correctly, they eventually melt the ice and fall into the water shouting, "Aaaaah, what a refreshing dip it is."

My head turned hot, my brain felt disconnected from my nervous system. I rubbed the surface of the drum, kept my eyes closed, breathed for heat, and floated across a congenial sea like a doomed mountaineer falling into the final stage of hypothermia. The instrument vibrated so intensely that water spattered six inches up into the air. A swell struck the drum. I swayed to compensate. The cold water jolted my spinal column.

A gray whale approached to check out the source of this unlikely sound. There was so little warning. One moment I was completely alone, then the body of a forty-foot animal rose to the surface in front of me. My eyes squinted to take the full measure of this object. Covered over with barnacles, the creature registered to my mind less as a whale, or even a living animal, than as a stone wall that filled my field of vision. The wall spouted a fountain. A wave interceded, suddenly lifting me on a ridge of moving water sixteen feet above the animal. Far to the east, the green Bolinas ridge rolled toward the thin beige strip of the beach as if reflecting the swells I rode. I gripped the outriggers of the drum and peered downward to watch the whale tip its body sideways. We made eye contact just as I glided down into another dark canyon.

The eye was right beside me; the feeling was intimate, nearly too close for comfort. The walls of water deadened the sound as thoroughly as they enclosed the view. I paused in my playing to give full attention to that eye. But the Ferris wheel of the ocean jostled me back onto the crest. I gazed upon the sharp prominence of Point Reyes Headland but could discern none of the hundred or so whale watchers I knew were watching through binoculars at this moment of first contact.

Sucked down into the trough again, I was greeted by a blow whose fragrance reminded me of gum disease. The whale's mouth gaped open, revealing rows of the wiry, comblike baleen. I bowed my head as if the whale's gesture was a display of finery, although to my uneducated eyes it appeared far more odd than beautiful. With no discernible sign of movement, the whale drew so close I could have reached out and touched it. It blew again, lifting its flukes so high into the air that I craned my neck backward to witness the sight. From below, they appeared to be sleek and massive wings blotting out the sun so completely that, had they belonged to a bird, I would have feared them as a shrew fears the abrupt shadow of a hawk. The flukes slipped beneath the waves. I gaped at a slight ring of turbulent water, fully expecting giant bubbles to break all around me and capsize the drum. Nothing happened. I unhooked a diving mask dangling from one of the outriggers and pulled it over my head before dropping my face below the surface. As the whale passed beneath, it relieved itself with a mighty venting of feces that ebbed and flowed through the water like smoke lingering in the air after fireworks.

No more than a minute elapsed from the moment I first spied the whale. Yet now, after twenty-five years spent investigating the draw of the charged border, this singular event, more than any other, has kept me returning to meet the cetaceans again and again.

A helicopter lifts me, along with six journalists, out to the site of the gray whale rescue. It lands, disgorges its passengers, and lifts off to pick up another load of reporters and saviors waiting in Barrow a few miles away. The hush of the winter Arctic rushes in from all sides. There is no wind this morning. I pick up my bag full of underwater acoustic gear, a tape recorder, and a half-size guitar, and saunter over to the scene of the action.

Three whales bob up and down in a round black hole rimmed in white. They lie on the surface for a full two minutes, breathing easily with cavernous two-second-long exhalations. A prolonged three-second breath signifies a change. Together, the whales dunk beneath the ice, disappearing completely out of sight and sound, and for such a long period of time that we might easily forget what on earth has impelled us onto this formless Arctic ice sheet in the first place. My eyes wander over the theater of the rescue operation. To the south, two great chopping helicopters unload journalists and cameramen directly onto the ice. To the east, a three-foot-high escarpment of solid ice runs along the shoreline all the way out to the horizon, looking as if the last wave of a long-forgotten summer had frozen as it curled in upon itself. To the north, a white plain of sea ice charges unbroken. I blink, unable to locate even the hint of a landmark.

Turning my body another ninety degrees, I notice, far to the west, twenty eggmen clutching chain saws along a series of newly dug channels. Cindy has informed me that, two days ago, the local Inupiats, most of them whalers, sat by and giggled as marine biologists, oil company laborers, and national guardsmen began cutting three-foot-square slabs of ice and lifting them onto the adjacent ice surface. After a day and half of backbreaking labor they managed to cut out two small breathing holes. Yesterday afternoon, these same Inupiat enacted a friendly coup d'état against what they considered to be the incompetent, albeit well-meaning, authority of the U.S. government. They commandeered the chain saws and took over the digging of the channel. The Inupiat avoid lifting the two-hundred-pound blocks of ice, and simply slide them under the main body of the ice with a stick. Already today, the loud wail of the chain saws has dwindled to a faraway buzz. The Inupiat-dug channel stretches a momentous half mile from the whale's own breathing hole.

Of the holes dug two days ago, one has already frozen over again; the other was recut earlier this morning and is now kept open by the electrically induced bubbling of two donated deicer machines. Without the machines even the whale's current ice hole would have frozen over days ago. I take several steps backward to take in a larger view of two breathing holes located a hundred yards apart. A few hundred yards beyond that begins the cut channel running all the way out toward the horizon.

When I arrived on-site this morning, I asked Mark Fraker, one of the marine biologists in charge, why the channel didn't start right at the second breathing hole so the whales wouldn't have to swim a few hundred yards under the ice just to reach it. "A few hundred yards is no big deal for a gray whale. We decided not to cut too close to the whale hole, because we felt the noise of the chain saws might provoke the whales to flee in the opposite direction. Without the luxury of several alternate breathing holes, they'd drown for sure. The hard part is getting them to realize that both the second hole and the channel are actually there. Hopefully, you can provide the signal for that."

The whales are still underwater, neither in the breathing hole with the two deicers nor at the second hole without a deicer where a thin layer of ice already shrouds the surface. Ten men propel themselves toward the hole without the deicing machines. They stop, bend over the black water as if praying to the god of whales to guide these animals toward this hole. If the whales do not discover the channel before the workers leave the scene at dusk, the half-mile-long cut will assuredly freeze overnight, and an entire day's work will have been in vain. If the whales discover the channel, they'll undoubtably swim its entire length. The optimistic Inupiat have already cut a huge breathing hole at the channel's opposite end. The plan is that the deicing machines will keep that single hole open overnight, while the channel and the holes closer to shore are allowed to freeze. The interspecies brigade of whales and chain sawers can continue their dance tomorrow morning, eventually cutting a channel all the way out to the open lead, five miles offshore. But the whales have to cooperate.

The smallest of the three whales surfaces in front of me. The ten men start waddling toward us. The second whale surfaces, then the third. One of the rescuers groans, followed by intermittent shouts of encouragement. "Come on, you whales! Why won't you try out the other hole?" I have been informed that the ocean at the breathing hole is barely thirty feet deep, slightly less than the body length of the largest whale. I step forward to join several human beings at the rim of the black water. "You would think they'd feel cramped." "You would think they would have an ounce of curiosity to explore all that noise made by the chain saws." Then someone pops a wonderful question: "Where do you think the whales go during their three minutes underwater?"

The man standing to my right clicks his tongue. "Go? What's that supposed to mean?" I chuckle, recognizing the existential lineage of the question. Does a falling tree make a noise if no one hears it? American Indian tribes like the Cree believed that whenever animals venture out of sight of human observers, they take off their creature costumes, revealing bodies and souls identical to our own.

All the TV journalists want to file their reports standing at the same spot in front of the whale hole, so a queue has formed consisting of crews from around the world. Now it's the turn of a reporter representing Australian broadcast news. He steps gingerly to the lip of the hole, composes himself, directs his cameraman to pan across the landscape before settling on his face. The man speaks, accentuating certain words by jerking his head to and fro in the ticlike gestures favored by TV newspeople. He describes the drama of a multimillion-dollar rescue mission that has bogged down because of the whales' unmitigated lack of curiosity. While the camera eye fixes on the reporter from one direction, I am delighted to notice the baby whale nudging her chin against the edge of the hole as if seeking a better vantage to hear the sounds uttered by this two-legged. "How odd that the local Eskimos who usually kill [head jerked hard toward the left shoulder] and eat [pause, lifted eyebrows] whales, should be working so hard to save [entire head thrust forward like an ancient Egyptian dancer] these three individuals."

But why is this man railing on so? Like everyone else here, I am certain he has been briefed by the biologists at the research station. The local Inupiat kill a few bowhead whales each year as part of a strictly regulated hunt. They have never hunted gray whales. The reporter has, in effect, trivialized several thousand years of Inupiat culture for ten million Australian viewers. The Aussie concludes his report. His crew steps aside.

A British reporter steps up to the rim, unzips his hood, takes off his knit cap, runs a comb through his honey-colored hair, and unbuttons his coat to display a white dress shirt and a blue necktie. Then he begins. "Can they justify the expense of more than a million dollars, and a hundred volunteers out here on the pack ice, to save three gray whales, while they permit children in the Sudan to die of starvation?" By the time he finishes this soliloquy, his cheeks have turned purple. An assistant rushes in to place an outsize Russian lamb's-wool hat over his skull, wind a down muffler around his neck, zip his coat, and pull up his hood.

The Englishman's commentary clarifies a conviction shared by most of the journalists on-site. If his majority opinion is anthropocentric, the minority opinion he rails against might be called mythical, and summed up this way: How wonderful that, at least once in a great while, we lose our heads enough to permit something as imaginative as an interspecies love affair to have a life out of all proportion to its monetary value.

Joseph Campbell taught that myth is an essential aspect of human culture because it awakens the human psyche to the unexplainable dimensions of the universe, converting an inscrutable mystery into a grounded order through the creation of icons and heroes.[7] Seen in this light, a rescue operation mounted in the far northern antipodes of the planet grounds the inscrutable forces of nature through the icon of three stranded gray whales. When nature is larger than life, humans are not quite so afraid of the dark. What do three gray whales teach us? It is a question voiced very few times over the several days of the rescue. Here is perhaps the best answer as it appeared on the editorial page of *The Hartford Courant*: "The creatures' plight stirred global sympathy. . . . The caring doesn't compensate for any human shortcomings, but it generates hope that this element of human nature will be seen more often."[8]

Last night I was invited to join a group of rescuers and journalists for dinner at Pepe's, billed as "the world's most northernmost Mexican restaurant." We were filling up on chips and salsa when it was revealed to me that marine mammals get stuck in the ice around Barrow every winter. Even as we rescue three gray whales at one hole, there is another hole located several miles offshore that contains a slaughtered bowhead whale. But the Eskimos eat bowheads, and no one in Barrow is interested in publicizing that event. I also learn that if there were no predictable Arctic larder of frozen critters, the threatened polar bears would have a very difficult time making ends meet through the winter. Our dinners arrived. "Does that mean," I asked while inhaling the complex fragrance of salsa verde, "that we starve polar bears when we save gray whales?" Everyone at the table reacted with a mixture of sighs and meaningful grunts signifying that no one had the answer.

Bill Hess, who publishes an artful magazine serving the Inupiat community of the north slope, explained in some detail how the rescue was born. A local reporter wrote up the story in the Barrow newspaper only because the whale hole was located so close to town. This led to a second story in the Anchorage daily, leading to a syndicated story by UPI, leading to the TV networks, and so on and so forth around the world. It finally accrued enough power to prompt President Ronald Reagan to offer the U.S. Army to help save the whales. As syndicated columnist James Kilpatrick finally described it, "The story had taken on the kind of irresistible momentum that defies objective analysis."[9]

Where peaks rise, chasms plunge. As we sat around the huge circular table enjoying our enchiladas, my hostess from Greenpeace voiced the wish that this galvanized community could somehow influence the Japanese policy makers who subsidize the killing of endangered whale species under the loophole known as "scientific whaling." The few Japanese biologists in the employ of whaling companies insist they need several hundred whale cadavers each year for purposes of dissection. When the anatomy lesson is over, the whale bodies get recycled, through an established network of whale brokers, to various fish markets and restaurants throughout Japan. The *science* of so-called scientific whaling is a sham and a standing embarrassment to the international community of whale biologists. The U.S. government could stop it but chooses not to. Back in the early 1970s, the U.S. Congress passed a farsighted law called the Pelly amendment that demanded, among other things, that the U.S. government impose trade sanctions against any country ignoring international whaling accords. Unfortunately, the same U.S. president who has sent the army into Barrow to free three whales refuses to uphold the Pelly amendment against "scientific whaling."

The two P.M. helicopter has carried the majority of news reporters back to Barrow. Accounts of today's activities have to be written and sent off via modem or satellite to make it into tonight's newspapers and telecasts.

From that perspective, anything that occurs on the ice after two P.M. may as well not happen for millions of TV viewers and newspaper readers. Now that I am on the verge of starting my own job, I feel strangely liberated not to have reporters peering over my shoulder.

There remains a single reporter who soon corners me. When I agree to an interview, he pulls off his mitten, extracts a tape recorder from up his sleeve, turns the tape over, pushes the record button, slides the recorder up his sleeve again, and finally pulls on his mitten. I stare at the small microphone dangling from his sleeve and imagine my words traveling through a needle directly into his veins. He holds the microphone in front of my face, clears his throat, and asks what I plan to do here.

"I will transmit guitar music into the water—"

"To communicate to whales?" he interrupts.

"Not exactly. I have no inside information about how to talk to whales, if that's what you mean."

"Do you really think they'll respond?"

"Gray whales are curious. I've attracted them to a sound source several times over the past few years."

"What kind of music, please?"

"I'll start with a simple drone on the guitar. If that doesn't work, I'll try playing recorded music into the whale's own hole. I'm just going to make it up as I go along. You know, until something works."

The reporter informs me he plans to stay out here until dark, just to see how the music turns out. He seems blithely unhurried, strangely unconcerned about meeting the deadline that cleared the site of journalists a few minutes before. "What paper do you write for?" I ask.

He points a finger due north then hooks it in a nosedive. "I represent a different time zone, which is why I have a different deadline. I'm from the Voice of America. This interview will be broadcast late tonight, when it's the middle of the afternoon for people listening across Eastern Europe and the Soviet Union." I nod, then turn in a circle to catch the panorama one more time before the sun sets. Off to the southwest, bright rainbows of ice, called sun dogs, have precipitated on either side of the sun. When I turn back to the journalist, he is already walking away.

The engineer who built my underwater sound system has warned me that it will not function below zero degrees Fahrenheit. When I voiced this concern to Cindy Lowry, she made sure I was provided with a heated shed on runners. I asked that the shed be placed beside the empty ice hole midway between the whale hole and the channel. I am gratified to notice that someone has cleared the hole of ice. My plan is simple: to play music into the water. If the whales investigate the source, they will discover the channel, hopefully swim its length searching for an outlet. At the north end of the channel they encounter not the ocean, but the large, de-iced hole. Tomorrow, the Inupiat start cutting a new channel. By then, the whales will have figured out that the channel is their only salvation. If they don't, I'll play again tomorrow.

I walk across the ice to the shed, open the door, step inside, and get hit by a blast of warm air scented with kerosene fumes. I pull off my mittens and my hat, then realize that the initial sensation of steamy warmth is relative. The thermometer stuck on the wall hovers at thirty-three degrees. There's not much to the shed; it's just a nailed-together four-by-ten enclosure with a wooden floor and a single window. A lit kerosene heater rattles and hums in the corner. My own suitcase full of sound gear sits on a waist-high shelf beside two twelve-volt batteries, a plastic cooler, and a large cardboard box showing a Federal Express label. I place the cooler and the box on the floor and start assembling equipment.

A snowmobile stops by the door. A man is shouting, "I need a bite to eat! I'll be back in ten minutes." The door is hurled open. An Inupiat man dressed in a traditional sealskin coat and polar bear pants steps inside. He is obviously startled to notice that someone he doesn't know has taken over the shed. The room has turned into a maze of electrical cables and connectors. Undeterred by the clutter, he pushes against the net of wires in order to close the door. Now he pulls off his hood and his mittens. Steam rises off him like off a hot tub. He notices the tiny electric guitar leaning against the wall of the shed. "Oh yeah, I heard about you. You're the guy who's gonna play music to the whales." I turn to face him. A huge grin lights up his handsome face. I smile. He pulls the cooler from under the shelf. "I won't bother you long. I just came for a sandwich." He opens the cooler. I stare at it. He follows my eyes. We both register the unspoken joke of an Eskimo needing a cooler in wintertime. "It's not what you think." He chuckles. "It keeps the food from freezing." He chooses ham and cheese, closes the lid, unwraps the wax paper, and starts munching away. I retreat to the far corner to wire the two twelve-volt batteries to each other. He's looking at my tiny electric guitar. "Hey, I never saw such a tiny guitar. What's it do?"

I pass it to him. It's the same instrument I used on the *Lamarck*, barely eighteen inches long, a white, solid-body, soprano guitar. "I only use it for playing music with whales and dolphins. They hear higher pitches than we do, so it's tuned an octave above a normal guitar." He fingers an E-minor chord, but it sounds dissonant. I reach in my pocket for a glass bottleneck. "It's tuned to an open D. Try rubbing the glass over the strings. It sounds quite nice."

He does so but can't hear much without the amplifier. He holds it up to his ear and tries again. "That's Johnny Winters's sound. Hey, that guy plays wild, don't he? You gonna play Johnny Winters to the whales?"

"I'll just play a drone. I don't want to scare them with anything too rough-and-tumble." I finish connecting the battery and screw the water-proof connector of the underwater speaker into the system box.

He finishes his sandwich, lifts up the lid on the cooler, finds several candy bars, which he stuffs into a pocket underneath his coat. He places one on my guitar case and winks, watching me intently as I finish wiring up the system. Then he sighs. "Well, I wish you good luck with your music. If you need to move the shed, just ask anybody with a snowmobile. We can pull the shed wherever you like." He yanks on his hood, makes his exit. The snowmobile starts; the whine dwindles into the distance.

Wiring complete, I run a quick diagnostic test. Turn on the main power, watch the little diodes light up. I set the volume on the guitar and the preamp, play a single note, listen intently as a faint, tinny whimper emerges from the speaker. It doesn't sound like much through the air, but it's plenty loud underwater. I put on a pair of headphones, listen to the ripping sound of my finger rubbing against the hydrophone's surface. Everything seems to be functioning. Without bothering to put on a hat and gloves, I pick up the underwater speaker and the hydrophone and carry them outside the shack. The two components are dropped fifteen feet down into the black, icy hole. I tie them off to the shed runners and step back inside my warm nest. I was outside for all of a minute, but I can barely bend my fingers. I hold my hands over the heater to get them working again.

Yesterday, when I arrived, I was shepherded into a room where several scientists, military personnel, environmentalists—but strangely, no Inupiat—sat around a table plotting today's tactics for saving the whales. Cindy was the only woman present. They sat me down and handed me a chocolate doughnut and a cup of hot chocolate. The biologist in charge asked me precisely what I planned to do out on the ice.

"If these trapped whales hear a clear musical response to their own rhythmical grunts and clicks, who knows, I may get them to leave their hole to search out the source of the sound."

"Hey, do I get to bring my flute along?" interrupted a man in creased chino pants. It got a chuckle all around. A man in a whiffle haircut asked if I had brought along any gray whale recordings.

"No, I didn't. However, I did bring a cassette of the South African a cappella group Ladysmith Black Mombazo. Their music seems ideal for this situation. Lots of whispering voices singing exquisite harmonies. No sharp edges anywhere. I can't think of a gentler music to transmit to these traumatized animals." I looked up and smiled. Not unexpectedly, the men in the room started eyeing one another as if I had just informed them that I would transmit music recorded on a recent spaceship trip to the Pleiades. Cindy rose to recommend that I first transmit a recording of gray whales, which was made in Baja by a senior scientist from the government's National Marine Fisheries Service. "Let's all agree to try the gray whale tape first. The idea is that our grays will be tricked into believing there are other whales just a few hundred yards away."

"Oh, I don't know," I answered sharply. "These whales may react better to something strange than to any prerecorded cassette of grays. You should let me do what I know how to do best."

Everyone agreed that, so far, nothing else was working. Had I proclaimed that I would conjure up a fifty-thousand-year-old cetacean-ascended master with a third eye pulsing like a strobe light to channel the whales up the channel, the rescue leaders would have felt obligated to try that as well. In fact, my little white guitar seemed to fit right in with the other props of this theater of the absurd: the oil-drilling equipment, de-icing machines, chain saws, commando helicopters, a steel skycrane right out of *The Empire Strikes Back*, a hundred-and-eighty-five-ton ice-breaking barge, a seven-ton ice-breaking needle, an eleven-ton Archimedes screw-wheeled ice-breaking pontoon vehicle. Now that none of the above props have worked at all, the stage is set for the next act on the program, an interspecies musician wielding a homemade underwater boom box. He starts his set by announcing, "It won't be too difficult to get the whales out of the hole. We just need to play some good old South African a cappella choral music."

Amicably, we arrived at a plan of action. I could play whatever I wanted, but only after I first tried the gray whale sounds.

In the heated shed, I don a pair of headphones, hand a second pair to Cindy, who has joined me, and tap on a toggle switch to power up the underwater sound system. The headphones receive only sounds picked up underwater through the hydrophone. Likewise, any sound generated through the system—whether a cassette or a live guitar—is transmitted only through the underwater speaker. Nothing is transmitted in air. The two of us listen intently to the acoustic environment under the ice. All is silent except for a distant whine. Searching for a source, we agree that it is most likely produced by chain saws slicing through the ice a half mile in the distance. I pop the gray whale cassette into the tape recorder and push the play button.

Our ears are greeted by an overbearing whoosh accompanied by a whiny hum. I press the stop button, fast forward for twenty seconds, try again. The whoosh and hum are just as loud as before, although we now hear a distant gulping sound bleed through the feedback. I slowly shake my head at Cindy. Whoever made this tape broke two cardinal rules of underwater audio. First, clear recordings cannot be made while a ship is under power. The overbearing whoosh is turbulence caused by a hydro-phone being towed through the water. Second, the technician forgot to double-check his wiring; the hum is an ungrounded electrical connection. The gulp is probably a gray whale, but it's embedded so deeply in the ship's noise as to make the recording unusable.

I turn off the tape, calmly announce to Cindy that the recording is use-less. She's out of her element and offers neither protest nor guidance.

Without another word, I plug in the little guitar; make a single quiet sound; adjust the tuning, the volume, and the EQ; and then start to strum a drone in the key of D major. Although I have no explanation, many animal species seem to favor this key when vocalizing among themselves.

Not this time. After fifteen minutes strumming a drone in the key of D, and another fifteen minutes slowly sliding a bottleneck up and down on the middle D string, I stop playing. Outside the shed window, the sun is reduced to a slice of light on the horizon. The Arctic day is short in mid-October; it will be dark in less than an hour. I shut down the system, start piling on clothes to go outside. Cindy insists that I remain right where I am. "Look, we don't have much time. Why not fast forward the gray whale tape to a different spot and try again? Maybe it's not all feedback. Who knows, maybe the whoosh is a gray whale vocalization."

Understanding her frustration, I smile wanly but say nothing. I step out into the cold to pull the speaker and hydrophone out of the water and secure them inside the shed. Cindy steps outside to inform me she's going to check if the overnight holding area has been completed. I watch her leave, then clomp across the ice to the hole where the three whales are lollygagging on the surface. The two adults, described by an on-site biologist as "young adults," look fairly healthy. The yearling looks more beat-up than ever. One of the larger whales, probably a female, swims close to where I stand. She looms out of the black water so close to my face, she takes my breath away. I could easily reach out a hand and touch her, but decide against it. The feeling of camaraderie, no matter how fragile, is too powerful to risk.

Although whale behavior varies immensely from species to species, many whale lovers tend to lump the intellectual and communicative abilities of every cetacean into a single category. A few of the media pundits have described these animals as veritable Einsteins, generic whales who would certainly be in oceanariums electrifying audiences with clever tricks if only they were a bit less bulky. In fact, the gray whale, *Eschrichtius robustus*, is a relict mysticete whose ancient line sired both the rorquals and the rights, related to the blue whale in much the manner an eohippus relates to a modern horse. Grays never sing glorious songs like humpbacks, nor do they whistle and echolocate with the playful precision of a bottlenose dolphin. One on-site biologist has responded to the misbegotten image of this brainy generic whale by pronouncing Snowflake and her two cousins "instinctoids" who graze on muck and whose brains are hard-wired to respond to a genetic code that, among other things, stipulates that members of their species spend half their lives migrating between the Arctic Ocean and the lagoons of Baja California. Back and forth, up and down the coast like pelagic yo-yos.

I peer deeply into a dark brown eye heavily folded at the corners, and feel vulnerable to reading too much comprehension in her gaze. Or too little. There are no other people nearby. I have this beauty all to myself and feel grateful for the private audience. The female stares back at me through an eye the size of a softball. Her mouth is half open, displaying her baleen. It is a wondrous organ, a fibrous tangled net emanating from a black tusklike frame. I smile. She opens and closes her mouth four, six, eight times, then drops a bit lower into the water.

I open my eyes wide and peer at her like a character in a Japanese *kabuki* drama. Is her life guided by instinct? If so, her movements up and down the coast are rightfully called a migration. But if she reasons, we might just as easily label her travels a pilgrimage. She studies me, unwavering. One thing is certain. Her eye is a gate I cannot open, leading to a labyrinth I do not know how to navigate.

She turns away. The other adult, a male, moves in to take her place. He, too, makes eye contact. Minutes pass. I take a step forward, grunt long and loud before starting a pep talk to the three whales. "Okay, you guys, I want you to pay attention. You've got to move out of this hole within the next hour or the channel is going to freeze overnight. Please, listen to what I'm telling you. I know it's only English and you don't know English. But try to catch my gist." I feel like a basketball coach explaining a pick-and-roll to teenage athletes. I sigh deeply, try again. "Come on, listen to me. It's your lives! You've got to do this, okay! Now do it!!"

If they don't pay attention to what I have to say (how can they possibly know what it means to pay attention) and learn the rules of this game (what rules? what game?), they will be dead within eight hours. What's eight, what's hours? Is it like darkness and then light? The big male blows loudly, like a vacuum cleaner turned on and off inside Carlsbad Caverns. Something intangible makes me wonder if he's more aware of the situation than the other two. He seems to be studying my lips as I speak, observing the movements of a mouth articulating gutturals and glottals.

His candid stare makes me feel he's right on the verge of opening his mouth to address me in English. "So, my two-legged friend, what precisely are you trying to tell me? You don't really think I'm going to respond, do you? I may be about to die out here, but I insist on the right to remain a gray whale to the bitter end."

I once spent a month with the New Zealander Frank Robson, one of the first gurus of the nonscientific school of cetacean communication. He was a good-humored barrel of a man who worked for years as a trainer in a local oceanarium. Frank rarely communicated his commands by word or by whistle, or handed his dolphins a food reward for tricks done correctly. He even forswore the trainer trick known as "fading," minimal twitches and hand signals, a slight shake of the head or a shuffle of the feet, that cues an animal for a set response even while remaining imperceptible to the audience. The tactic was perfected with a trained horse called Clever Hans, who seemed to be able to multiply and divide numbers, until it was determined his trainer was cuing him to start and end his stomping. When Robson wished to get his dolphins to do a trick, he told me he visualized the picture of them doing the trick in his mind, describing the mechanism in this way:

> A vibration that reflects. It's not unlike walking in the dark and stopping at an obstruction without actually seeing it. With animals it's a two-mind job. Until the mind that you are trying to reach is receptive to what you've got to transmit, it's hopeless.[10]

Robson concluded that most of us "have educated the ability right out of ourselves. We are hopelessly poisoned by our reliance on language as the primary means of comprehending our world."[11]

If Robson is correct, my words to the gray whales may not be spoken in vain. Intention has authority even though the big fellow shows no sign of recognition. Against my better judgment, I reach out a hand. The whale named Crossbeak or Siku or Ice moves forward a foot to nudge my mittened hand with his badly bruised snout. I close my eyes to visualize the game plan from the whale's point of view. The quicksilver shimmer of the ice hole falls away to the south. The dim translucence cast by eighteen inches of solid ice passes overhead for thirty seconds. Over there to the northeast is the bright undulating mirror of a second ice hole. Dangling from the rim is a gray wire attached to a saucer-shaped underwater speaker. I pat the whale's snout and sing a song from Paul Simon's *Graceland* album. My cheek firmly laid against the shagbark plane of the gray whale, I say, "Follow the song. Okay? You understand what I'm saying, don't you? Let the song take you to the place you need to go. I'm going back to the other hole now. I'm going to play this same melody underwater. I want the three of you to join me there. Okay?"

I walk from the hole back to the shed. The chain saws have stopped whining. The silence overpowers the scene. The chill air hurts my cheeks, nose, lips, my fingertips. I pull open the door to the shed and am nearly bowled over by the stench of kerosene vapors. I leave the door open to clear out the fumes and step outside to dangle the speaker and the hydrophone over the edge of the ice and into the water. I reenter the shed, close the door, put Ladysmith Black Mombazo onto the cassette player, put on the headphones, and listen to the music as it sounds fifteen feet underwater. Whispery, proud male harmonies fill my ears, chanting a song about the struggle of living in poverty under a warm South African sun. On and on the voices sing. The choirmaster, Joseph Shabalala, warbles in his shining alto. The chorus starts to exhale together. "A-huuut, A-huuut, A-huuut, A-huuut."

Fifteen minutes pass in the shed. Keeping watch at the tiny window, I notice the sun has transformed into a small point of red light glimmering on the southwest horizon. Not much time left until dark. I have been told that a few people may remain out here all night but that most of the work crews will return to Barrow until morning. I rub my scalp, realize that my plan to attract the whales to a musical source has utterly failed. I munch on a candy bar and decide to try plan B: to repulse the whales from their own hole. There are a few ways to approach the problem. I could broadcast sounds that badger them. History relates the curious tale of a Scottish chieftain who took the sweet-sounding Celtic bagpipe and altered the timbre to produce a far more shrill tone. The new instrument granted the clans a tactical advantage on the battlefield by disorienting the sensibilities of the enemy. I have a tape of Scottish bagpipe music in my cassette bag.

Or I could play a tape of orca vocalizations. Men who fish herring on various rivers in southern Alaska employ an underwater sound system called a "beluga spooker," which broadcasts a tape loop of orca sounds. Beluga whales, who enter the rivers to prey on herring, turn about when they hear orca sounds wafting at them from around a bend. Because orcas also prey on gray whales, the sound transported into the whales' hole seems certain to make the gray whales flee their hole. But I worry that the gray whales may become so frightened that they will keep swimming without bothering to search for another air hole. It's not a good choice.

There's no more time for deliberation. I shut down the system, pull in all the loose wires, pile on my coat, hat, mittens, and step outside into the sizzling wind. I trudge a half mile out to the end of the channel, walk all the way back again, trot laterally away from the rescue operation, spend a few crazy moments enchanted by the sun dogs dancing across the sky, and then return to the shed. I flag down the first snowmobile that passes nearby. It's the same Inupiat man who gave me the candy bar. "Will you drag the shed over to the hole the whales are in?" I implore.

"No problem," he answers, quickly hooking the shed hitch to his machine. He revs the engine a few moments, then starts pulling the shed slowly until he stops beside the whales' ice hole. He jumps off his vehicle, unhooks the shed. "So, my friend, have you had any luck?" I shake my head, then turn away to unwind the cables to the hydrophone and underwater speaker before dropping them into the water.

Several of the Inupiat chain sawers gather around as if waiting for an explanation about the wires and the guitar. It's the first time they've seen me, and they seem excited about the possibility of playing music into the water. "What kind of music is it?" asks one man. "What you gonna play for the whales?"

"It's a men's a cappella chorus from South Africa. They call themselves Ladysmith Black Mombazo."

Everyone laughs, although I believe their response is more a reaction to the very idea of playing music into the water and not from my specific choice of song. "The whales really love that rock and roll," declaims one man, laughing gaily. "You can bet this music gonna get them dancing down the channel." I do not need to remind these good-natured men that at least three times during the past two days they have draped plastic tarps over the open hole in an aggressive attempt to prevent the whales from breathing, and thus forcing them to swim to the other hole. But the whales kept surfacing violently into the plastic, pushing the tarp upward with each thrust until, finally, the wind delivered it from their midst.

I step inside the shed, followed by two of the Inupiats. I hand each man a pair of headphones and explain that everything they are about to hear is produced underwater. They listen a moment; hear nothing, but then register a slursh as one of the whales creates turbulence against the hydrophone. I twist the volume control of the tape recorder to less than half of what it was at the other hole, sigh deeply, and push the play button. I notice the faces of my two companions brighten, a sign that the harmonies of Ladysmith Black Mombazo have begun to course through the dark water.

The whales dive out of sight.

I step outside the shed. Stand alongside eight or nine Inupiat watching the empty, smooth water. A minute passes. The crowd grows to fifteen people. Two minutes pass. Several people shout out at once, "Look, there they are! . . . Too mu-u-uch!" The three whales have resurfaced at the other hole. Who could imagine that human beings dressed in so many layers of clothing could jump up and down in sheer delight? I rush into the shed and turn off the tape. The whales immediately dive again. A minute passes. We are all scanning the water for some sign of them. Suddenly, they surface right in front of us. "Oh no!" someone shouts. "Turn the music back on!" Everyone starts yelling at me to play it again. Not thinking anymore, I press the play button.

The three whales dive together. No one speaks. Everyone darts their eyes back and forth between the two holes. Two minutes pass. Three minutes. Where have they gone? Finally a keen-eyed rescuer shouts, "Look! There they are. Way down there." He points his finger a good quarter mile down the length of the channel. Yes, I see them as well. We all see them; one whale blows, then another one. The whales have found the channel! Success! Everyone is smiling broadly; a few people are jumping up and down. I am patted on the back several times.

We all waddle across the ice toward the channel. By the time we arrive, the whales have already found their overnight home of open water at the far end of the channel and have turned about, now dashing vigorously back and forth along the channel's entire length. They seem to be as delighted by their liberation as we are. There is nothing more for me to do but return to the shed, disconnect the sound system, pack it into its metal suitcase, and lug it across the ice to the main command hut to wait for a snowmobile ride back to Barrow.

Something is amiss. Someone reports to me that the yearling has not been sighted for over ten minutes, although it may be too dark and the channel too long to be certain of anything as ephemeral as a whale spout. I distinctly remember seeing the yearling return to her original hole after the music had been shut off that first time. Perusing the channel one last time, I plainly see the two adults. All eyes start to search the channel for a sign of a third whale. Nothing! If it is true that the yearling is gone, then it must have happened when the whales dove the second time. Although the yearling could have surfaced at the second hole, she might have tried to keep up with the two adults. Already listless, she must have exhausted her limited store of energy. Drowned.

I returned home late the next day to newspaper headlines tolling the death knell of a gray whale. Every report mentioned that the two remaining whales inexplicably left their death trap sometime during the night. No one could offer a reason to explain the move. No American newspaper made mention of the eggman who had arrived on the scene bearing an underwater music maker. No one disclosed Paul Simon's evocative lyric, sung by Ladysmith Black Mombazo, as the source of the whale's liberation. Over the next few days, the two remaining whales easily kept pace with a much larger team of army chain sawers as they continued their marathon jog toward the open sea. Three days into that journey, forward progress came to an abrupt halt as diggers and whales reached a thick pressure ridge in the ice. A Soviet Icebreaker arrived on the scene and punched a safe passage all the way out to the open sea. The gray whales were last seen setting a course south into the Bering Strait.

So, the gray whale rescue came to an upbeat conclusion in the form of a stunning collaboration between the U.S. and Soviet militaries. On such a note, this myth finally revealed its form to be a perfect circle. Just as we humans had to save the whales, so, undoubtedly, did the whales also make their best effort to save us.

6 THE DOLPHINS IN THE LAKE

The dolphin has especially developed a very well functioning third-eye chakra, which makes this animal clairvoyant in a rather far-reaching manner. Together with the throat chakra and the whole sonar system this third-eye is a receiver of cosmic wisdom and messages from the spiritual realms, and the dolphin is able to forward these messages to human beings. That is why so many people feel so deeply affected when meeting dolphins, whether they live in dolphinaria or in freedom in the seas. . . . You could say, that the dolphin is here on Earth to help human beings on their way, by reminding them of the important connection between innocence and spiritual wisdom.[1]
—BIRGIT KLEIN

The Australian Aboriginal people inhabiting Groote Island in northern Australia tell a story of a time in the distant past, what they refer to as *dreamtime*, when the Earth was inhabited by spirit beings called *indjbena*. Some *indjbena* looked like dolphins, although smaller in size. They lived in the deep waters beyond the reef, throwing themselves high into the air, turning and twisting in the breeze, then landing with a loud splash. Dinginjabana, strong and bold, was the leader of these spirit dolphins. His mate, Ganadja, was cautious and curious. Rather than spend her days sporting with her own kind, she preferred to visit the *yakuna*, or bailer shells, who crept slowly across the ocean bottom in their spiral houses. In those days, the *yakuna* were considered by all the other *indjbena* to be the wisest creatures in the ocean. Although Ganadja never saw as much of the ocean as Dinginjabana, she became wise about the ways of the sea and its creatures.

Dinginjabana was jealous that she spent so much time among them. "Don't visit the *yakuna*," he scolded, "or you, too, will become fastened to the bottom of the ocean." When Ganadja refused, Dinginjabana teased the *yakuna*, swimming into their colonies, swishing his powerful flukes, dislodging the shellfish from the coral.

The leader of the *yakuna*, Baringgwa, called his kin together to discuss the unprovoked antics. "The dolphins show no courtesy. They rarely speak wisdom, yet they talk more than all the other creatures together."

One day Dinginjabana swam up behind the leader and dislodged him from the coral. As Baringgwa spun down the reef face, Dinginjabana warned, "Stop your criticism or next time I'll toss you onto dry land." The *yakuna* understood well that Dinginjabana had a temper that he could not control, and they became fearful of this threat against their leader. Baringgwa decided to put some fear into the dolphins. The next time they teased the *yakuna*, Baringgwa shouted, "Be careful. When I shout the name 'Mana,' the tiger shark will surely come to our rescue." Tiger sharks were fierce enemies of the dolphins, sleek creatures with row upon row of razor-sharp teeth. The first time Baringgwa called the name 'Mana,' the dolphins forgot their game and swam away. But when they saw that nothing happened, they returned to torment the *yakuna*.

One day, fresh winds ruffled the waters. Several young dolphins frisked in and out of the waves beyond the coral reef. "Let's find Baringgwa and toss him into the air, then try to catch him before he falls back into the water," suggested Dinginjabana.

Ganadja tried to stop them. "You must not torment the *yakuna*," she pleaded. "They will not stand for it again." Dinginjabana flew into a jealous rage. He swam away to find Baringgwa, dislodging the *yakuna* leader from a rock and carrying him in his mouth to the surface. When Ganadja realized she could not dissuade Dinginjabana, she swam to the bottom to console the other *yakuna*.

All the other dolphins, young and old, male and female, joined in the game of tossing Baringgwa into the air. "Mana!" he shouted. "Come and protect me." The dolphins did not listen. Their eyes turned to the sky to watch the spinning *yakuna*. While he flew high in the air, Baringgwa noticed black shadows appear below the dolphins. "Run for your lives," he shouted again, "Mana is here." But the dolphins only laughed at him and kept their eyes to the sky. A great slaughter ensued. The waters around the reef turned bright scarlet. Dinginjabana himself was sliced in three pieces as he tried to swim away. Ganadja cried out in terror as she saw the head of her mate float down beside her. One of the great sharks heard the scream and swam to investigate, but the *yakuna* clustered their shells over her body. Of all the *indjbena* dolphins, only Ganadja was spared the massacre.

Several months passed. Ganadja gave birth to a son, whom she named Dinginjabana. The younger Dinginjabana grew so large that, from that day forth, no adult dolphin ever feared the sight of Mana again. Dinginjabana was the first member of the bottlenose dolphin tribe we see swimming close to shore today. More time passed. The souls of the slaughtered dolphins became hard and dry, then were reborn on dry land as the first human beings.

One day, after all her many children had grown, Ganadja swam close to shore to satisfy her curiosity about these new creatures. She recognized the spirit of her husband, Dinginjabana, living inside a man. Stranding on the beach, she worked her way across the sand with several heaves of her flippers. The man gazed upon this dolphin stranded on the beach and recognized his wife. Ganadja gave a joyful cry and took the shape of a human woman. That is why when we see dolphins stranding themselves today, we can be certain they are searching for their human soul mates.

Dinginjabana and Ganadja had many children who were the ancestors of the entire human race. That is why in our hearts we all feel dolphins are our kin. The dolphins also know this, which is why, of all the wild creatures, only dolphins seek out people.

I am invited, along with my wife and two young daughters, to join ten other people in a weeklong dolphin workshop held on a secluded island beach north of La Paz, in Baja California. Our leader is Carolyn Pettit, forty-six, who has been leading "dolphin-facilitated swims" for five years. She is a vivacious redheaded woman with flashing green eyes, a former therapist for the terminally ill, who returned to school in her thirties to get a master's degree in marine biology. Carolyn refers to her current calling as *a dolphin channel.* "I always wanted to make a difference," she declares to the group assembled on the sunny foredeck of a large trimaran carrying us to the remote island where we'll live for the next week. "I never found the handle until dolphins entered my life. The first time I swam with them I knew there was something electric about it that I had to share with other people. They make my job easy. Everybody feels good around dolphin energy."

In a few respects, Carolyn is cut from the same cloth as Steve Templor. Both serve as play-by-play commentators of the charged border, two cetacean professionals who seek the jolt of recognition that comes whenever a noticeable pattern leaps from the random field of marine mammal behavior. But their viewing platforms are different. In the biologist's world, humans stand at the apex of a Darwinian pyramid built on intellect. The perks of living life at the top of this pyramid include a clear conscience while shooting darts, a projectile that distresses whales but whose utility remains legitimate as long as it increases human knowledge. That Steve's own conscience wavers indicates that the timeworn pyramid is currently being reappraised by the young turks who comprise the upcoming generation of behavioral biologists.

Carolyn's influences are more diverse than Steve's. The meditation she espouses finds it roots in Buddhism. Seeing God in everything is distinctly Hindu. She quotes the medieval nun Hildegard of Bingen, and the Lakota shaman Black Elk, to explain why modern people must honor a spiritual linkage to other species. She acknowledges St. Francis of Assisi and the Bushmen of South Africa as past masters of the fine art of communicating with animals. When all these influences mingle inside Carolyn's mind, what emerges is a modern, "future-primitive" expression of *animism*, the most ancient expression of human spirituality, teaching the essential belief that all natural phenomena are alive and all living creatures have souls. Animism shows nature to be a congregation of spiritual cousins, *indjbena*, if you will; some members are ill-behaved, some cooperative, others are tricksters, gift givers, communicators. All are peers, all possess wisdom. Humans are the best at being human beings, just as worms are the best at being worms, and coyotes make the best coyotes.

In this view, nature is emphatically not a pyramid, but rather a vast and mysterious intellect Carolyn calls by its modern, paradigm-shifting name, Gaia. Gaia's essence flows bountifully from the Earth like myriad springs gushing from a cliff face and flowing into a huge lake. Carolyn has convened this workshop to show each of us how to surrender to the flow. Our objective is to float downstream to the lake without drowning. Once there, we must continue swimming to attain a suitable place to view Gaia unimpeded by the shadows that loom along the shoreline.

How do we find the lake? Carolyn quotes Ishi's famous dictum that "human beings are smart, but not yet wise." She believes we need a totem animal to serve as our mentor. A totem is an animal, a plant, or even a rock we treat as a member of our immediate family, like an older brother or sister whose steady presence in our lives affirms a sense of belonging to the community of nature. A totem is a navigator able to guide a person who has strayed too far from the lake. A totem speaks to us directly, although only a believer can plainly hear the advice. Carolyn's own totem is the dolphin. She swims with them in the sea, so that they may invite her to swim with them in the lake.

It would be a mistake to dismiss Carolyn's worldview as "New Age" and therefore ungrounded. She may be a bona fide mystic, but she is neither anti-intellectual nor disdainful of logic. Carolyn can spout cetacean behavior as well as Steve Templor. But she is an artist, not a biologist. She adds improvisatory twists to her dissertations, much the way Eric Clapton appends extra notes onto a common melody to make it his own. "If you insist upon reducing nature to hierarchies," she tells us as we tip our heads back to gather the hot sun to our faces, "then by any quantitative measure of brain and nervous system, cetaceans reside at the top of the pyramid. Their powers include psychic energy as well as intellect."

I am learning to understand Carolyn's "psychic energy" to be, variously, a place, a vitality, a talent, an ethic, and an attribute of nature. It exists everywhere. Those who perceive it live in a world where the air itself tingles. They detect portents in star patterns, are able to hear the animals, the trees, even the rocks conversing among themselves. Having seen it, found it, listened to it, they grant authority to intuition. These seekers relish the fact that information about psychic energy resides in first-person anecdote rather than data. The lines that separate subject from object, metaphor from reality, and yearning from observation are never so finely drawn as the biologists insist. No landscape is firm. The Earth, its vistas, and its denizens continually shape shift in synchrony with each person's altered perception. Within Gaia's lake, synchronicity itself is an everyday occurrence.

This relativity of perception means there can be no experts, only points of view. Whereas Steve Templor finds deep contentment declaring, "I have the answer," Carolyn is equally satisfied to announce, "I feel its energy." To her, learning the slippery truth about whales and dolphins is not a straightforward result of careful observation and good note taking. To know the cetaceans is to open one's heart to the energy fields she insists emanate from them more clearly than from any other animals, humans included. Every person feels this charge to a certain extent. How else to explain the six million people around the world who will go whale watching this year? It's not just marine mammals they want to see. They seek a hit from an energy field found only at the charged border.

The difference between Steve Templor's marine biology and Carolyn's shamanism is a religious distinction. Both believe their worldview is the only real one. Steve's certainty is essentially mechanical, masculine, yang. Carolyn's is communal, feminine, yin. Steve once assured me that "out there" remains the same no matter who observes it. A branch dropping in a forest makes the same sound no matter who hears it or even if no one hears it. Carolyn disagrees. "Out there" is emphatically different from observer to observer. The branch makes a sound if no one hears it. And everyone hears it differently.

A biologist may gather a thousand distinct data points to explain one aspect of dolphin behavior. A hundred other biologists may concur. To Carolyn, their judgment is valid, but only as a statement of the scientific point of view. A different point of view will produce an equally valid explanation because the sleek gray shape we call a bottlenose dolphin is a construction our brain manufactures from input provided by crude human sense organs. The viewing process is analogous to peering at a computer screen. Most people see the text, ignoring the building-block pixels that compose them. Biologists look a bit deeper than most people, perceiving text and pixels. Carolyn perceives the text and the pixels, but also the excited molecules that compose the screen's images. Consider this metaphor another inadequate explanation of psychic energy.

The skipper has turned off the engine. He raises the sail and steps below to liberate four bags of corn chips, which he serves with a smoky *chipotle* salsa. I munch a handful, then close my eyes to listen to the rhythm of many teeth crunching chips over bass notes played by the wind that's puffing the sail. Carolyn talks about pixels and text "upholding the dominant culture's belief in *objective observation.*" She mouths that last phrase with the same derogatory tone Steve Templor reserves for *anthropomorphism.* "No one is objective because no one can stand outside the world and watch the goings-on unaffected. That would be like playing at Greek gods, peering down on nature from the clouds of Olympus. If we want to know the dolphins, really know them, we have to stop playing and start acting like gods. These are creatures of vibration as much as of blood and bone. Until more people begin to see the dolphins this way, I harbor little hope for our species' survival."

With my eyes still closed, I ask Carolyn why scientists don't perceive the dolphins as she does. "From the time we're born," she responds, "we're taught it's useful to interpret the world on a solid, informational level. Psychics perceive the world differently—not because they possess different receptors—but because the cultural programming of their brains was never complete. They are modern shamans, what anthropologists refer to as wounded healers."[2] Ironically, this term suggests to me that anyone who belittles Carolyn's shamanic talent further corroborates her hold on that entitlement.

People lie on the top deck, some stare at the sky, others drape arms over the gunwales. I grow sleepy on the gently rocking boat. The water gurgles and hisses past the hull, providing serene music to my ears. Carolyn continues, now in a near whisper. "The dolphins are here on the planet to guide us onto the next plane of existence. They provide a channel to the etheric entities who recently arrived on Earth from the Sirius star system."

My eyes pop open to gaze upon a spinnaker I can't recall being unfurled, forming a pleasing bowl of wind directly above my head. I must have fallen into a half sleep because my ears clearly remained attentive. I sit up, gaze into Carolyn's striking green eyes. The Sirius star system? Is this another one of her metaphors? Perhaps, although, as I said, Carolyn refuses to draw sharp lines between metaphor and reality. Why specifically Sirius? Why not Venus or Pluto or Betelgeuse?

Her statement of belief is lifted directly from a delphic creation story told by the Dogon people of sub-Saharan Mali. The Dogon believed human civilization was carried to Earth thousands of years ago by a god called Nommo. When the Dogon asked Nommo his origin, he told them of a small planet circling the small binary companion star of Sirius, which astronomers today call Sirius B. Before Nommo arrived, humans lived like animals. Nommo taught our ancestors art, agriculture, architecture, mathematics, writing. Today, a visitor in Dogon country can still gaze upon ancient petroglyph images of Nommo. He is seen half-submerged in water, a being with a blowhole and the opposing flukes of a blunt-nosed dolphin, perhaps a pseudorca, or a pilot whale. This rendering seems especially curious since the Dogon reside in the sub-sahel of Mali, a thousand miles inland from the Atlantic Ocean.

Another aspect of this story is even more curious. The ancient Dogon could not possibly have viewed Sirius B with the unaided eye because the star was discovered by astronomers using new, powerful telescopes at the beginning of the twentieth century. Actually, the Dogon never claimed they *saw* the star. Rather, Nommo told them it was his place of origin. He even went so far as to draw a map displaying the double helix trajectory of the two stars of Sirius revolving around one another in a fifty-year cycle. When Nommo's map is placed on top of recent computer-enhanced renderings of the same orbit, they make a match.[3]

Such an elaborate claim of extraterrestrial visitation is bound to attract critics. Astronomer Carl Sagan argued that the French anthropologists who first recorded the Nommo myth in the 1920s were preceded, fifteen years earlier in Dogon country, by a European explorer and amateur astronomer. At the time of the visit, Sirius and its dark companion were causing a stir in astronomical circles as the first discovered binary system. Sagan concludes that the worship of Nommo from Sirius B is nothing more than front-page astronomical news transcribed into mythic terms by a primitive tribe during a fifteen-year hiatus.

By any measure, Sagan's conclusion is inconclusive. He fails to mention that anthropologists have provided evidence that Dogon cosmology predates the telescopic discovery of Sirius B by hundreds of years. Other anthropologists link the Dogon priesthood to ancient Egyptian religion. Isis, goddess of Sirius, was the principle female deity of ancient Egypt. Osirus, her husband, was commonly depicted as Isis's "dark companion." Osirus was the god of knowledge, who brought agriculture and other aspects of civilization to the ancient Egyptians.[4]

I ask Carolyn where she learned about the dolphin connection to Sirius B. She stares dreamily into my eyes and answers, "The dolphins told it to me." I am sorely disappointed by her channeled explanation of a myth documented in several books about dolphin mythology, which I presume she has read. By personalizing the Dogon revelation, Carolyn wrenches it away from the realm of debate. The dolphins told her so. And that's that. I resist blurting out: "Carolyn, the dolphins didn't tell you that, so-and-so's book did." Remaining silent, I am left feeling uneasy that our boat's destination is the fantastic island of Frivolous, described by the Abbe Gabriel Francois Coyer in 1750, a place where the trees bend like rubber, the fruit dissolves in the mouth like foam, and the roar of the wild beasts of the forest is like the whispering of silk.[5]

The trimaran arrives at a glorious sand beach near the northern tip of Isla Espiritu Santo, thirty miles north of La Paz. The skipper drops anchor. Two inflatables and several kayaks shuttle us and our mountain of gear to shore. Everyone dons a hat with a brim and dark sunglasses to cope with the intense light. As much as the sun, the silence of the desert environment overwhelms my senses. As I run to the edge of the beach to gather up a stray daughter, the sound of my footfall reverberates with every step, tricking me to sense an invisible walking partner. We assemble our tents at the back of the beach. Closer in, next to a boulder the size of an elephant, a kitchen is constructed from a remarkable collection of folding aluminum tables, chairs, and shelves. The food bins are placed in the cool shadow behind the rock. Setup complete, the skipper bids us adieu and sets sail back to town. He will return for us in seven days.

After lunch, the group gathers on the white sand beach to stare at the jagged purple-and-orange-striped spires of the Gigante mountain range that loom on the horizon fifteen miles across the Sea of Cortez. We are nine women, three men, and two little girls. This tally upholds my suspicion that the pursuit of dolphins interests women far more than it does men. This is substantiated by a hunch of mine that surrender is an experience sought more often by women than by men. And for every woman out in the water surrendering to dolphins, there is a man caught up in the market-driven capitalism that results in the dolphin entertainment industry, the dolphin military budget, and the slaughter of millions of dolphins in the cause of tuna-flavored cat food. And very few women. It seems the story of the world.

Actually, rattlesnake dancing aside, there may be no other human/animal relationship in which a wild animal is permitted to exert such reckless control over assenting human adults. If a few more people went off manifesting their version of the animal vision quest with other species, one might assume that the world would become a kinder and gentler place. Except, as it stands, these sorties remain the dolphin's burden alone. For just one example, the African safari does not exist without Land Rovers and rifles. No one pays $2,000 to trek onto the savannah to graze with zebras for a week, hunt with lions, pick over bones with jackals.

Carolyn sits down in front of us for orientation. Much of her rap is geared to issues of safety, paying attention to cactus quills on land and stingrays in the water. She leads us to a nearby tide pool to point out the identifying characteristics of five species of starfish and three sea urchins. Sitting around the tide pool she informs us that we may observe sperm whales, grays, and even blue whales from shore here at this time of year. Like a collector saving her best baseball card for last, she drops her voice to inform us that a year ago, she observed two unidentified individuals of the rarest genus of all, *Mesoplodon*, cruising along the shore at dusk.

Mesoplodons are considered rare because humans don't see them very often. I close my eyes and, in the spirit of Carolyn's relativistic view of observation, invent an alternate explanation for their aloofness. If whales communicate, and if they are intelligent, perhaps the elders of the *Mesoplodon* genus observed the demise of their cousin cetaceans and made the strategic decision to avoid the human species. They prosper, today, in the middle of every ocean, tens of thousands, perhaps hundreds of thousands of scamperdowns and Hubbses, Trues and dense-beaked diving for squid and reproducing their kind in the only place a cetacean Eden has a chance of existing: far from the charged border.

Carolyn passes around a cut-up pineapple and gives us a lesson in human/dolphin history. She tells us the tale of Pelorus Jack, a grampus or Risso's dolphin who accompanied steamers between the north and south islands of New Zealand for twenty-four years from 1888 to 1912. Jack leapt and dashed about the boats, eventually becoming a major tourist attraction witnessed by the likes of Mark Twain and Rudyard Kipling. When someone took a potshot at him, he was awarded special protection by an act of Parliament. It is reputed to be the first time a law was enacted to protect an individual wild animal, as opposed to a species or population.

Carolyn straightens her back and beckons us to close our eyes and breathe deeply. Ten minutes pass before she whispers to us, "We advance into a higher field of dolphin-evolved consciousness where beings of light reside. Many of you have already evolved to this awareness through channeling and dreams, but during this week we will physically visit many new realms of life to sense, on a cellular level, the three-dimensional world as an omnipresent four-dimensional reality." She pauses a moment, during which my literal mind struggles to render this cosmic rap into everyday terms. According to Einstein, the fourth dimension is time, possibly rendering the "omnipresent four-dimensional reality" into a polysyllabic synonym for the old hippie axiom: "Be here, now." "Physically visiting new realms" suggests we get to swim in the ocean with dolphins, rather than just dream about swimming with them as many in this assembly have been doing for years.

The dolphins off Isla Espiritu Santo play a role similar to Odysseus's sirens. They call sweetly to us across the waves, filling our heads with visions of a sensual paradise just beyond reach. One significant aspect of the myth has altered in the three thousand years between Homer and Carolyn. We trust these sirens and, therefore, no longer need to lash ourselves to a mast to avoid a face-to-face meeting. We can dive in and have fun. Except most of the people in our group display an aversion to the word *fun* to describe our time together. A week spent among a friendly group of strangers swimming with dolphins and camping out on a warm sunny beach in Mexico is couched, instead, in a language more apropos to the

Vedas than a holiday cruise brochure. We are not on vacation. This is a workshop, a retreat. We are pilgrims, not tourists. We have arrived here not to swim in the water, but to enter a four-dimensional realm where we will be healed. Even the white sand beach, presently being hollowed into twelve peaches by the force of gravity pulling against twelve pairs of buttocks, is a sacred border beyond which we encounter beings of light.

Dolphin-facilitated swims occur along the Kona coast, the Bahamas outer banks, the west coast of Ireland, the Dominican Republic, the Florida Keys, the Red Sea, several places in Japan, Portugal, Tenerife, Bali, Gibraltar, southern France, Thailand, Costa Rica. In the words of a brochure published by one well-known dolphin channel, Joan Ocean:

> The dolphins are assisting us to change the vibrational frequency of our physical matter through tones, directed rays of light, and adjustments to our belief systems. As spiritual people we are already open to these experiences, only needing to be guided into the parallel realities and refined states of living that exist close to our heart, around us.[6]

Carolyn asks us to open our eyes. In front, a flock of twenty pelicans dive-bombs on sardines. "Watch how each pelican straightens its long beak, then rolls its neck to the left the moment before it hits the water." We sit quietly to observe them plummeting from a great height. Some in our party have never seen feeding pelicans before, and stare openmouthed at the sheer exuberance of the behavior. Sure enough, she's correct! "On the rare chance that you see a pelican dive to the right, it's like finding a four-leaf clover. Make a wish. And don't forget to thank the pelican for its gift." For me, this anecdote sums up Carolyn's unerring ability to merge the keenly observational with the cosmic. She will keep these polar opposites in harmony through the memorable week of our workshop.

Next morning, just after dawn, eight pilgrims, including Carolyn and myself, set off from shore in the hope of meeting dolphins. We push Boogie boards in front of us for added buoyancy. Two people don wet suits; two others opt for nudity. Carolyn has designated the center of the bay, two hundred yards from shore, as our interspecies meeting place. There we wait, immersed in the calm sea, a group of human heads garbed in goggles, with snorkels jutting upward at odd angles. A quick dive displays a separate world where blue hands and bluer feet paddle an isometric dance. That the flat sand bottom lies twenty-five feet below brings home the fact that few among us would willingly swim so far from a strange seashore without a purpose. I chuckle to realize that only in the water is sputtering and spitting not considered bad manners.

Thirty bottlenose dolphins round the corner of the bay and head straight toward us. They stop a moment, then start swimming back and forth twenty feet from us. "They've come to see us," shouts Carolyn. "Greet them with your hearts!"

I find myself feeling cautious about her mantra of dolphin synchronicity. They do this for us when we open up to them. If they hadn't arrived so promptly, Carolyn would no doubt have concluded that our transmitters weren't tuned. It was our fault. We didn't call, so they didn't answer. Her certainty reminds me of psychic healers who insist we subconsciously invite disease into our lives. We bring on our illness, *and* we bring on our dolphins through the same tenacious act of will. But just as the former proves a cruel and unnecessary burden to lay on the head of dying cancer patients, so the latter seems an unnecessary burden to place on these marine mammals.

A bottlenose dolphin rises to the surface a body length in front of me. I am hardly immune to its majesty, first drawn to the silky gray skin drawn tight over eighteen-inch-long cheeks. The siren calls. If only I could draw close enough to rub my hand along its long cheek, I would be satisfied to do it just once. The animal is staring right at me. Its flat brown eyes are located on the sides of its head, but arranged in such an ingenious manner that the animal seems able to look forward stereoscopically, as well as sideways.

Directly above and between the eyes emerges a domed protuberance the size of a large cantaloupe, and appropriately called a melon. I know enough dolphin physiology to identify the melon as a fatty lens used to focus echolocation clicks. Having spent the past twenty-four hours listening to a discussion about the psychic abilities of dolphins, it is easy to understand how anyone might interpret this clicking sense organ to be a third eye, the seat of telepathic communication. The dolphin exhales, a sound more reminiscent of a luffing sail than of the cavernous sonorities produced by humpbacks or grays. Although I'm aware that evolution has rotated the dolphin's skull ninety degrees to our own, observing the blowhole's position near the back of the head remains a disorienting sight. If my nose grew between my shoulder blades, why not toes on my knees, or ears sprouting from hips. A sharp one-second sucking sound followed by the clack of its air valve closing tells me that this dolphin is about to dive. I stick my head into the water, watch it barely flick its flukes to glide smoothly toward the open sea.

It flicks a second time, veers to the right to surface in front of Glenna, a twenty-nine-year-old ceramicist from Ojai, California. Glenna goes beyond Carolyn in her certainty about dolphin intentionality. Sitting at the campfire last night, she stated flatly that the dolphins who frequent this bay have called us here. They have chosen, not just anyone, but us. Sticking my head in the water to watch five dolphins swim in a tight circle along the ocean bottom, I admit to some doubt. Cetologist Kathleen Dudzinski has informed me that this bottom-hugging tactic is "avoidance behavior or at least a distance-increasing mechanism."[7]

Trying to unravel Glenna's logic, I conjure up an image of these same animals forming a similar configuration two months ago. They force a stream of air from their blowholes in the manner of humpback lunge feeders, although when dolphins blow bubbles it may actually indicate an aggressive exchange between young adults. The bubbles slither to the surface, growing larger as the water pressure decreases. Within the first set of bubbles, I see myself trying one activity after another in an attempt to brighten my dull life. In the next bubble, my mailman delivers Carolyn's trifold brochure. In the next one, my wife and I are sitting at the dining room table discussing our mutual desire to spend some time in sunny Mexico swimming with dolphins. In the next bubble I board an airplane with my family in tow. The last bubble bursts into the air, displaying a diorama of our present group of eight sitting in front of the campfire agreeing to meet the dolphins this morning at dawn.

Whether we clothe ourselves as scientists or mystics, the rule makers and pattern finders among us feel in touch with life only by keeping a score card that offers some measure of control over what otherwise seems an aimless universe. Glenna shouts raucously to Carolyn, "You knew they would come this morning, didn't you?" As I sometimes turn off the play-by-play watching sports on TV, now I swim twenty yards from the group to meet the dolphins without having the experience marred by chatter about coincidence control.

My petty annoyance passes the moment lighthearted laughter strikes my ears. This happiness clarifies a belief harbored by all dolphin swimmers: that danger cannot possibly intercede within the orbit of interaction. Some of these bottlenose dolphins are ten feet long, yet no swimmer expresses the slightest hint of fear. The charged border is a safe haven like the monasteries in the Middle Ages.

On one occasion in my own long career of interacting with cetaceans, that belief turned psychotic. In 1983, a hundred miles south of Puerto Vallarta, Mexico, I was the principal investigator of a communication experiment cosponsored by a Mexican resort and John Lilly's Human/ Dolphin Foundation. A small pod of spotted dolphins resided a mile from shore. One afternoon, the resort manager asked me to take a family out to see the dolphins. We motored out but found the dolphins feeding on a school of bonito; they paid no attention to us. The man looked at his seven-year-old son. "I want you to have a dolphin experience you'll never forget as long as you live!" He wrapped a life jacket around the boy, lifted him up, and threw him into the water. The boy started screaming and sobbing. I quickly fished him out of the water. Later that evening, the man found me to say, "Don't you know that dolphins are well known for rescuing humans?"

His comment upholds the myth that cetaceans are always friendly to humans. Not everyone agrees. Underwater cameraman Howard Hall has written of feeling more comfortable filming sharks than any of the great whales. A shark's temperament is guided by instinct, making it easy to anticipate danger before it happens. Whales are unpredictable. Hall was once knocked unconscious after inadvertently surprising a gray whale underwater, prompting his colleague, Marty Schneiderman, to call the zone where whales kick their flukes "the arc of death."[8]

To my knowledge, on only one occasion has the sense of sanctuary been violated by a delphinid. In 1991, Lisa Costello was swimming with filmmaker Lee Tepley off the Kona coast of Hawaii among a pod of pilot whales, the large, bulbous-nosed dolphin species. She drew close to a male that appeared to be resting on the surface and reached out to caress its head; a small plastic camera dangling from her hand bumped it.[9] The whale grabbed her by the thigh. As Tepley watched helplessly—but with his videotape camera running—the pilot whale pulled Costello down sixty feet and held her there for forty-five seconds before bringing her back to the surface. Her wound needed stitches to close. Nonetheless, she later confided to me that, given the chance, she'd swim with the same animal again in a minute.

Although most of us start out swimming straight at the dolphins, this gesture is quickly understood as futile. They move just out of reach and hang in the water as if challenging us to try again. The distance dwindles from ten feet to six then four. My own standoffishness to the rest of the group dwindles accordingly. Then the slightest shake of a fluke causes the animal who was nearly in someone's grasp to zoom twenty feet out of reach. "The best interactions occur when you swim away from them," Carolyn shouts to the throng. "They'll follow you. Believe me." Everyone does. The dolphins do. I watch Glenna turn to grab at an animal, although the action is reduced to slow motion by the friction of the water. The dolphin moves aside with only the slightest kick of its flukes. The entire pod retreats to the bottom to perform synchronized swimming just above the white sand bottom.

If this were the United States instead of Mexico, our futile act would be regarded as a legal infraction. In U.S. waters, the Marine Mammal Protection Act (MMPA) sets a hundred meters minimum distance for anyone trying to get close to cetaceans. As a measure to protect cetaceans, it sounds terrific on paper, although, most unfortunately, this law makes no provision for dolphins who choose to interact with human swimmers of their own volition. At Kealekekua Bay, Hawaii, people have been swimming a quarter mile from the beach for several years to spend a few minutes in the company of a local pod of spinner dolphins. Once the MMPA was approved, the swimmers found themselves harassed by agents for the

Department of the Interior, who sometimes went to the ludicrous length of hiding in the palm trees along the shore to get a good vantage to shoot video proof of swimmers breaking the law. Though many people have been cited, the swimmers continue the practice.

Some dolphin behavioralists accuse the swimmers of anthropomorphism, of putting the human agenda of friendly contact onto the dolphins. "The bay is one of the places dolphins rest during the day. They feed nocturnally, so they need a rest area to be able to forage efficiently. If they are displaced from it, the long-term effects may include a decrease in reproductive efforts. They may be in the area the swimmers are and not really wanting to be near the swimmers. . . . It may simply be a case of being in the same place at the same time."[10] Swimmers counter that the behavioralists' stingy depiction of dolphin motive is typically anthropocentric. The spinners actively engage the swimmers. Why else would they stay close for hours at a time? The bay is large. It would take little effort for the dolphins to move beyond the reach of any human swimmer. Like a tale told by Dr. Seuss, the feud inflates, anthropomorphs and anthropocents both insisting that their own interpretation is the only plausible one; neither group willing to entertain a third possibility: that the event in question is neither harmful nor premeditated.

The bottlenose dolphins resurface. I notice one animal projecting its snout upward directly below a woman's feet. She is naked and instinctively closes her legs. A moment later, perhaps just as instinctively, the woman reaches down in a futile attempt to touch "him." He (or is it a she?) zooms back to the bottom. Humans, bonobo chimps, and dolphins are three species known to use sex for reasons besides reproduction. That dolphins have sex often, with many different pod members, yet without ever exhibiting a trace of jealousy or aggression, is another staple of the modern canon. It may not be true. Sexual aggressiveness is one likely cause of the so-called "rogue dolphin phenomenon," in which a harassing individual is eventually evicted from the pod. Being social animals, a lone dolphin cannot survive for long without companionship so, as the theory goes, they gravitate to humans who relish their attention. There is a story, perhaps apocryphal, of a young woman in Italy who took her budding communication relationship with a rogue male into the realm of sexual intercourse. That the person who told me this tale did so without revulsion or even judgment, indicates the cultish stature dolphins hold among certain true believers.

All these accounts bolster my hunch that dolphin swims are far more sensuous than they are mystical, although I can endorse Carolyn's Tantric view that treats the two as synonyms. The sea is warm. Our adrenaline is flowing in ways that would never occur if we were watching these animals from a boat. Right here in the water, swimming amid the pod, we are as close to being dolphins as we will ever know. Their splashing makes me want to splash. Observing all that silky dolphin skin drifting past my out-look—sleek, shiny, svelte, muscular—makes it easy to understand why some members of our group find it so difficult to keep their hands to themselves. Gazing upon the erotic dolphin's grin makes me want to grin. What does it matter that this Mona Lisa smile is a hoax, an accident of evolutionary musculature? Peering into their pointed faces through the blue-green water makes me wish any lover in my life would have smiled upon me with half as much delight.

Jake, a balding forty-five-year-old advertising executive from Los Ange-les with a hairy chest and a baggy plaid bathing suit, announces to the throng that he's cold and tired. Would anyone else like to swim back to shore? Melissa, a thirty-year-old high school teacher from Phoenix who is swimming nude, and Joan, an athletic-looking white-haired fifty-five-year-old psychologist from Dallas, join him. Their departure verifies that this activity demands much physical strength and mental alertness. I am struck by the paradox of so much physical exertion accomplished in the cause of unmitigated surrender.

I grow cold, swim to shore alone, but remain seated on the lip of the beach to watch those who choose to remain in the water. From this vantage, their enthusiasm reminds me of myself the first time I swam with dolphins at Kealekekua Bay. This was years before the strange days of federal agents climbing trees at taxpayers' expense to videotape swimmers breaking the law by attracting dolphins to meet them. I swam two hundred meters from shore on becalmed, coral-studded, blue-green water. I wasn't much of a swimmer at that time, so I was happy to support my weight by cradling a musical instrument known as a waterphone, constructed from a stainless steel salad bowl welded to a pizza plate to form a hemisphere, with a vacuum cleaner tube projecting from the bowl to serve as a handle and as a mouthpiece. All around the lip of the instrument projected tuned brass prongs. Rubbing the prongs with a cello bow produced a sound like a violin immersed in a bowl of Jell-O.

It was 1976. I had never heard of anyone swimming with dolphins before, so a part of my media-cluttered brain imagined shark-infested movie-set oceans. Directly in front, twenty spinner dolphin dorsal fins rolled over the ocean surface in close formation. I had read John Lilly's accounts of communicating with captive dolphins, and, as a budding interspecies musician, I wondered if dolphins might be attracted to a person making music in their midst. I stroked the main tube of the waterphone with the cello bow. Cradling the instrument, I felt the vibration course clear through my body. As the spinners continued about their business of exploring the outer edge of the bay, I stopped bowing long enough to plunge my head into the water to listen. There was no sound besides the low, fading bellow of the waterphone. I altered my technique; produced shorter, more rhythmical sounds, tapping a palm directly on the prongs that rim the equator of the sphere. The beat issued clear and simple, five seconds of sound, followed by five of silence. Once again I stuck my head in the water. The sphere was vibrating so sharply it hurt my ears. The spinners kept their distance so I tried something else, struck the center tube with a mallet while simultaneously immersing various sections of the sphere. A ringing tone was produced, the pitch modulated by the immersions. It sounded a bit like cartoon music accompanying the throbbing of Wile E. Coyote's heart.

This time the dolphins responded by swimming toward me. At fifty meters they formed a circle, turning on an axis like Israeli folk dancers doing "Hava Negila." One at a time they broke from the circle, drew closer. It was difficult to judge distance accurately with my eyes six inches off the water's surface. Their eyes became visible. That smile! Several lifted their heads high above the water's surface to examine the source of the vibrations. I looked upon them as human beings dressed in dolphin suits. The image vanished when they blew, like champagne corks popping all over the surface of the ocean. I continued to draw long sliding notes from the throat of the waterphone. The sphere sounded like a church organ, then an Oriental gong. I dunked my head, opened my eyes. Seven blurry figures scooted past the edge of my vision.

Spinner dolphins vocalize at frequencies at or above the limit of our audible range, like the highest tones on a hearing test, but with the perceived gravity of intrigues whispered at the opposite end of a cathedral. So suddenly as to make my blood rush, one of the dolphins jumped six feet clear of the water. They were all jumping, spinning, somersaulting. And from the shore, so far away, the audience of human beings gathered to watch started laughing, clapping, slapping each other on the backs. Someone on shore blared out a "charge" on a trumpet. The dolphins jumped higher. At that moment, I understood why captive dolphins attract large audiences. They are born performers. If musicians, acrobats, and clowns had a totem animal, it would be a dolphin. Yet we reward their joyous talent by trying to own it, capturing them, placing them in concrete pools, and then making them do insipid tricks for dead fish and shortened life spans.

The spinners frolicked about for ten minutes, then moved off, formed their circle a second time. Gone. I suddenly felt cold, my arms sore from treading water, feeling much too far from shore.

Three days pass quickly on the Sea of Cortez. I spend hours at a time alone on a little hill overlooking the cove, assembling mandalas in the dust with shiny stones, feathers, bits of seashell; and observing the rest of the camp out in the water cavorting with dolphins. Some members of the group don't know when to come out of the water. Yesterday I watched Junie, a fifty-two-year-old physical therapist from San Diego, need help getting back to shore. She suffered cramps and hypothermia. Later, I overheard her apologize to Carolyn for wanting just one, then another fleeting encounter with the dolphins. Carolyn shrugged her shoulders, frowned, and murmured something about "know thyself." But most of us were shocked it had come to that. The dolphin as drug. A few camp mates exhibit clear signs of addiction denial.

Late in the afternoon, six of us, four women and two men, head off from shore, without Carolyn, to meet a pod of six spinner dolphins that are leaping high out of the water near the north point of the bay. Spinners are smaller and sleeker than bottlenose dolphins; their beaks are slightly longer in proportion to the rest of their bodies. But it is their leaping that best distinguishes them from their larger cousins. Like figure skaters performing a triple lutz, spinners may twirl six or eight feet out of the water and then fall back with a mighty splash. Though several theories have been advanced to explain the behavior, joie de vivre seems to be the only one that makes real sense. We swimmers quickly discover that the spinners are far more vigilant than bottlenose dolphins about keeping a distance between themselves and our outstretched hands. We swim toward them. They back off. We swim away. They stay where they are. They never face us directly, never draw close enough for me to describe the relationship as an interaction. The span between our two species dwindles slightly over a half hour. The promise of decreased distance keeps us from returning to shore. Two women hold hands to do a backward somersault that twists at the end so they surface facing in the opposite direction. The third time they do it, two dolphins somersault beneath their feet and end up facing them directly. The mirroring is uncanny. The somersaulters burst to the surface and whoop in response.

Junie suggests we hold hands and visualize somersaulting together without actually doing it. How will the dolphins respond to that? The three other women immediately agree. Wendell, a forty-one-year-old commercial airline pilot from Connecticut, and I, declare that we wish to enjoy the swim without the overlay of group acrobatics. As we swim away from the women, Wendell growls that it's one thing for dolphins to mirror human movements and quite another for them to perceive unspoken thoughts. He concludes that certain members of our group can't accept delight and intelligence without coloring it as a spiritual bond between species.

I disagree, and tell him so. A spiritual bond is an item of faith, not logic. The linkage is real for everyone who believes it. Wendell's observational skills are also at fault. These woman are relating to the dolphins with far more delight than we are. He and I turn to watch the experiment but are surprised to see the women swimming right behind us. When they catch up to Wendell and me, Junie explains that the dolphins disappeared just a moment after we left the group. I have no idea if dolphins are telepathic, but I strongly suspect they possess the social skills to identify Wendell and me as party poopers.

Wendell and I sit on the beach to discuss the legacy of John Lilly, who first described dolphins as "the humans of the sea." He asserts that Lilly's image of a cetacean as a swimming neocortex incidentally surrounded by flesh is a distortion, the reverie of a scientist who spent some years dissecting dolphins, and the ensuing years speculating about the mystic mind he conjectured must reside inside such a large brain. I disagree with him again. Whatever his failings as a dolphin authority, Lilly remains the first great modern explorer of the charged border. More than anyone else, he brought the myth of the intelligent dolphin into the mainstream. Without Lilly, Carolyn might still be a therapist. I might be bagging groceries at Safeway.

John Lilly started his career in the 1940s as a neurophysician for the U.S. National Institute of Health. Working with electrodes attached to the heads of various animals, he discovered that different parts of the male monkey brain controlled erection, ejaculation, and orgasm. Although his work may sound unconscionable in hindsight, it must be understood in the context of the time. Unwilling to comply with the CIA's demand to use his discovery for human brainwashing research, Lilly quit government service, although not before he discovered the mental capabilities of bottlenose dolphins. In 1958, he wrote:

> Young adult [bottlenose] dolphins have brains equal to humans in weight and, as they age, the brain weight and body length continue to grow to levels exceeding the average human size. The true porpoise (*Phocaena phocaena*) is limited in brain weight to the range of human children; the adult porpoise has a brain smaller than that of a newborn dolphin. . . . The absolute size of the mammalian brain determines its computing capability and the size of its storage (memory); the larger the computer the greater its power.[11]

Working on his own, Lilly found that dolphins reacted differently to electrode stimulation of their so-called "negative areas"—the seat of anger—than monkeys or humans. Dolphins do not (or cannot) express rage. His animals shook all over and attempted to terminate the stimulation by pulling at the electrodes. However, the same animals were able to control their "positive areas"—the seat of joys and appetites—with a greater discrimination than any primate. Lilly was most impressed by their ability to vocalize to obtain more positive stimulation, something no monkey was able to do. By the late 1950s, Lilly abandoned electrodes to investigate dolphin communication. He concluded:

> I cannot convey to you all the evidence for my feeling that if we are ever to communicate with a non-human species of this planet, the dolphin is probably our present best gamble. In a sense, it is a joke when I fantasy that it may be best to hurry and finish our work on their brains before one of them learns to speak our language—else he will demand equal rights with men for their brains and lives under our ethical and legal codes.[12]

In the mid-1950s, he bought two bottlenose dolphins and placed them in a pool/laboratory constructed in the Virgin Islands. In an experiment now legendary among dolphin aficionados, Lilly's assistant, Margaret Howe, set up living quarters beside the enclosed pool, and ceased all contact with the outside world for several months. During that time, she taught the dolphins a few words of English. In the late 1970s, Lilly tried a similar experiment with two dolphins named Joe and Rosie. The objective of Project Janus,[13] as it was called, was to create an intermediary language comprehendible by both species. Lilly's programmers invented a computer-generated language composed of human speech, visual signs, and dolphin whistles, which were associated with objects and actions. When the experiment failed to fulfill its promise, critics charged it was an exalted training regimen, words and actions bartered for fish. Lilly had serious doubts that the promise of scientific knowledge was enough reason to keep Joe and Rosie in captivity.

As Project Janus ended, I met John Lilly and his wife, Toni, and argued that human-centered experiments produce human-centered results. After five years of intensive training in captivity, with nearly a million dollars spent, two dolphins had learned to vocalize like a human two-year-old. Using humor, Douglas Adams describes this impasse in *The Hitchhiker's Guide to the Galaxy*:

The dolphins had long known of the impending destruction of the planet Earth and had made many attempts to alert mankind of the danger; but most of their communications were misinterpreted as amusing attempts to punch footballs or whistle for tidbits, so they gave up and left the Earth by their own means. . . . The last ever dolphin message was misinterpreted as a surprisingly sophisticated attempt to do a double-backward somersault through a hoop while whistling the *Star Spangled Banner.* In fact, the message was this: "So long and thanks for all the fish."[14]

I suggested to Lilly that we try to attract wild dolphins to a meeting area located near shore where he could set up a lab on a raft to conduct the next phase of his language experiment. But the animals must be able to come and go as they pleased; no holding them with nets, or coercing them with food rewards. I proposed music as our lure. In 1983, the Careyes Project began, named after the resort a hundred miles south of Puerto Vallarta, Mexico, where we conducted this six-month experiment in human/ dolphin community. My partner in this venture was my wife, Katy, who is an excellent swimmer.

Every morning we'd load up our Boston Whaler with underwater sound gear, masks, snorkels, and fins and proceed to search for dolphins. The boat covered a lot of territory, and before long we spied the mottled dorsal fins of spotted dolphins neither interested nor uninterested in our motorboat. We turned off the engine, plugged in the wires connecting hydrophone to headphones, electric guitar to underwater speaker. I played whatever music entered my head at the time. The dolphins changed course, ventured within a hundred feet of the boat and echolocated in the tones of a creaky door. Katy donned snorkling gear and jumped into the water. The dolphins sometimes ventured within ten feet. After a few minutes, the dolphins regrouped and swam away. We zoomed after them. When we stopped again, the dolphins occasionally stopped as well, which caused the process to repeat.

After six weeks, no interaction had lasted more than ten minutes, so we overhauled our method. We decided to stay out of the water until the dolphins accepted our presence. We chose a specific meeting place a mile offshore from the cove where Lilly hoped to build his laboratory. We played music from this spot every day, starting at nine A.M., whether we saw dolphins or not. If they showed up and then left, we never chased them. From then on, until the conclusion of the project three months later, the dolphins came to us 80 percent of the time.

The dolphins invented a game we quickly mastered. After a short musical interaction, they would appear to leave. When they reached a line-of-sight distance from us, I stopped playing the guitar. One day, my sudden silence apparently prompted them to return to the boat. I played again, which made them turn away. When I stopped, they turned and came back again. I describe this interaction as a game because it involved rules and prescribed results. It evolved. One morning, we heard a new sound emerge from the hiss of the ocean, randomly percussive, like a hundred typists pecking madly at their keyboards from an office on the ocean bottom. A local fisherman informed me that the sound was made by a species of grunt as part of a seasonal courtship ritual. Next morning, I cautiously played a rough approximation of the "fish rhythms" by damping the strings and striking them with the edge of the plectrum. The ocean came alive with the calls of hundreds of vocalizing grunts. Then a new voice joined the fracas. Three spotted dolphins soon surfaced right next to the boat.

I responded to the random clicks with a polka: one-two, one-two. The dolphins responded to my rhythm with a counterrhythm: one-two-three-four . . . onetwothreefour. I started playing the Johnny Mathis standard "Misty," in sync with the dolphin's rhythm.

Ocean current hissed against the hydrophone. Hundreds of grunts clicked randomly. Dolphins kept a steady one-two-three-four . . . one-twothreefour. Our interspecies ensemble reminded me of the band in the barroom scene in *Star Wars*. Then Katy dropped into the water for the first time in months. The dolphins swam to her, copying her in-water movements. By the end of the morning, we were convinced we could establish a human/dolphin community based on music and dance.

The sponsors were not enthused. I emphatically rejected their attempt to turn the dolphin meeting place into a tourist attraction. They countered that the budding interspecies relationship would never reach the shore during the allotted six months. Money had been raised for a language facility, not for an improvised music and swim program based on back-and-forth games and fish rhythms. Despite much abstract rhetoric about dolphin intelligence, Katy and I were the only ones interested in letting the dolphins control the terms of the relationship. The project soon ended.

John Lilly's writings fortify Glenna's certainty that dolphins are enlightened beings. One evening, with the entire camp lounging around a campfire of deliciously fragrant mesquite smoke, watching a large dolphin fish sizzle on the grill, she argues this point vehemently with Wendell, who has, over the past few days, emerged as the community's resident rationalist. He turns quietly rude, prodding Glenna to clarify her terms. "The only enlightened behavior I've seen is dolphins avoiding your hands."

As Glenna becomes undone by her certainty, and then distressed by Wendell's condescending tone, Carolyn shocks us all to attention by blowing hard on the whistle that dangles from her neck. "Sorry 'bout that," she drawls. "But I hate listening to you guys carry on." She hands spatulas to the two of them. "Sure, our attraction to dolphins is cosmic," she adds while directing them in a neat-and-clean turning of the twenty-pound fish. "But language doesn't express it. Calling dolphins enlightened is like calling them intelligent. The words mean too many things to too many people."

Linda, who is in charge of the foil-wrapped potatoes, hasn't said much of anything to anyone all week. Now she abruptly announces that she plans to develop her own dolphin swim program. "It's not as easy as it looks, honey," answers Carolyn, her eyes closed tight to avoid the smoke. "You've had remarkable luck. My last group had just two short encounters in ten days. Most of them didn't feel they got their money's worth. One woman asked for a refund."

"You'd think the desert would provide satisfaction enough," replies Wendell, munching on a *sopapilla*.

Carolyn gazes at the shadow of a sharp bluff reflected by the fire. "For me, the desert provides as powerful an energy source as the dolphins. But people have to unload their expectations before they're ready to substitute. Last year, when no dolphins showed up after five days, I proposed to the group that we hike into the hills to spend twenty-fours alone with nothing beside a tent, a sleeping bag, and a canteen full of water. Everyone was afraid the dolphins would arrive the second we left." She pauses, pours herself a cup of tea. "Dolphins showed up for twenty minutes on the last day of that trip." She chuckles. "But it was a memorable twenty minutes."

Our own group is not so tied to this beach. Yesterday, five of us kayaked up the coast. At the tip of the island, in a channel formed by a small off-shore islet, we encountered a colony of Baja sea lions, a rare species indige-nous only to the southern Sea of Cortez. The skipper of the trimaran had told me that the colony was nearly wiped out in the early 1980s by a Japa-nese trawler fishing illegally in the Sea of Cortez. When the boat was boarded by Mexican authorities, they discovered several sea lion pelts among a shocking number of marlin and tuna carcasses. All three species have been slow to recover.

The sea lions were delicate animals not much larger than harbor seals. Someone threw them an orange. The sea lions pushed it back and forth to one another with their noses. We pulled our kayaks onto the beach and jumped into the water to start an interspecies ball game. I grabbed the orange, threw it high into the air. A sea lion retrieved it, dragged it to the bottom, and then let it rise to the surface where Melissa grabbed it. The sea lions spiraled through the water, often swimming upside down, some-times stopping directly in front of our faces, displaying the longest eyelashes framing the prettiest black eyes. Everyone kept their hands to themselves.

We tired of the game, swam to the islet, and switchbacked up to a grass-covered plateau to discover a small colony of blue-footed boobies sitting on eggs. Boobies are master minimalists, who merge the usually distinct tasks of defecating and house constructing by squirting a ring of white feces on the ground to denote the boundaries of an illusory nest. The males do their fair share of egg sitting and chick tending. Sitting on a ledge covered in brilliant yellow lichens, we observed the sea lions still playing with the orange in the sea below. I asked the group how swimming with dolphins felt different from swimming with sea lions. Jake declared that the sea lions were more fun. They weren't so tentative. Joan sharply disagreed, felt uneasy the moment she entered the water. The sea lions seemed too much like dogs playing a game of fetch the stick. She couldn't relate, always worrying that they would become overexcited. When I asked if they did anything to frighten her, she answered, "Not exactly. But I felt they would have, if we stayed a few more minutes."

Pat, who is a public relations director for a large publisher, agreed with Joan, adding that there had to be some reason *lion* was part of their name. "It's just a name," responded Jake. "Male sea lions have a mane like a lion."

"People used to call orcas killer whales," I added. "In the 1950s, the U.S. Coast Guard published a manual warning boaters to avoid 'the killers' at all cost. Today, our perception of the same animal is entirely different. Kayaking in close proximity to orcas has become a booming business in the Pacific Northwest."

"It's not just a matter of a name," replied Pat. "Swimming with dolphins *feels* friendlier than swimming with sea lions. Like Carolyn says, words don't express it. They show me their compassion mind to mind. And I love them dearly for it."

Herodotus was probably the first writer to recount the peculiar habit of dolphins of showing concern for the welfare of human swimmers. He told the story of Arion, a gifted musician who won a contest in Sicily and was traveling home to Corinth with his prize. The sailors on board coveted the treasure and threatened to kill him. Arion requested to play his kithara one last time; his tormentors agreed. Facing the sea, he strummed a song, described by Herodotus as distinctively high-pitched and high-spirited. At its conclusion, Arion boldly mounted the gunwale and threw himself into the waves. But dolphins had been attracted to the music. They carried him to safety. When he returned home to Corinth, Arion had the thieves arrested and recovered his treasure. Today, there are so many documented instances of dolphins rescuing human swimmers that one may assume the myth of Arion to be a true account of the time.

Critics of the dolphin-swim phenomenon might refer to Pat's declaration of extrasensory contact as an expression of *Dolphinism*. These skeptics concede that dolphins demonstrate great exuberance playing with humans, a trait they share with dogs and, as we have just witnessed, sea lions. Granted, dolphins have a large brain, and a well-developed neocortex, which is posited to be the seat of reason in human beings.[15] They may even have a grasp of language. But they do not exhibit mind-to-mind power. Doubters view Dolphinism as one more narcissistic reflex of our own species longing to find its animal heritage in similarly endowed, hairless, large-brained mammals. People who contemplate Utopia in the dolphin's smile are no different from astrologers who find answers consulting a haphazard arrangement of stars in the sky. Both are irrational, both prone to self-deception, both seek solutions by avoiding the tangible in favor of the ephemeral.

Treating dolphins as gurus is also a form of celebrity worship, cut from the same cloth as fans who give deference to the opinions of sports stars instead of listening to the immediate needs of their husbands, wives, children. Some critics even complain about the environmental favoritism demonstrated by dolphin celebrity. A donor gives huge sums of money to relocate a single celebrity orca like Keiko, while the donor's immediate environs remains polluted.

The promise of Dolphinism has been captured in dozens of films. These are of a different genre than the cetacean "nature films" that fill up Steve Templor's schedule. Pretty people, often celebrities, dive into crystal-clear waters to reach out to dolphins, who make passes at them to the drone of an airy sound track. The swimmers resurface, expressing awe that such a miracle could be happening to them. The film formula sometimes juxtaposes images of dolphins at oceanaria, to demonstrate that swimming with wild dolphins is a different experience from swimming with captive animals. Some of the films assert that captive dolphins can be used positively in healing, although more of them offer the MacLuhanesque paradox that one cannot be healed by inflicting pain on the healer. This growing film genre of lighthearted people swimming with smiling dolphins may also be understood as the sunny flip side to all the crisis management depicted in so many environmental documentaries illuminating the darkness found wherever resource-hungry people pick at nature. With the dark side so utterly gloomy, is it any wonder that the light side often appears lightweight?

Lightweightedness occurs because of the immense difficulty any filmmaker faces while translating the subtle anecdotal energies of the charged border onto a TV screen. Most people look silly underwater. Blue arms flail, cheeks and eyes bulge, noses and snorkels let loose with the occasional bubbly fart. Nothing much happens besides the occasional dolphin filling the same frame as goose-pimpled human bodies in bathing suits. An occasional touch between species is treated as if it was Will Mays's over-the-shoulder catch in the 1954 World Series. The elusive dolphin smile that drew the audience in at the start does not alter, finally revealing itself as a frozen mask. An earnest narrator insists that this clumsy exercise is a life-transforming experience of global import. But the audience increasingly perceives the dolphin's evasive maneuvers as evasive maneuvers. The films fail for much the same reason flailing bodies in a pornographic film can't evince love. In fact, the fleeting glimpse of a dolphin swimming just out of reach *does* prompt transcendental experiences in swimmers, and quite often at that. But communion is not a spectator sport.

After a week swimming with dolphins every single day, members of our little community have developed shticks to optimize the swim experience. Some display obeisance to their rationalist roots by paying attention to dolphin demeanor. These naturalists keep journals in which they write for hours at a time, trading observations about patterns of behavior with one another the same way my daughters trade seashell fragments. "Did the spinners come closer today than yesterday?" "How much closer, would you estimate?" Individual animals are identified by comparing their markings to the hundred or so line drawings of animals contained in a large spiral-bound notebook assembled by Carolyn over the past two years. One bottlenose dolphin is named Nicky in honor of a nick from the trailing edge of a dorsal fin. A spinner is called Cookie because of a curious circular scar on its cheek, identified as the bite mark from a cookie-cutter shark. Each day's observations add to our growing sense of familiarity, and our discussions reflect this newfound intimacy. "Did you see what Nicky did with Joan this morning?"

Other members of our group display the advanced symptoms of celebrity worship. The fans linger longest in the water. They display their blue lips and their shrunken fingertips as signs of devotion. Junie is the worst of the lot. She squeals constantly whenever a dolphin looks at her directly, yet seems incapable of understanding the basic lesson that one gets nowhere by reaching out to an animal, that the dolphins must initiate contact or they simply won't play. She confessed during last night's group meeting that she'll be dissatisfied unless she gets to touch a dolphin. Yet if our group camped on this beach for ten years, swimming with the dolphins every day, I feel certain that Junie, with her passive aggressive neediness, would be the last one to touch a dolphin.

Finally there are the mystics, members of a small flock Wendell refers to as "the first church of dolphins." These devotees enjoy close encounters in the water as much as anyone else. But physical meetings serve mostly as a prelude and a verification of the real work that occurs inside one's mind, heart, and plexus. Carolyn calls her four-person congregation together by striking a gong every morning half an hour before dawn. They assemble at the water's edge to meditate for an hour. It starts out much the same as a Buddhist prayer: with instructions about how to unload the trash can of one's mind. But unlike Buddhists, who work hard to make sure the trash remains empty, these mystics leave the lid open in the hope that a dolphin's thoughts will gain entry. Does it happen? They insist it does, although, significantly, the experience is important enough to them that they don't dissipate its power by sharing its content in an open forum.

I sit at the tide line, dangling my feet in the water, drawing the mountain range onto a page of my journal. Carolyn emerges from a swim with an apricot-colored silk scarf tied around her ankle. "What's the scarf for?" I ask, shielding my eyes from the strong afternoon sun.

She stares over my shoulder at the drawing, then sits down beside me to dangle her own feet in the water. Five long minutes pass before she answers. "One dolphin I connect with in meditation asked me to wear it to identify myself among all the other swimmers."

"Did it work?"

She wraps a towel around her shoulders, rises a moment, then sits directly in front of me. She stares deeply into my eyes. "It really worked. One bottlenose dolphin with a little groove at the tip of her dorsal fin stayed close to me for the entire swim. At last, I feel certain she's the one who talks to me."

I place my book and pen on the sand, and give her my full attention. "What does she tell you?"

"She thinks it's good I bring people here. She's learned a lot about humanity by interacting with us. But she doesn't want me to do it more than one week a month. This is her home. She's asked me to respect that."

I sigh, then tell Carolyn a story from the Careyes Project. One morning, Katy and I invited a couple, Fred and Betsy, to join us on the boat for a morning. When we reached the meeting place, Fred lay faceup on the floor of the boat with a hat covering his eyes. I played the guitar for half an hour, but the dolphins didn't show. When I stopped, he removed his hat and stated matter-of-factly: "Three dolphins told me they'll be arriving from the south in ten minutes." Then he bolted upright with a quizzical expression on his face. "Actually, it wasn't *ten* or even *minutes*." We waited. Fifteen minutes later, three dolphins appeared from out of the south.

"Fred was right," responds Carolyn, wiping tears from her cheeks. "Dolphins have a clear sense of time but not our specific measurement of it." I smile, intrigued by her precise manner of qualifying the terms of this telepathic experience without judging it.

We sit in silence, two nature lovers content to watch the shadow climb up the bluff overlooking the cove. "What do the dolphins tell you about their powers?" I ask.

"They are seasoned travelers who migrate freely between the solid Earth realm and the vibrational realm."

"Say it another way?" I plead. "I don't always understand your language."

She smiles gently, and her face relaxes although her voice turns earnest. She chooses her words carefully. "When the channeling begins, the dolphin takes over my physical form. My knees lock together. I feel like I'm losing my legs. Or she might use my mouth as a blowhole. She breathes so hard that sometimes I feel my lungs are going to explode. But she settles down, so her message can channel through me telempathically. Obviously, she doesn't speak English, but my subconscious is tuned well enough to translate her message."

"What does she tell you?"

"That we humans need to see ourselves as spiritual entities who inhabit physical bodies for just a short time. My dolphin friend doesn't care if she dies tomorrow. When her time in the ocean is over, she will go somewhere else, and do something different. Just like us. Except we don't accept it and she does.[16] Am I making sense?"

"You used this word, *telempathically*. What does telempathy mean?"

"The Hawaiian channel, Joan Ocean, made it up. Telepathy plus empathy equals telempathy. It's the bond that occurs when two beings are communicating mind to mind. Sometimes the bond itself is the message."[17]

"Do you ever see dolphins as animals?"

Carolyn wraps the towel around her shoulders. Her face tightens; then she sighs deeply. "Why do I get the feeling you think my work is escapist?"

I pull my head back to take the full measure of her accusation. A minute passes as I compose my response. "I can't criticize anyone else's sense of the sacred without imposing an order on it that's just as limited as the order I criticize. My own feelings about dolphins change every time I see them. Right now I'm thinking they're playful sea mammals, and I was just curious if you ever see them so simply."

From the kitchen, Glenna calls Carolyn to help locate a pot of leftover lentils. She grimaces a moment, then cracks her back. "I have to go fulfill my job as camp counselor." She rises to walk up the beach, leaving me alone with the orange sun of evening beating on my nose. Carolyn is correct to defend her otherworldly convictions. Mainstream psychological literature contains few studies of channeling that don't uncover some pathology as the driving impetus.[18] Likewise, traditional cultures that rely on channeling for their perception of the sacred have always been discounted as less enlightened than our own. Anthropologist Paul Reisman might as well be commenting on Carolyn's guardedness when he writes:

> Our social sciences generally treat the culture and knowledge of other peoples as forms and structures necessary for human life that those people have developed and imposed upon a reality which we know— or at least our scientists know—better than they do. We can therefore study those forms in relation to "reality" and measure how well or ill they are adapted to it. In their studies of the cultures of other people, even those anthropologists who sincerely love the people

they study almost never think that they are learning something about the way the world really is. Rather they conceive of themselves as finding out what other people's conceptions of the world are.[19]

After a dinner of lentils served in a delicious green sauce, cheese tacos, jicama sticks, and Corona beer, we gather around the campfire for Carolyn's evening lesson in human/dolphin cultural history. Two nights ago she told us of the *Oannes*, an ancient race of gods who possessed the body of a fish or dolphin and the head of a man. Before the advent of Mideastern civilization, the Oannes appeared on the shores of the Persian Gulf to hold discourse with local fishermen. Like the Dogons' Nommo, Oannes bequeathed the locals a knowledge of art, architecture, and agriculture, which eventually led to the Sumerian ascendency. Priests of Sumeria took to emulating the Oannes beings, by donning a curious cloak with fins, flukes, and a pointed snout for a hat. Some mythologists believe the Egyptians borrowed the costume, which influenced Aaron, high priest of the Hebrew Exodus, who also wore a peaked hat. In Greece, priests wearing a similar hat worshiped the sun god, Apollo, who was considered the father of dolphins. When the early Christians took up the costume, the dolphin's-beak hat evolved into the pope's mitre. Today we see the same curving dolphin smile in the groove that wraps around the dome of the bishop's chess piece. In France, where the king called himself the heir to Apollo's heavenly throne, *Dauphin* was the name given to the prince.[20]

Tonight Carolyn's subject is the Australian Aboriginal concept of *dolphin dreamtime*, a concept that coalesces totem with genealogy. Ask an Aborigine what his "dreaming" is, and he will respond with the name of an animal, a feature of the landscape, a plant, or a constellation. This answer alludes to his personal ancestry, his clan's family tree, the basis of his sacred rituals, and the place his spirit lived before he was born. Honoring the terms of this dreaming assures the continuance of life for himself, his children, and his clan.[21]

The Aboriginal people who told the story of Dinginjabana regarded the bottlenose dolphin as their dreaming. Living by the sea, they observed these near-shore cetaceans for thousands of years, and ultimately developed a body of knowledge about dolphin behavior that was as sophisticated as the sum of marine biology, although the ultimate objective of their science was tribal security and personal power, not information.

Talking to the dolphins eventually led the Aborigines to the extraordinary process known as cooperative fishing. The deceased shaman Larry Langly has left us hints of the technique:

> When I was a small boy, I used to go fishing with my uncle who had studied the dolphins for many years. When he called to them, usually three dolphins would spread out at the sides of the boat and another one at the back. They would then make a field of sound and drive a whole mob of fish up onto the shore. He knew so many sounds and the exact way to do it; and sometimes he would take up some salt water in the palm of his hand, and clap his hands together in a certain way to tell the dolphins what kind of fish he was hunting for that day. There are many kinds of dolphins in these waters: the white ones, they live in the sweet water. In the salt waters you find grey-silver ones and black ones.[22]

Another anecdote is related by one of the last Aboriginal shamans, Jackson Jacobs, while being filmed for a television documentary in the 1960s.

> One day we were walking along Ggodiggah near Walpardi. My Daddy sang the sacred song even though there was only one dolphin there. I went away, I never believed my Daddy. I didn't take any notice of him singing. I had my own spear and so I went up on the hill and there were all the boys there. And this one boy, he comes over and says, "Hey! You look over there. All them dolphins are everywhere!!" Where they come from I don't know. And at that time we were all hungry because we had no fish. And all of a sudden I couldn't believe my eyes. All the fish, black everywhere in the waves. And my Daddy was singing the song for the dolphins. He walks along the beach and he whistles like this (makes a slow vibrating whistle). . . . And after that my Daddy does this (slow clapping). And the dolphins come right up and my Daddy threw that fish to the dolphin.[23]

According to the Aboriginal elder, Bill Smith, it didn't matter if the dolphin pod was beyond visual or audio range when Jacobs's father sang his song.[24] Singing was neither the mechanism nor the message of correspondence, but a ritual that prepared the shaman for mind-to-mind communication. Imagining the pose of a shaman in trance, eyes closed, head bowed, it is not difficult to understand why the experience was translated into English as *dreaming.*

Jacques Cousteau documented cooperative fishing among the Imragen of Mauretania in northwest Africa. Men of the tribe stand up to their knees in the shallows and beat the surf with sticks. The first time the Imragen permitted filming, they attracted a pod of orcas. Cousteau speculated that the orcas appeared in the hope of snaring a few dolphins. A few days later, they tried again. This time, a pod of bottlenose dolphins appeared and corralled a school of mullet into a net assembled in the shallows. The Imragen set up their cookfires on the beach and ate dinner while the dolphins frolicked offshore.[25]

I once showed Cousteau's film to a gathering of fishermen and children at Iki Island. In the discussion that ensued, I asked Mr. Yamaguchi if he would prefer cooperative fishing to his own violent relationship with the local dolphins. He answered that if the local dolphins were taught to help fishermen catch yellowtail and squid, the offshore banks would become a desert in a matter of weeks.

Each morning after breakfast we hold council. An osprey feather is passed from hand to hand to serve as our "talking stick." Anyone with a story to tell, a logistical concern to share, a joy or a sorrow to commend, is given the opportunity to share. Only the feather holder may speak. By midweek, the interpretation of dreams receives the lion's share of attention.

One bright morning John takes the feather, studies it a moment as if the words he is about to speak are coded into its black-and-white chevrons. He sighs deeply, then relates last night's dream. He was floating in the middle of the ocean among a pod of sperm whales when, from out of nowhere, a disembodied eye zoomed in to scrutinize him. Cradled within folds of heavy skin, the eye peered down at him from above, then plunged directly into his skull, where it surveyed his cerebral landscape like a spelunker mapping a cavern. John was able to watch the eye and yet perceive what the eye, itself, was seeing. Finally, a whale surfaced beside him and invited him to explore its mind.

John's voice turns to a monotone as he reveals that the whale's mind did not reside in its head. The huge brain was a radio receiver tuned to a source of blinding white light located he knew not where, and transmitting music composed of unimaginably dense polyrhythmical clicks. John watched the white light focus first into wave patterns, then into a vague three-dimensional geometry that slowly morphed into a recognizable craggy seamount. He realized he was watching the eternal night of the abyss as a sperm whale must see it. A giant squid with huge saucer eyes loomed out of the darkness, extended its tentacles studded with frightening claw-rimmed suckers, and snatched an eel-like creature with a hinged jaw full of needle teeth, and chartreuse lamps dotting its fins. When the whale opened its mouth to show its own eel-like tongue, the squid moved forward. John woke up.

The osprey feather revolves around the circle. It progresses quickly through two more dreams, an anecdote about oranges and sea lions, a testimonial to last night's dinner. Then it stops a while to allow Junie to deliver her daily lecture about the wonder and awe of swimming with dolphins. Today she concludes with a question, "Can anybody still doubt the powers being unleashed offshore?" The stick passes to Melissa, who briefly assures Junie that no one here harbors doubt.

When the feather arrives in my lap, I sigh deeply, and stare at it. Junie's evangelism leaves me feeling like a casualty of Tourette's syndrome, where sowing discord seems the only viable behavior. I take ninety seconds to uncork a long-hidden horror story of Iki fishermen gaffing newborn dolphins for dinner. As long as others in the group feel obliged to invoke third eyes and fourth dimensions, I feel bound to keep some balance by bringing Mr. Yamaguchi's profoundly dark cloud into the sunny circle of this field of dreams. Thankfully, when I finish, no one comments on either my imagery or my game.

It is our last day living as a dusty biblical troupe on the lip of the desert in the Sea of Cortez. When the council ends, some camp mates walk down to the shore to peer longingly into the bay, like lovers waiting for their

188 · THE CHARGED BORDER

paramours to return for one final meeting. But the dolphins don't show. At lunch, I mention to the group that if the dolphins arrive this afternoon, it might be worthwhile to try something different. "What do you have in mind?" asks Joan.

"We could try to attract the dolphins to us. Stand in waist-deep water and click stones, and sing together. If they're as interested in us as we think they are, then according to the Aborigines, the dolphins may come. If they don't come, then we learn something about our powers of persuasion."

"You don't think they're interested in us, do you?" pipes up Glenna.

"I'd just like to try something different, that's all. But now that you ask, these animals do seem wary. I haven't seen much of the mirroring of movement I've witnessed many times with spotted dolphins in the Bahamas. They don't hang around as long as orcas on the British Columbia coast. Nor have I heard of any instances of game playing."

"Why do you have to grade the experience?" complains Joan, frowning. "This one's better than that one. That one's worse. Whatever it is that's going on here, everybody else is completely turned on by it."

Before I can respond, Carolyn comes to my rescue by putting the original question back on track. "What if we try your experiment and the dolphins don't come in? At what point are you willing to call it off?"

"I think if we decide it's worthwhile, we do it either until they join us or until they leave the bay."

"But it's our last day," sighs Glenna. "I want to swim with the dolphins, not do an experiment. I don't need that kind of a reality check."

"If we had more time, we could try a lot of things," replies Carolyn. "I agree with Glenna. It is our last day."

We put the matter to a vote. My suggestion is soundly defeated.

Late in the afternoon, a pod of fifteen spinner dolphins appears in the middle of the bay. Everyone in camp swims out to meet them; even my daughters, ages five and seven, buoyed by life jackets and Boogie boards. As we arrive, the dolphins break into smaller groups of threes and fours to swoop in a graceful arc to the bottom. There they choose to linger, far beneath the grasp of even the best free divers among us. Watching them hug the sand, I acknowledge that they are certainly beautiful. But after so many days serving as an audience to such beauty, then hearing this passive role described as interactive, I hunger for context, even if it means grading it.

Feeling the cool touch of the sea all over my body, I recall an experience from Careyes. Katy and I noticed six huge dolphins of an unknown species leaping to such heights and landing with such splashes that it seemed the sky must be venting itself of meteors. We motored to meet them, doused the engine, grabbed our masks, snorkels, and fins and, without pause to consider who they were or what we were about to do, jumped fearlessly into the water. They were sixteen to twenty feet long, black, snub-nosed. Pseudorcas. The pod came to an abrupt halt, then turned. One animal zoomed within inches of my face. It opened its toothy jaws and shook its head as if laughing raucously, then disappeared to be replaced by another animal. Then another. One in particular turned its head back and forth to scrutinize me more closely. The dark, featureless eyes flashing before me were every bit as curious and flabbergasted by the experience as I was. I gush to relate that the dolphin peered through the face mask to grant my deepest longing of what it means to attain communion with another sentient being. I was at its mercy, terrified yet trusting that my fear was unjustified. The machine-gun echolocation clicks pattered all over my body while the pod's swooping whistles added an edgy sound track to my growing sense of submission.

How did it end? As quickly as the pseudorcas appeared, they kicked their flukes and simply vanished from our sight. Katy and I climbed back into the boat. Out of breath. Stunned. Not a word to say. We scanned the ocean. They were already far away, heading south down the coast at twenty knots. We never saw them again.

By contrast, these cute little spinners gliding along the bottom in groups of three and four choose to keep their distance from us, although the margin occasionally dwindles to a body length. But even if they drew beside me, I would not feel elated. It is not proximity I seek, but correspondence—a clear signal that some sound or movement they start can only be completed by a commensurate action from me. It is what I sought that first time, cradling a waterphone to meet spinner dolphins off a beach in Hawaii. It is what I found swimming with pseudorcas. By comparison, the structure of our entreaties with these spinner dolphins is too delicate to pull me out of myself. Carolyn proclaims that she gives no power to dolphins that they don't already have. But to know their energy, we must first open ourselves to receive it. My own thoughts stray to irony rather than certitude. If dolphins are as intelligent as their devotees insist, these spinners would have to be as confused about our motivations as we are about theirs.

When the spinners finally venture from the bottom, they bless us with a quasi–close encounter. I am jubilant to observe my little daughters, Claire and Sasha, spread-eagled like waterbugs on the lake, splashing with excitement, yelling "Daddy" and pointing their fingers at the dolphins just in case I may have forgotten where I am. At such a moment, it makes little difference that some formerly glimpsed revelation eludes me this time around. I make up for it by swimming with my family and friends among dolphins. I thank the dolphins for granting such simple pleasures. Like everybody else here, it keeps me smiling until my cheeks ache.

7 SIX HONEST SERVING MEN OF LEARNING

A pine needle fell.
The eagle saw it
The deer heard it
The bear smelled it.
—TLINGIT PROVERB

Many animal species communicate, although correspondence is generally limited to instinctual signals expressing danger, territory, and courtship. A dog growls at a perceived threat, a frog croaks at dusk, a male bird of paradise clings to a branch upside down while preening his feathers. Signaling as acquired behavior is much less common. A dog is trained to bark at a deer, but not at a sheep. Redwing blackbirds possess regional accents they pick up from their parents, causing a blackbird from Maine to ignore the call of one from New Jersey. Ravens, mynahs, and mockingbirds mimic the sounds in their environment for reasons that may include impressing a potential mate, hoodwinking predators, and playing.

Baby orcas learn discrete vocalizations referred to as dialects. These calls vary from pod to pod, even among pods that inhabit the same waterway. When orcas interact physically with one another—chasing, nipping, pushing, the kind of thing we call play in humans—they occasionally improvise melodic phrases they seldom if ever repeat again. Some scientists interpret these frequency-modulated gestures as an example of vocal creativity.[1] When humans do much the same thing, we call it making music.

Blue whales rumble at volumes louder than a commercial jet at takeoff to broadcast their location and probably their heading to other blues. They vocalize directly at a thermocline, using it as an underwater PA system to amplify and echo calls over distances measured in oceans. A U.S. Navy listening post in Long Island has recorded blue whales vocalizing loud and clear seven hundred miles away in Bermuda.[2]

Some of the most complex examples of animal communication occur within species that stand relatively low on the evolutionary scale. The best-known example is probably the honeybee's waggle dance, first observed by Karl von Frisch in the 1940s. Von Frisch established that their dance (regarded as an art form when humans do it) communicates sun position (astronomy), a system of measure (mathematics) and precise direction (navigation). It even communicates the desirability of a food source (denoting a syntax composed of adjectives and adverbs). One variant of the waggle dance communicates the location of standing water that is used to cool an overheated hive (thermodynamic engineering). Another dance alerts the bees that their hive is irreparably damaged. They are directed to commence a swarm,[3] in effect, the dancer declaims, "Sisters, gather round; watch my footwork. Most of us need to form into a search party. We'll leave tomorrow at sunup, fly off in every direction. Our mission is to locate a new hive cavity. Whoever finds an appropriate site, send out a pheromone to signal the rest of us. We'll pass the word around, and delegate some individuals to inspect it. If you all agree, we'll start constructing the new hive immediately. But some of you need to stay behind. You have the critical job of protecting the queen. When the new hive is built, you can transport her to our new home."

Most entomologists explain the diverse messages of the waggle dance as an advanced form of instinctual behavior, arguing that honeybees comprehend the footwork of the damaged hive dance even though none of them have experienced it before. If it is instinct, then the bees' ability is analogous to a human child emerging from the womb, not only cerebrally prepared to acquire language, but possessing the syntax and vocabulary of a specific language bound up with specific tasks. It is as if French babies were born speaking French and baking French bread. Of course, people who have never baked French bread learn to do it all the time by reading a recipe. Whether or not the syntax of the waggle dance is instinctual or acquired, honeybees clearly use it to communicate (and possibly even devise) solutions to community issues on a task-by-task basis. Actually, the argument against acquired behavior in social insects is mostly a presumption based on what biologists expect, given the insects' tiny brains.

In the 1920s, South African naturalist Eugene Marais spent ten years studying termites and ants, concluding that colonies are best understood as a composite organism possessed of a group purpose and even a group mind. Individual workers are not individual entities, but cells of a higher organism, yet with no awareness of the greater strategy of this group mind. Marais believed the queen's reproductive function is the main focus of this intellect, although she herself is not in control either. He observed that the tasks of the group were communicated through some unknown mechanism comprising elements of syntax and vocabulary, now known to be chemical fragrances called *pheromones*. When Marais enclosed a termite queen within a tiny steel-plated prison, the colony continued to flourish. When he killed the queen inside her prison, the community ceased to function. If another termitary existed nearby, the queenless workers drifted to it, where they immediately began carrying out the functions of the new group mind, indicating that they spoke the same pheromone language. But if the disinherited termites were brought to a nest further away, the newcomers were always killed, implying that the new group mind spoke a "foreign language."

A few animals use sound to communicate a vocabulary. In response to the sight of a weasel invading the coop, a bantam hen emits a high-pitched *kuk-kuk-kuk*. If the invader is a hawk circling overhead, she'll shriek a single long note.[4] In 1980 biologists Tom Struhsaker, Robert Seyfarth, Dorothy Cheney, and Peter Marler discovered that vervet monkeys in Kenya also possess a vocabulary based on the predators in their life. A certain grunt is the actual word for eagle. When it is vocalized, all the vervets in earshot scan the sky. A bark means leopard, prompting the monkeys to scamper to the top of a tree. Other sounds express territoriality, kinship, and social standing. As in some human languages, meaning varies depending on who is speaking. When a vervet infant screams out the word signifying a certain predator, only its mother responds directly. The other monkeys react to the mother, recognizing whose baby is in distress. Until these discoveries, linguists generally agreed that the use of sounds as symbols (i.e., words) was a unique trademark of human communication.[5]

While communication among species is common throughout nature, communication *between* species is much less frequent. The alarm call of a robin attracts robins, but also blue jays, orioles, and catbirds, who help drive off the predator. The birds arrive not out of curiosity, or because of some universal sensibility to pain and suffering, but because certain alarm calls mean the same thing to several bird species. The timbre and frequency of that particular call overrides territorial protocol.

Horses and their riders communicate in subtle ways, combining vocals, touch, and body language to disclose direction, pain, fear, and joy. Recent studies also verify what pet owners have known for ages, that communication occurs regularly between humans and canines. Dogs bark to let us know they want food. They scratch the door to tell us they want to go outside. Animal rights advocate Dr. Michael W. Fox writes that dogs are masters of nonverbal interspecies communication as well, ascertaining as much about human happiness, submission, and aggression by reading our postures and facial expressions as we learn about them from watching their tails wag, their ears press back, and their necks bristle.[6] What develops is a dialogue of sorts. We reply to a dog's tail wagging by giving her an affectionate pat. She rolls on her back, communicating allegiance. We kneel to rub her belly, confiding intimacy. She growls contentedly, prompting us to the kitchen to get her a dog bone. She sits up, barks firmly. We throw her the bone.

Rudyard Kipling observed "six honest serving men of learning and intellect: *what, where, who, when, how, and why.*"[7] Dogs, parrots, elephants, and even pigeons have been documented communicating *what, where, who,* and arguably, *how.* But they all lack the other two servants, *when* and *why,* which is the reason Dr. Fox stops short of recommending a dog's interaction with its master as an intellectual dialogue. Dogs can be taught to tell *who* precisely *how* and *where* to throw *what* stick for them to catch. But no dog can communicate *why* she prefers that stick over another one. Beyond the *when,* of right now, no dog has ever asked a person to feed it tomorrow. Even the dogged quality of unconditional love, as exemplary an expression of loyalty as exists on Earth, can be explained as an instinctual allegiance to a pack leader transferred to a human master.

The science of interspecies communication is in its infancy and saddled with more controversy than it probably deserves. Among cognitive scientists, the idea of animals holding an abstract conversation with us is met with knee-jerk disapprobation as often as with professional inquisitiveness. Credibility seems a cultural issue as much as a scientific one. This subject is born of children's stories and traditional myths, deeply influenced by our dreams, and distorted by long-lost gut feelings from childhood, the end of the world as we all once lived it, the destruction of the kindred worldview replaced by the advent of the objective revelation. This loss, our loss, fosters an innate resistance to objectification, which explains why some critics seem to regard the subject as anthropomorphic by default.

Scientific success stories do exist. Koko the gorilla has been taught nearly 2,000 words of spoken English. As her language skills increased, her ability to communicate emotions and concepts has leapt far beyond the rote mastery of words. Koko adopted a cat as a beloved pet and expressed grief when it died. She even learned to fib, using sign language to distort tutor Francine Patterson's perception of reality, then skillfully resorted to Kipling's *why* when Patterson expressed misgivings. When Koko was asked by a journalist if she was an animal or a person, her response was "fine animal gorilla."[8]

Bottlenose dolphins at Hawaii's Kewalo Basin Marine Mammal Laboratory have learned sixty words and basic grammatical rules that allow them to understand hundreds of simple sentences. The command "person (subject), surfboard (object), fetch (verb)" is understood as "bring surfboard to person," while "surfboard, person, fetch" is interpreted as "bring person to surfboard." The dolphins also understand the word *creative*. When they are separately commanded, "tandem, creative," they find each other, presumably agree on an action, then respond in tandem, perhaps spitting water and pirouetting, or whistling and lifting their tails high.

Alex, an African gray parrot, identifies seven colors, five shapes, forty objects, and numbers up to six, all in plain English. When professor Irene Pepperberg showed him a green bottle and a green hat, and then asked him what was the same about them, he answered "color." Asked the difference, he answered "shape."[9] Alex also connected words together to communicate (and satisfy) his own curiosity, learning the words "carrot" and "orange" by essentially asking a researcher eating a carrot what color it was and what it was called.[10] Alex's achievement amounts to a cognitive heresy,[11] demonstrating that the neural threshold of consciousness is not limited to beings with human-size brains. If a parrot with a brain the size of a pea can string words together to verbalize inner thoughts, exhibiting nearly as much intellect as a signing gorilla or a nodding dolphin, perhaps beings with brains (or nervous systems) commensurately less complex than a parrot's—millipedes, octopi, even oak trees and slime molds—are privy to Kipling's serving men as well.

Most scientific experiments presume a species's intellect is best demonstrated through its ability to respond to some form of human language;[12] acting on words and accomplishing rote tasks in return for the necessities of food and companionship. When researchers are unable to fit an animal's oftentimes "round" response into the "square" superimposed structures they develop to facilitate analysis, they conclude that the animal who just failed their elegant, but human-focused, language test lacks the ability to communicate symbolically. That may also explain why success often seems anticlimatic: an adult dolphin or chimp whose communicative achievements mirror those of a three-year-old toddler, and whose personality traits include the toddler's lack of discipline and inability to concentrate on any one task. Despite her impressive 2,000-word vocabulary, even the twenty-six-year-old adult gorilla Koko—who has spent most of her life living and communicating with humans—is described by her tutor Francine Patterson as "having behavior much like a small child."[13] Paradoxically, this same failure may explain why no test animal has ever been treated as a co-respondent or designer of a scientific experiment in interspecies communication.

The research might obtain different results if the methodology emphasized collaboration rather than animals mimicking human intellectual patterns. Clearly, a dialogue that adapted to both species' preferred syntax, vocabulary, behavior, and environment would demonstrate not only how and what an animal can learn, but what it already knows as well.

Unfortunately, no animal, wild or captive, can possibly uphold the zealous control deemed so essential by the scientists who administer communication experiments. Yet only strict control produces replicable data, say researchers, and without it, scientific credibility evaporates. Journalist Wyatt Townley concludes: "It's a Catch-22 situation. Relinquishing rigorous control nurtures communication even as it invalidates science."[14]

Research with captive cetaceans probably receives the most criticism. For instance, the signals used at Kewalo Basin are *hand* gestures, a curious choice that guarantees that handless dolphins can never develop a dialogue with their trainers. While boosters describe the sophistication of the syntactical commands, critics assert that the animals themselves can achieve only a single goal—the receipt of a fish to eat. Nor do dolphins have any natural motivation to manifest such commands as "fetch the Frisbee to the hoop." More criticism is leveled over the real-world applications derived from the research. Navy scuba divers don luminescent gloves to train dolphins in the retrieval of ordnance underwater, a technique perfected at Kewalo Basin. Animal rights advocates charge the navy with using dolphins for underwater surveillance where they are trained to attack on command. The navy denies it.

Horace Dobbs, who administers Project Sunflower, the British program that places severely depressed patients into the ocean with wild dolphins, believes that captive cetaceans have no inclination to reveal the depth of their intellect to captors who reward displays of ingenuity with dead fish and endless rounds of identifying objects. In a remark aimed to draw attention to what he believes is interspecies slavery, Dobbs calls captive dolphins "dumb niggers," that mask their keen intellect as a basic survival strategy.[15] Gregory Bateson, who spent some years attempting to communicate with captive dolphins, wrote that the world is not a collection of things and functions devoid of association, but a dynamic web of relationships bound together by communication.[16] He asserted that dolphin language research would never succeed as long as it denied the full spectrum of social behavior and communication. Kathleen Dudzinski, who has studied wild dolphin behavior in the Bahamas and Japan, comments that delphinids "employ posture, context (behavioral activity), contact, vocalizations, and other external referents (e.g., age, sex, associate

IDs, bubbles, and more) to convey information. Just because they may also understand the concepts of syntax and grammar does not mean they use (or need) it in their daily lives."[17]

Despite these shortcomings, there are some important reasons bottlenose dolphins remain a favorite subject for captive communication research. Along the coast of North America, several populations of bottlenose dolphins inhabit near-shore, shallow environments. This preferred habitat makes them the easiest and least expensive species to capture. That also explains why they adapt so well, and breed so successfully, in shallow swimming pools. Their large brain assures a deep well for future researchers to draw inspiration. In 1863, Thomas Huxley postulated that the more complex a species brain, the more evolved it is. Using the best evidence of his time, he concluded that the human species has the largest brain and is therefore the most intelligent. In 1960, H. J. Jerison proposed encephalization—the ratio of brain volume to a body's surface area—as a better criterion for measuring intelligence in species. Jerison placed the human species at the top of his hierarchy. John Lilly undermined both conclusions by showing that the brains of several odontocete species are both larger and more encephalic than human's. However, recent research has found the tissue in dolphin brains lacking a crucial layer that, at least in humans, contains many neuronal connections.

The dolphin brain evolved to its present capacity at least fifteen million years ago. If Huxley, Jerison, and Lilly are to be taken at their word, then fifteen million years ago the dolphins had evolved an intelligence greater than humans. Today, Lilly refutes captivity and quotes James Thurber to describe the knowledge he feels we should be seeking from dolphins.[18]

> I observed a school of dolphins . . . and something told me that here was creature all gaiety, charm, and intelligence, that one day might come out of the boundless deep and show us how a world can be run by creatures dedicated, not to the destruction of their species, but to its preservation.

Scientists who study cetacean vocalizations in the wild, point to the beluga whale as a potentially better candidate for communication studies.

Belugas were called sea canaries by nineteenth-century whalers for the way they chirp and chortle among their own kind. Almost all beluga calls are audible to a human ear. They are also among the few cetacean species to naturally vocalize in air. Becky Kjare, a Canadian biologist who made an extensive study of beluga vocalizations, concluded that the species produces more different kinds of sounds than any other whale or dolphin.[19] Listening to them vocalize to one another at Lancaster Sound in the Canadian High Arctic, I was reminded by their discourse of a raucous party heard through the walls of an apartment building. I intuited that the revelers were indeed talking coherently to one another, although individual words could not be discerned.

The species is notoriously uncooperative at learning the standard fare of oceanarium antics, like jumping through hoops. Of nine beluga whales born in captivity, only two have survived even a week. The video of one such birth and death, at the Tacoma Washington Point Defiance Zoo, had the look and feel of a mercy-killing administered by its mother. Another otherwise untrainable beluga, confined for years in a tiny pool at the Vancouver aquarium, spent hours a day making faces through the glass at children who made faces in response.

The charged border itself casts an ethical tension over language experiments with captive cetaceans that Francine Patterson and Irene Pepperberg never needed to address. In the dolphin lab at Kewalo Basin, Hawaii, two graduate students accused the program director Louis Herman of cruelty to animals. Late one night they bundled the two dolphins into a pickup truck and freed them into the ocean. One student was eventually found guilty of stealing the research center's property. Herman announced that such highly trained animals could never survive in the wild; yet by admitting that, he inadvertently demonstrated how exploitation damages an animal's native intelligence. The two dolphins had been taught many ingenious signals, although, having land animals as teachers, they never learned about currents, predation, or how to relate to other dolphins.

As someone who has played music with several different cetacean species over a twenty-five-year period—including bottlenose dolphins and beluga whales—I wonder if their complex vocalizations are actually closer to music than language. Acoustic information may just as easily be communicated through sonic algorithms based on melodies, harmonies, and rhythms as through words. Like nineteenth-century railroad workers employing the cadences of a work song to perform a group task, certain whistles may provide a rhythm for scattered pod members to roll across the surface in synchrony, as I have witnessed orcas do in the straits of British Columbia. And like the whistling language of Basque shepherds, vocalizations certainly help pod members keep in touch with one another across distances. If my interpretation is credible, then attempting to translate a delphinid's musical/symbolic calls into English may be as futile an endeavor as trying to translate a Beethoven symphony into English.[20]

Some cognitive scientists believe that a species' ability to acquire language gauges that species' intelligence. The connection may be false, because intelligence itself defies a universal definition. *Webster's* defines the term as the ability to learn or understand from experience, to acquire and retain knowledge.[21] Yet street intelligence in the Los Angeles barrios must be graded differently than the intelligence displayed in the physics labs of UCLA just a few miles away. The question has even been asked whether more intelligent people get higher or lower marks on intelligence tests.

If cognitive scientists cannot pin down the capability in humans, they are much further from forming a valid definition that includes animals. The nature philosopher Michael Fox may offer the most workable, if not transcendent, definition when he writes, "A lot of people confuse intelligence with trainability. I turn it all around and say, there's no one more intelligent at being a butterfly than a butterfly."[22] According to Fox, controlled scientific experiments in nonhuman cognition are ultimately flawed because they judge animal intelligence only in terms of *human* intelligence. Louis Herman's experiments, for example, focused on the dolphins' ability to reflect a human proficiency to apply information to a task.

This flaw also hinders cognitive science's best-known test for determining a species's *sentience* (defined as the capacity for feeling or perceiving consciousness).[23] A researcher anesthetizes an animal and then paints a spot on its body not visible to self-examination. Upon awakening, the animal is placed in front of a mirror and then shown the spot in its reflection.

A species is considered self-aware if it reaches to touch the mark on itself rather than on the mirror. Until very recently, only the great apes passed the test. Naturally, much fanfare resulted in 1991 when the Hawaiian-based Project Delphis coaxed a bottlenose dolphin to observe a blemish on itself after first observing it in a mirror and, by doing so, became the first nonprimate to attain membership on "the sentient list." Animal right-ists have concluded, with some irony, that in order to be deemed sentient, the dolphin was first captured, caged, isolated, drugged, marked, and interrogated to teach its experimenters something akin to a declaration that the sky is blue. Alex the parrot is not officially considered sentient, although he learned the word "gray" after bidding a researcher to tell him, in plain English, the color of his own reflection in a mirror.[24]

Animals are wise beyond the systems of language we impose upon them, intelligent beyond our training regimens, creative beyond the behavioral tricks we watch them perform. The most conscious forms of communication—Koko's fib, for instance—are circular and transparent. While it is happening, both parties simply feel it and are thus able to respond intelligibly. Sentience cannot be properly measured any more than creativity can be measured. Or love. This conclusion suggests that animal intellect—the outward expression of sentience—may be an issue of philosophy more than science. Is the creator of a complex tool, such as the atom bomb, more intelligent than the creator of a simple tool, such as the spiderweb? The web is eminently utilitarian, a wonder of design, light on resources, and, most notably, has ensured the survival of its creator for a hundred million years. It harms nothing besides the spider's immediate prey. It is easily reconstructed when damaged. If the architect of the atom bomb is deemed more intelligent than the architect of the spiderweb, the obvious next question sounds like something out of *Alice in Wonderland*: "Is it more intelligent to be less intelligent?"

Some visionary scientists argue that both sentience and communi-cation are universal in nature, operating as one aspect of the "nonlocal" mind. As in John's sperm whale dream, the brain may not be the seat of the mind but, rather, the conduit of consciousness, what the Hindu mystic Yogananda referred to as a radio receiver linking us to some as yet poorly understood external cosmic record where all knowledge and wisdom reside. Every species possesses the ability to tap into any part of it, although the size of an animal's receiver limits how much can be held at once. When a parrot is taught to think like a human, it also learns to tap into the human part of the nonlocal spectrum.

This is not only the dream of mystics. Nonlocal communication was investigated in the 1930s by Einstein in an unsuccessful attempt to unravel the means by which quantum mechanics is able to predict the interaction between subatomic particles far beyond (even light-years beyond) one another's normal sphere of influence. Several modern consciousness researchers, including biologist Rupert Sheldrake, M.D., Larry Dossey, and philosopher Ken Wilbur, have studied nonlocality in an attempt to understand such disparate phenomena as species morphogenesis, instinctual behavior, disease remission through prayer, and the basis of herbal knowledge. The investigator of psychic phenomena, Russell Targ, pleads for humility when he states that contemporary science possesses neither the tools nor the methodology to explain the true nature of separation between organisms.[25] The Gaia hypothesis postulates that some as-yet-unknown communication linkage among species is responsible for stabilizing the chemical composition of the Earth's atmosphere for a billion years. For Gaia to be true, communication must be the norm rather than the exception in nature.

This view, an alternative to orthodox science, is the basis of a growing ethical and ecological perception of nature. In many ways, it takes up a very old cause and recasts it as conservation biology, deep ecology, and other terms familiar to its adherents who hardly offer a unified front: artists, animal rights advocates, scientists, philosophers, mystics, healers, ministers, telepathic pet owners. What they share is a compassionate, humble relationship with all organisms on Earth, rejecting the anthropocentric society for a biocentric one, scrutinizing nature's many "parts" not as objects, but as relations, extended family, each with a unique gift. The animals deserve our empathy, our compassion, and our ear, but that doesn't mean any of them will ever talk to us in English. Nor are they human beings in animal suits.

Many who hold this view side with Gaia by asserting that communication is far more common in nature than biology warrants. Whether it occurs at any given moment has less to do with methodology than with a sensitivity to listen. It depends on how willing we are, as individuals and as a culture, to seek out the unknown, push beyond the quantifiable, and adopt new ways for studying the possibilities. Orthodox scientists contend that this view is anthropomorphic. But perhaps their criticism is a handy obfuscation that serves to uphold a dogma that keeps humans above and separate from the rest of nature. Transparent communication is nurtured best in an atmosphere of mutual respect; if that means "attributing human characteristics to an animal," then so be it.

Those who promote this interdependent perspective are not unscientific; they stretch the boundary of science. While the old guard of interspecies communicators works to keep data free from personal interjection, the new guard pursues goals that are experiental, ethical, and shamanic. By reporting back to the greater culture, they hope to reconnect ethos to mythos, culture to nature. The difference between the two approaches emerges as a distinction of kind rather than degree.

The practices of traditional culture confirm the virtues of interdependence. Native people observed other species closely, seeking practical insight to help meet their own life challenges. Unhampered by the hierarchical organization that positions one species above or below another, they had great freedom to learn from every species.[26] By contrast, our anthropocentric society has not yet learned that the prevailing "separate but not equal" worldview is killing the planet and us along with it.

A cautionary tale told of the Kalahari Desert Bushmen illustrates both sides of the coin. The Bushmen's millennia-old oral history reveals many instances of animals mauling or trampling humans, but not one instance of a lion killing a person or a person killing a lion. In the 1950s, Western anthropologists visiting the area noted the eyes of many lions glowing just beyond the cooking fire. The animals would cease their roaring when a Bushman hunter sauntered off to the edge of camp and asked them to keep the noise down so children could sleep. Human and lion shared a watering hole, one using it by day, the other by night. This peaceful coexistence changed when ranching was introduced and cattle began to share the watering hole without regard to schedule. At first lions kept their distance, as if cattle were an extension of the human family. But eventually they attacked. Ranchers reciprocated by shooting the lions, and within a few years lions had killed several Bushmen.

The traditional Bushmen knew they were incapable of controlling lions, and they developed an interspecies protocol to optimize their chances of survival. Today, technological hubris prompts many to declare we *can* control nature. Fortunately, a growing number of ecologically minded people recognize that, like the traditional Bushmen, our own society must develop a conciliatory relationship with nature if we are to survive. Although the anticipated drift toward biocentrism—defined as life lived with nature (not humans) at the center—seems wildly revolutionary to some, its goal is mild in practice, mostly insisting that each one of us meet nature halfway.

Examining this drift closely, once again we notice cetaceans swimming at the center of a human cultural adjustment. As the Industrial Revolution was fueled on the bodies of whales, and the environmental movement gained impetus from a passionate crusade to save the whales, so today a growing number of people are being persuaded to let both the symbol and the social behavior of cetaceans inspire and guide them toward ecological community. Some in the cultural avant-garde, like Carolyn Pettit, believe cetaceans serve as a harbinger for a new totemic spirituality. Yet no matter how this seminal totemism/biocentrism/Gaia consciousness eventually informs the greater culture, all the signs indicate that the charged border will remain a hotbed of influence in the years to come.

8 GETTING INTO THE GROOVE

When the planet herself
sings to us in our dreams
will we be able to wake ourselves and act?[1]

—GARY LAWLESS

Most visitors to Orcananda dive into the frigid waters of the strait some-time during their stay in camp. They row a dinghy out to our anchored forty-foot boat, step outside the gunwale, and commence a fierce scrutiny of the water's surface. Most let loose a shriek as they release the railing. Those of us on shore look up to glimpse the shouter suspended in midair, followed by the plunk of a body interrupting the water's plane. A three-second silence is followed by the diver breaking the surface and issuing a whoop of satisfaction, then rushing back to the boat ladder. One summer, a visitor to Orcananda boasted he could swim all the way from the boat to the shore. He rowed, climbed, scrutinized, shrieked, dove, surfaced, and whooped. But halfway to the beach his arms lost all feeling. His breathing turned frantic. He made it, but his body was blue as the sky. No one kidded him. Everyone knew he was in over his head.

The children who join the Orcananda community each summer don't "swim" much, but they play along the shore, overturning rocks searching for crabs, bending their bodies deep into tide pool crevices. When the wind comes up, they shiver, change into dry clothes, have a hot cup of cocoa by the campfire, then head back to the shore. On a low tide early in the morning, a mama and baby black bear may lumber out of the forest to the cove directly across from our own to spend some time overturning rocks searching for a crab breakfast. The kids line up to watch the bears. The bear cubs stand to full height to watch the kids.

Most every afternoon, the kids will talk an adult into taking them out fishing on the inflatable boat. Except they don't fish for long. The first time a seal pops its dark-eyed face from the water, the kids beg the skipper to motor closer. Or they ask to float over kelp gardens to search for urchins, anemones, and eighteen-inch-wide sea stars with twenty or more arms. Once, when my eldest daughter Claire was four, she sighted an octopus occupying a crevice just inside the cove. The other kids leaned over the pontoon of the boat to get a better look. One boy shouted, "It's not one octopus, it's three!" He was right, but also wrong. Tentacles started peeking out of the rocks everywhere we looked, but they all belonged to the same animal, perhaps twelve feet wide. The beast stared up at our boat through eyes so ancient and wise that someone suggested it studied us more meticulously than we studied it. It made me wonder why we devoted all of Orcananda's resources to communicating with orcas, and none to octopuses.

Living with wild animals is not always a joy. One summer, a guest named Jill walked off alone to a creek to wash her hair. Returning to her tent, she nearly stepped on a cougar crouched on the trail stalking three little girls playing nearby. Jill took a step backward, but tripped over a log. The cougar pounced, took her head into its jaws, raked her thigh. She screamed, a sound so fraught with terror that those of us who heard it hope never to hear it again. We made noise to rescue Jill, who survived with a few memorable scars to show her grandchildren. The cat was shot by our boat captain without group consensus, a bad bit of business that disturbed everyone, especially Jill. Cougars inhabit the meadows of the high country. No local we talked to had ever heard of one visiting the shore. So much of the western Canada coastline has been clear-cut that the cougars are forced to seek out new territory. New prey.

The presence of so many children in camp grants Orcananda a different ambience than the four or five other orca research stations strung out along this strait that separates our little island from the rugged east coast of Vancouver Island. The children's participation is critical to understanding our special brand of nonscientific research. The whales swim past our little cove several times a day in their matrilineal pods consisting of a grandmother, her sons and daughters, and her daughter's sons and daughters, etc. The young orcas, *juveniles* as biologists refer to them, get to vocalize with us whenever they wish. It seems appropriate that our family groups conduct communication research with their family groups. Does it matter if a child can't actually play a musical instrument? I suspect the orcas don't judge human musical virtuosity.

We choose the orcas as the subject of our musical experiment in interspecies communication because, in contrast to almost all other dolphin species, orcas vocalize nearly all the time in a frequency range within the confines of human hearing. They vocalize so loudly we sometimes hear them, although still a mile from the cove, fifteen minutes before we see them swimming our way. These whales cruise close to shore in an inland sea located two hundred miles north of Vancouver. Biologists call them *residents*, which simply means they swim back and forth in the same waters for months at a time without ever leaving. These residents feed primarily on salmon, which migrate through here in great abundance.

Resident orcas talk to one another in two distinct modes: the frequency modulated whistle and the pulsed click train. "Frequency modulated" means melodic. The pulsed click train is rhythmical. In other words, the orcas use musical concepts to communicate among their own kind. To hear orcas call back and forth to one another, and then interact with them, Orcananda's sponsoring organization, Interspecies Communication, Inc., has assembled a sound system with underwater recording and transmitting capabilities built inside our trawler, which is anchored in seventy feet of water just inside the cove. A single switch powers up a keyboard, a few microphones, and an electric guitar, all of which are plugged into a mixer and then run through a fifty-watt amplifier and outputted to the underwater speakers. This sound system is basically a telephone line to the whales. To optimize stereo separation, hydrophones (underwater microphones) dangle forty feet apart off the bow and the stern. The underwater speakers suspend starboard and port at midship. If we like the conversations we hear, we tape them for posterity.

If it's little children using the orca telephone, the whale's innate loudness and edgy abruptness can breed either excitement or fear, and sometimes both simultaneously. A few children bang on the synthesizer with their tongues hanging out, consumed by the pose rather than by any sounds they make. When a whale vocalizes, they bang more often. When the whales turn silent, the banging turns frenetic as if fury can communicate the children's need for interaction. Neither the notes they play nor their choice of rhythm correlates much to what the whales vocalize.

"Do you think that's what the whales like?" I ask.

"Yes," a little voice pipes in, "the whales like it when we play music with them." When I demonstrate various ways to synchronize their sounds to the whale's vocalizations, the children try it once or twice, then fall back to banging. How could I expect anything different? These young children already reside in a world where animals are aware, communicative, and possessed of rich emotional lives. The results they find playing to Orca don't sound the least bit like Bambi harmonizing with Thumper. When the offshore pod of resident Keikos fails to join in singing "chopsticks," the children's attention wanders. They gaze longingly out the window at their beloved tide pools and rocks—even at their beloved orcas rolling through the waves right next to the boat.

Some parents who come aboard presume that the orcas will naturally be drawn to young children. They invoke a naive view of the charged border as a Peaceable Kingdom, where innocence is always celebrated and hard work disdained. Whales are compassionate and wise; they love us and they love our children even more. When the orcas fail to respond, these parents wonder what could possibly be wrong. Maybe the studio isn't child-friendly? They turn up the thermostat, hide the synthesizer, and lead the kids in a rendition of "Row, row, row your boat." The children sing enthusiastically. Who can deny its cuteness? But it makes no difference. The whales' rubbery, bone-jarring screams remain child-unfriendly and aloof.

Playing music with orcas is better understood as an expression of conceptual art than as a variation on an Edward Hicks painting. To keep going at this work, a musician must revel in counterintuitive phrasing, dissonance, and nearly unbearable stretches of silence. The slightest hints of synchronized rhythm become the pen and paper of our correspondence. Those of us who persevere for more than an hour, more than a week, until, finally, we visit Orcananda every summer for more than a decade, celebrate a radical paradigm that insists animals are sentient beings both capable and amenable to aesthetic interaction. Most people feel no such motivation. Most musicians find the sonic rewards too few and far between and the intellectual rewards too unmusical.

A few children become interested in the details of the charged border at about age nine. One day a boy asks to use the keyboard to work out a phrase he heard an orca singing the night before. A girl spends the day composing a song to sing after dark through the underwater speakers. These children are often as naive as the younger children in their choice of music, but now they have acquired the essential trait of perseverance. They realize an interaction may not take place the first time or even the tenth time they try. They have an inkling of what it means to honor the process of close listening. An adult is delegated to gather up these initiates just after dark and row them out to the big boat, where the sound engineer sits them down in front of a microphone. Everyone on board waits, makes small talk and popcorn. An hour or two may pass. But the orcas will come. They swim past our cove between nine and midnight. It's happened that way almost every single night for eight summers in a row.

We hear them vocalizing through the speakers, sounding like a cross between an elephant and a soprano sax. They are still a mile or two up the strait. I turn on the mike switch. The child starts singing, concentrating hard to draw the whale closer, getting into a mutual groove. The rest of us keep our mouths shut, offering no cues about what the whales "might like to hear instead." To limit the player's experience, not to mention the orcas' experience, seems prejudicial and pompous. We have uncovered no evidence—at least in the vast realm of Western music—that a whale responds better to Bach played perfectly by a virtuoso than to some deter-mined girl singing "Come little orca, won't you play with me, sha-lalalalala-la-la." We've tried it both ways. Sometimes one gets a response. Sometimes the other. No matter what transpires, adults who attend these sessions agree that the experience is both touching and profound, display-ing the formative human mind engaged in the creative process of reaching out to another species for the first time.

My rationale to permit both children and nonmusicians access to the sound system is sometimes judged "unprofessional" by those who insist we attach scientific rigor to this long-term study. They recommend we focus the sound transmissions to a few pure tones spawned on a sine wave generator, monitored on an oscilloscope, perhaps modulated in accord with the pods' specific direction of travel, and activated to coincide with the turning of the tide. They tell us to combine these controlled transmissions with visual cues, such as a flashlight turned on and off in synchrony with certain notes. It all seems worthy, and I would gladly fit any valid experiment into our schedule if someone would simply administer it, *and* agree not to interfere with the music-making regimen. There lies the problem. Scientific control is like virginity. You either have it or you don't.[2] That our work prospers without control is an important reason Orcananda attracts artists and musicians, not cognitive scientists and behavioral biologists. We are laypeople whose relationship with the whales is more an affair of the heart, the ear, and the gut, than of the mind and the spreadsheet.

Those of us who have observed many people play with the whales over several years have reached an admittedly unprovable conclusion about the orcas' response. These whales are attracted primarily to music makers who are having a good time. While the orcas display no special interest in compositional virtuosity—for example, a soloist rendering Mozart with great precision—they seem highly attuned to soloists and ensembles who play with soulfulness. Musicians call this expression of passionate ease *getting into the groove*. The mechanics of rhythm, harmony, and timing take on substance greater than the sum of its parts. It carries the players aloft on the flow of the music even as they perform it. What affects the players likewise affects the audience, turning the sensuous experience communal. George Will has written that "to be in a groove is not to be mechanical, it is to be an animal, with the grace that only something living can have."[3] It is for this reason that the groove seems capable of mitigating the species barrier as easily as it cuts through the performer/audience barrier.

It is not only the Vancouver Island orcas who respond to human music. Offshore at Peninsula Valdez National Park in Argentina lives a pod of orcas who have developed a dramatic feeding protocol, cruising the shallows and then literally beaching themselves to grab young elephant seals that are sunning on the gravel shore. The orcas then roll back into the water with the seals clamped tightly in their jaws. It was with these reputed "bloodthirsty" orcas that national park warden Roberto Bubas spent several months sitting along the same shore playing his harmonica. The orcas gravitated to him, finally drawing close to listen attentively to the musical offering. Bubas was fascinated by the response, and he concluded that the orcas possessed an awareness of his musical aesthetic. Spectacular photographs were eventually published by a Spanish magazine that showed the orcas lying in the shallows so close to the harmonica-playing Bubas that he might have reached out and touched them.[4] In a classic example of paradigms in collision, his supervisor censured him for "taming" the wild orcas and banished him to a remote inland area of the park. The rebuke begs the question of what, if any, *positive* relationship between species his supervisor would have permitted.

At Orcananda, we impose a few rules to guide interspecies etiquette. First, we conduct our musical experiment only after dark. One does not presume to play and record underwater music with orcas during daylight without contending with considerable noise pollution from boat motors rumbling and whining along the freeway of the strait. Biologists and whale-watching boats tag behind the pods from sunup to sundown and, as the Bubas example forewarns, we do well to avoid their scrutiny. Second, we never chase the whales; instead, we play our music from a boat anchored at the same spot year after year. If they don't come to us, the interaction doesn't happen. Third, our objective is interspecies communication, so we never transmit *recorded* music into the water. Although a whale may certainly respond to a recording, a recording cannot respond to a whale. Fourth, we never retransmit whale sounds; for instance, using a digital delay unit to reflect an orca vocalization back into the water again. Such technology offers nothing vital to the communal ground we nurture.

Flautist Gene Groeschel visited Orcananda one summer bearing an elk call made from a round paper membrane stretched across an aluminum lozenge and played by placing it against the roof of one's mouth. Humming vibrates the membrane, which is modulated by moving the tongue. In the mouth of a virtuoso like Gene, the elk call bore such an uncanny resemblance to the local orcas that other musicians were incapable of discerning between a whale and the elk call. Although the orcas never showed any special interest in the elk call, I asked Gene to retire it for the same reason I reject electronic echoes. It was the only time I ever made such a request.

Over the years, musicians have discovered various techniques to facilitate interspecies music making. Foremost is the routine of adding rhythmical silent spaces to an improvisation as an invitation for a whale to fill in the hole. If the orca vocalizes only in the allotted space, most people regard it as a response. Sometimes it is, although congruency is not always what it seems. For instance, a player may hear an orca call a phrase, E-D-E, and respond by repeating the same notes. The orca vocalizes the pattern a second time; the player likewise mirrors the phrase again. Back and forth it goes. Then the whale turns silent. A waiting game ensues. Usually, the musician loses patience, repeats the phrase again, first slowly, then faster as if a concerted rush of sound is what it takes to get the orca back on track.

Except the whale was never off track. It was never responding to the music and would have made the same sounds even if the musician hadn't played anything. This simultaneity of response is of the same basic ilk as Paul Winter's affable studio compositions that include animal calls as overdubbed elements. However, a lack of correspondence does not necessarily mean the player made a "mistake." We are musicians, not cognitive scientists. To use another example, accompanying the wind can be a worthwhile musical endeavor, even though none of us considers it communication. If it sounds good, we like to hear it, record it, and encourage other musicians to try it. But it is not interspecies communication.

Pointing this out to a newcomer often leads to dispute. "What do you mean I wasn't communicating? I heard it! The whales were talking to me!" One may well ask why so many players persist in confusing orca karaoke with real-time communication. The mistake is partly a function of a charged playing environment. Our studio is a rocking boat anchored in a wilderness cove. The sessions occur late at night, often with a hard rain pounding on the roof. The candlelight we favor to conserve electricity casts an eerie glow over the proceedings, contorting shadows. When the wind blows, the waves come up, the boat rocks, the floor moves, sometimes enough to knock a musician from one wall to the other. The underwater audio system displays innumerable pinprick lights flashing on and off. The speakers resound with colossal gurgles, oddball kerplunks, the banging of a dinghy, the glissando whoosh of an anchor line flexing against the hull, the obscure croaking of bottom fish. The total effect is disorienting, so much so that certain water noises have prompted listeners to examine their clothing for signs of wetness.

Then the whales arrive. From far away, their whistles resound through the speakers like a saxophone chorus playing a bebop refrain. Certain calls occasionally rise above the fray, slithering, soaring, and dive-bombing with the wild abandon of a Charlie Parker solo. Other calls seem to balance this boldness; they fold in upon themselves like a dainty flower closing its petals at sunset. A musician plays a few tentative notes in response. The whales turn silent for a minute or two. When we hear them vocalize again, it is much louder, a sure sign they have moved closer. If they come close enough, the orcas start echolocating the boat, perhaps trying to discover the source of the music. At two hundred feet, the clicks remind us of a woodpecker knocking on a tree. At twenty feet, they sound like a machine gun fired directly into the boat cabin.

Now the orcas are whistling at such a loud volume their calls seem to explode into the darkened room, settling in like an army of occupation. The overall sensation is not so much that the orcas are close by and vocally active but, rather, that one of them has inhaled the boat with all of us inside it. We feel like latter-day Jonahs and Geppettos, although if not precisely swallowed whole into the belly of the whale, then certainly our ears are being sucked inside the moist lips of its vibrating blowhole. With it vocalizing at the volume of a loud rock-and-roll band, every sound an orca makes (and some it doesn't) suggests linkage. When a skilled musician mimics their calls with aplomb, no one aboard is left unaffected. By the time the whales have made their exit, everyone feels spit out, exhausted, quenched . . . and witness to a bona fide encounter. At such a moment, the question of whether the dialogue was genuine or counterfeit seems moot, a sorry attempt to superimpose an analytical frame over a profoundly emotional and spiritual experience.

One might imagine it takes nothing more than a little practice to tell the difference. It takes more than that. These respondents really are whales, a truth that confounds a player even as it hints of a secret knowledge. Climbers of Mount Everest describe a death zone above 25,000 feet, a place with so little oxygen that the human body operates by remote control, guided by sheer will because no one trusts their senses. A similar, although more benign, perceptual warping occurs on our boat. Although I have devoted twelve summers of my life exploring music with orcas, I would have never learned the difference between interaction and simultaneity by paying attention only to the sessions as they unfolded in real time. I learned it, instead, by studying recordings of the same events in the comfort of a home studio. The knowledge came to me in a rush, like glimpsing a face hidden within the folds and textures of a surrealistic painting. The moment I heard the difference, I heard it ever after. Unfortunately, the distinction hinges on a close listening of musical inflections, and defies a literal explanation.

Though describing the signs of interaction may be difficult, the techniques that foster communication are straightforward. A developed sense of courtesy is fundamental. Start off playing quietly. Treat the music as an invitation. Visualize the bond of time and place as a sanctuary filled with music. Feel what it means to get on whale time. If the orcas start to leave, give them up because the interspecies ensemble has no chance to form. Don't *try* to communicate; it's a contradiction in terms that impedes nexus. Remain humble to the fact that music—especially "beautiful music"—is a judgment call, and a species-specific presumption. The sounds a musician casts into the water may just as easily be interpreted by an orca as an intrusion, or even worse, as the acoustic analogue to poisoned meat set out to kill coyotes. The orca who draws close to a sound session today may have to dodge a fisherman's bullet tomorrow. This is not conjecture. In 1986, 80 percent of the orcas in these waters possessed bullet scars. Much of the violence was perpetrated by fishermen who perceived the salmon-eating whales as a threat to their livelihood. Fortunately, the advent of ecotourism has caused this wanton gunfire to diminish markedly.

The repetition of a simple musical phrase outside the whale's own repertoire sometimes gets a startling result. I once spent two nights repeating the same twelve-bar blues riff on an electric guitar. On the third night, a young bull, known as A6[5] to researchers, joined in by improvising over the chord progression. Like a jazz instrumentalist playing a solo, the orca kept his accompaniment harmonically and rhythmically consistent, making the chord changes on the correct downbeats. His phrasing was notably austere, perhaps fifteen notes in the verse, although not unlike the sparse trumpet solos favored by Miles Davis during his *Bitches Brew* period. Did A6 vocalize with the intentionality of Miles Davis? Actually, his performance seems too much in the groove to be interpreted as anything else. A Japanese film crew recording the event giggled when the orca started responding. By the end of the verse they were sighing in disbelief.

As the second verse started, A6's solo imposed itself on my brain as human/whale communication of historic proportions. Under such weight, the interaction faltered. I initiated a burst of single notes with the intent of extending the fragments of his solo. But with the chord structure essentially vanished, there was no framework for the whale or me to track. Within four more bars A6 resumed his normal pattern of vocalizations, and soon departed the area. Perhaps this novel interaction would have ended just as suddenly if I had not lost concentration. Nonetheless, I will always wonder what might have transpired had I not committed the blunder of trying to own the moment rather than surrender to it. This "soloists" interaction never happened again. That it occurred at all, and with such fluid grace, makes me suspect that A6 could have repeated it any time he wished.

Over the next few years, working alone, I discovered a simple technique to test my thesis of interaction versus simultaneity. D-C-D is a common orca phrase heard in these waters. The opening D note slides slowly down to a C and then quickly up to the final D. I discovered that playing the riff a whole tone higher opens a door of opportunity. About one in every ten tries, a whale would rise to the occasion by mirroring my alteration: E-D-E. About once in every 500 tries, a whale treated my melody as the start of a pattern, responding another whole tone up: F#-E-F#.

I next discovered it was not "the orcas" playing with me, but two whales in particular that gravitated to the boat whenever we transmitted. One was a male with a slight angular notch cut toward the tip of its dorsal. The other was a female with a distinctive nick cut out of the backside of her fin. It was A6 and his mother, A2, who was affectionately called Nickola by local biologists. Nickola was generally regarded to be the most outgoing whale on the entire coast, and the subject of many stories told about her interactions with researchers. Nickola initiated contact and nurtured it. Over several years A6 developed into the most inspired soloist, inventing melodies that occasionally attained a fluid density reminiscent of a jazz solo. There were nights the two whales remained to vocalize with us long after the rest of their pod had departed the immediate area. We would hear their pod mates calling with urgency, as if informing mother and son that it was time to move on.

Orcas, who inhabit every ocean, vary their vocalizations from locale to locale. The hundred-odd orcas belonging to the three pods of Puget Sound vocalize often, but sound decidedly unmusical when compared to the two-hundred-odd orcas who reside off the northeast coast of Vancouver Island. The northern pods' vocals also vary from family to family. It seems no coincidence that the members of A-pod make the most musical sounds to my ears, since they are also the whales most interested in interacting with my music.

I journeyed alone to meet A-pod for four years. Then, under the able guidance of community organizer Virginia Coyle, in 1983, a group of friends and colleagues assembled each summer in the little cove to formalize what came to be called the Orca Project. We named our campsite Orcananda, as a friendly parody of the communities that spring up around Hindu gurus. Each August for the next eight years out of nine, we moored a forty-foot cabin cruiser in the same tiny cove on an uninhabited island across the water from the northeast coast of Vancouver Island. Our cove was not ordinarily visited by the orca pods. If they ventured inside, we believed that our music attracted them. Each year we invited as many as twenty-five people to join the project.

For three summers in a row, we invited Tibetan lamas to chant their Buddhist prayers directly through our sound system and into the water. On a few occasions, the orcas related to this chanting in a manner we never experienced from other broadcasts. One or two whales would lag behind as their pod continued traveling up the strait. These animals would stop whistling, swim up to the boat, and float silently above the underwater speaker as if studying the chants. One rainy night, Lama Tsenjur sat at our galley table cutting a strange figure in his burgundy robes, eating popcorn and chanting "om mani padme hum" into a microphone. The whales passed by the cove, then seemed to disappear. I stood up, opened the hatch, and stepped outside to stare into the black night. "I am so sorry I frightened away the whales," murmured the lama, ending his chant. At that moment a whale blew in my face, then vocalized a single shriek so loud and so close to the hydrophone that it blew out one of our speakers.

My own musical experiments drifted away from western musical forms toward the ancient ragas of India. A raga begins with a drone that remains constant throughout the composition. Very gradually—in fact to some Western ears the process can seem so gradual as to appear tedious—a melody is introduced. It is said that gaps in the melody originated to offer sonic breathing room for the birds who gathered to sing when a raga was performed outdoors. In my case, orcas replaced birds. I tuned the guitar to a modal D, playing the drone on the lower strings, and the melody on top.

One summer, our group arrived at Orcananda to witness a rare event in the orcas' year. Several pods had gathered into what is known as a *super-pod*, to mingle and mate as a single extended family. During the next three days, forty-seven whales traveled back and forth within a few miles of our camp. Their incessant vocalizing filled the waterway with sound approaching the harmonic density of a symphony. On the first night, I slipped a bottleneck over the little finger of my left hand to improvise the raga "Jinjhoti" (the same song I would later perform aboard the *Lamarck*), in the key of D-major. Two whales arrived, dashing between the anchored boat and the shore, breaching and frothing the water with their flukes to stir up the bioluminescent plankton. The cove lit up from within. Next afternoon, I played the same raga again. All forty-seven whales responded by circling just outside the cove. At one point, fourteen orcas spyhopped in unison in a chorus line a hundred yards from the boat. When I hit the major third, the F#, several whales responded in unison, also in F#. Musical interactions continued unabated over the next few days. When the extended family of whales finally disbanded, my playing was no longer able to engage any of them.

The question has been posed whether this music with orcas is inter-species communication or "just avant-garde music." In fact, the best examples of communication express clear harmonies and rhythms and are therefore the most musical. Music itself communicates physical and mathematical properties, including frequency, rhythm, amplitude, and harmony. It also evokes a rich spectrum of unquantifiable concepts such as emotion and community. As a recorded medium, music demonstrates a unique capability to engage a distant listener as intensely as the on-site players. To deflect the covert criticism of the "just music" label, I have learned to hand the critic a recording of various orca sessions with the comment, "It's music; if the communication is there, you're going to hear it." To this bold statement I would add one caveat. Whatever the verdict may be, there is nothing "avant-garde" about it. Indigenous people have been talking and singing with animals since before history.

Oceanariums visited these waters regularly during the 1970s to capture juvenile orcas for their shows, a process that resulted in the death of many whales. As I write, only one of the unfortunate local whales, called Corky, remains captive at San Diego Sea World. Corky seems a living testament to the greed that prompts the oceanarium industry. She has been pregnant seven times during her captivity, but not one of her offspring has survived more than a few weeks. Here in the strait we see Corky's matrilineal family traveling these waters just about every day. Her mother, called Stripe by local researchers, is forty-seven years old. Siblings include Fife, born in 1992, Ripple, born in 1981, and Okisollo, born in 1972. A valiant effort to free Corky was undertaken in the mid-1990s. Advocates proposed a "halfway house" on a netted-off cove just three miles up the coast from Orcananda. Corky would be taught how to catch live fish and swim to a local research station for regular medical checkups. Hopeful rescuers point out that Corky still "talks" her family's unique dialect. Distinguished orca researcher Dr. Paul Spong heads the campaign and has repeatedly petitioned Sea World to set up an underwater telephone line between Corky's pool and the strait, to test the simple premise that mother and daughter may still recognize each other's voices. The oceanarium refuses and, in all regards, does not budge from the basic hard line that Corky remains its property unto death.

Corky's is not the only orca tale told by the human residents of this rugged British Columbia coastline. Many of these stories involve whales trying to communicate with humans. Regard an entry in the log of Paul Spong's Orcalab, a place sometimes described as an *embassy*, a meeting area where scientists and environmentalists come to study and discuss the orcas. One night in the mid-1970s, caretaker Jim O'Donnell was sleeping in the hand-hewn cabin overlooking the strait when he was awakened by the strident call of an orca. Orcas rarely vocalize in air, and for that reason Jim left his bed and walked to a point overlooking the water. There, his flashlight beam revealed a pod of orcas bobbing on the surface. In Jim's words:

> One of them has a strange sound after each breath—like a long low growl—like something is wrong. I hold up my hand and shine the light on it and on my face. The orcas stay very still except for the loud breathing. Then I feel a conversation in minds or mind. I am not sure what is happening. I seem to remember a short discussion and apology. What is happening here? I felt good. I felt bad. Something is wrong with that one. I left it with as much love as I could get together.

The next morning a colleague dropped by the lab to report hunters shooting at the orcas the day before. When the man who approached them protested, the hunters threatened him. Jim's late-night encounter with the orca pod took on new meaning. The pod had visited their "embassy." The whale with the growling breath was wounded, perhaps in its lung. Jim telephoned the Mounties. Unfortunately, the police were not sympathetic. Informed that hunters who take potshots at local wildlife are a low priority, Jim pointed out that the hunters threatened his friend as well. That was a different story. A police boat was dispatched, the hunters were found, and they were told to leave the waterway before they were arrested for attempted murder. Jim remained uneasy:

> Now what? Incident forgotten? Where is the orca with the long low growl? I am sorry. Please forgive our ignorance.[6]

Jim O'Donnell's log entry implies that the orcas have a clear sense of cause and effect. By displaying their pain to a human they recognize as an ally, they influence other humans. The notes also make an explicit allusion to human/orca telepathy. A similar suggestion is sustained in the tale of an overwrought Japanese photographer who motored his Zodiac up and down the strait from dawn to dusk seeking shots of orcas. The whales, usually abundant, had left the area. On his last morning, the photographer packed his gear, and sat glumly on a piece of driftwood at the water's edge, waiting for his float plane to arrive. A single orca entered the cove and swam into such shallow water that its white belly rested on the beach pebbles a few feet in front of the man's camera and tripod. When the man finished off his roll of film, the whale turned and swam away. The float plane arrived a moment later. The photographer later commented that he had been visualizing that precise situation when the orca arrived.

While such stories paint a picture of *Orcinus orca* as a compassionate and potentially extrasensory being, it seems essential to keep in mind that there is a good reason why this largest member of the dolphin family is also called *killer whale*. The name was handed them by old-time whalers who witnessed the species attacking baleen whales. In Greenland, Eskimos shaped their kayaks to resemble killer whales, a reverse camouflage that struck such fear into the heart of the seal that it climbed out of the water to avoid the whale, only to be speared by the hunter. Killer whales have been documented dispatching a hundred dolphins during an afternoon's forage, without feeding on more than a few animals. In a shocking variation of Aboriginal cooperative feeding, an orca pod in Australia aided whalers by driving humpback whales into a bay where they could easily be harpooned. Once the humpbacks were dispatched, the whalers rewarded their helpers by throwing them the tongues—a favorite orca food.

A group of biologists working in a bay along the west coast of Vancouver Island once observed a minke whale swimming uncharacteristically close to shore. The thirty-foot minke is a baleen whale, a plankton eater, easily identified by a broad white band on the dorsal surface of its flipper. This minke lolled on the surface and remained still for several minutes. A pod of killer whales rounded the point. The males advanced. One grabbed hold of the minke's lower jaw, while another one pushed its own body tight up against the minke's blowhole. Together, they pulled the minke underwater until it drowned. The females advanced, grabbed the minke's enormous tongue, and sliced it from its mouth, turning the waters of the bay red with blood. After the orcas finished their meal, they pulled the corpse underwater a second time. Several minutes elapsed before they were next sighted departing the bay. When the biologists motored to take a closer look, they noticed the minke's dorsal fin, apparently severed in a single four-foot-wide bite. The minke's carcass lay in shallow water, curiously flayed from end to end. The hide was never found. Two months later, the same observers chanced upon another minke carcass, also flayed, tongue eaten, dorsal fin severed, body otherwise unmolested.

The biologists at the scene theorized that the tongue, and perhaps the skin as well, offered the orcas a change of diet from their usual fare of salmon, citing the fact that the Inuit of Canada's MacKenzie River delta have long favored the skin of beluga whales as a major source of vitamin C. The minke's complacency might be explained as disorientation activated by loud orca sounds. I once witnessed a pod of pseudorcas swim noisily into a wide bay. Within moments, several sailfish in the vicinity rose to the surface and held their sails stiffly erect. The fish were so dazed they permitted me to motor up to them and run my hand along their sails. It took them five minutes to regain their senses.

The orca pods living in Puget Sound and eastern Vancouver Island are primarily salmon eaters who are often observed in the company of minke whales, for whom they pose no threat whatsoever. These residents are distinguished in the scientific literature from other orcas called *transients*. To understand the difference between them, it is perhaps more accurate to regard them as distinct cultures, rather than as subspecies. They are alike in all matters of anatomy, but are as behaviorally distinct as Jains and Norwegians. We interact musically with residents who whistle constantly in their limited travels through the inland waterway set between Vancouver Island and the mainland of Canada. Transients rarely whistle because they rely on stealth to capture their prey. They are nomads who travel far and wide to feed on other marine mammals, including seals, sea lions, and several species of cetaceans, both large and small, that venture across their path. Transients have been known to attack surfers, although they always seem to release them after identifying the rubbery black beings held in their mouths as humans rather than sea lions. The minke attack was the work of transients. In the Pacific Northwest, transients are sometimes seen traveling in the same waters as residents, although genetic studies have shown that these two cultures of the same orca species have not interbred for at least 100,000 years.[7]

Thomas Kuhn, in his landmark book *The Structure of Scientific Revolutions*, comments that scientists will always be imperfect in their ability to objectify nature because every observation is colored by limitations in human sensory apparatus as well as by intellectual bias. Kuhn's infallibility rule applies well to the charged border. The interpretation of the dispatched minke whale varies depending on who makes the assessment. An ethologist I consulted on the matter agreed with every conclusion extended by the biologists at the scene. It was an act of predation by a pod of transients that resulted in a gourmet meal. The minke was either stunned or at least resigned to its certain fate. The tongue was eaten on the spot. The skin was collected to be consumed later. The disk was severed to permit the clean removal of the skin.

When I described the same chain of events to a theater director, he began with the expected disclaimer: "Of course, I'm not a scientist," but then offered a provocative analysis that focused on the lack of frenzy and the hint of synchronicity established between the minke and the orcas. The event closely reflected Native American ritual. At Tenochtitlan, an Aztec maiden was sacrificed at the altar, her heart torn from her body to be eaten by a priest who then flayed her, donning the skin for a ritual dance to the hummingbird sun god, Huitzilopochtli. The theater director concluded that the event was a ceremonial sacrifice rather than a gourmet meal. I asked the ethologist his impression of the theater director's conclusion, to which he replied, "He doesn't know whales." The theater director said much the same thing about the ethologist: "He doesn't know ceremony." In a recent study of wolves, biologist Bruce Hampton concluded that packs "practiced elaborate ceremonial rituals, gathering and singing before hunting, after eating, or at other occasions [during a full moon] thus promoting group cohesion.[8] The minke flaying conceivably falls into this category.

Northwest coast tribes, including Kwakiutl, Haida, and Salish, believe orcas comprise an advanced culture a step above human beings. But strip the aphorism of its poetry, and what remains? Is this step analogous to the distinction between a C-sharp note and a D? Or is it comparable to the difference between apes and humans? Some environmentalists interpret the step as the difference between a species who does not attack human beings even though it can, and a species who captures and trains orcas to jump through hoops. Mystics explain it as the difference between humans and angels.

This view of the unoffending orca is not precisely accurate. Antarctic orcas were once documented breaking sea ice to tip a photographer into the water, although the assault is more likely comparable to California orcas mistaking surfers for sea lions. When captors under contract to an oceanarium netted a cow orca and her calf in Bellingham Bay, Washington, a bull responded to the distress calls by ramming the boat. Although the bull was shot and killed, the boat sank, pulling the net underwater and drowning the entangled whales. And at a Victoria, British Columbia, oceanarium, a trainer fell into an orca's tank after-hours. The orca dragged her underwater and held her there until she drowned.

Both Inuit and Northwest coast tribes stress that revenge against humans who do them harm is the only reason orcas ever attack human beings. The Inuit tell so many tales of orcas sneaking up on kayakers who harmed them that ethologist Randall Eaton believes the longstanding whaler's taboo against killing orcas is historically based.[9] Naturalist Erich Hoyt relates a story told by a Kwakiutl fisherman about a tribesman in Alert Bay, British Columbia, who shot and killed an orca, then brought the carcass to shore to exhibit to his neighbors. He was shunned by the entire tribe, the elders warning that "the blackfish [orca] will get you." The next time the man went fishing alone, he disappeared, the assumption being that the orcas killed him by sinking his boat.[10]

Most cetologists now agree that orcas possess a language of sorts. Members of one pod vocalize distinctively enough from members of other pods that each pod is said to have its own dialect. John Ford, the discoverer of dialects, is able to listen to a tape of a northwest coast orca and identify its pod.[11] In cataloging the various dialects, biologists sometimes rely on literary terms like "dialogue," "conversation," "song"—the same vocabulary employed in the theater. Research is under way to discover a vocabulary of individual orca phrases. One experimenter records orca movements from a vantage above an intersection in a channel. When the whales enter, they often vocalize, then move left, right, forward, or back as a unit. By recording these calls, the researcher hopes to discover the actual words for *left*, *right*, *forward*, or *back*.

Field biologists stop at Orcananda for conversation, tea, and the communal ambience provided by many children and their mothers. We fill their plates with fresh-baked salal-berry pie or smoked salmon, and listen to them express curiosity about the aesthetic focus of our inquiry. Occasionally someone confronts us about what they presume to be pseudoscience. But as *The Whole Earth Catalog* once wrote of the musical research of Interspecies Communication, Inc.:

> You can't call this pseudoscience. IC doesn't claim that this is any sort of science at all. The idea, rather, is to interact with other species in whatever way—scientific, artistic, shamanic—seems most appropriate to the situation. It is certainly a broader definition of communication than most researchers would accept. But the approach gives the animals a greater opportunity to shape the exchange to their liking than a purely scientific approach would allow.

We explain to doubters that our music is transmitted into the strait at a lower volume than their own outboards. And unlike almost every other research group, we let the whales come to us. Still, some critics contend that nonscientists should never be allowed to interact with the local orcas without scientific supervision. Once, that criticism turned venal. A boatload of Mounties landed on our beach to search our belongings and interrogate each person individually. When it was made clear that everyone in camp, including our Canadian skipper, was a volunteer, they relented, apologized for the commando tactics, and admitted they'd been "tipped off" that we were U.S citizens earning money in Canadian waters without paying taxes. We served them tea, during which they told us the complaint had been lodged by a local whale-watching entrepreneur who didn't like our nonscientific brand of research. We later learned that the plaintiff fumed every time he passed our camp and counted all the people who were watching whales without paying him.

I also get annoyed over certain types of research. This morning, a film crew we've watched harassing the whales all week long pays us a courtesy visit. The producer, Lute, and I find parallel driftwood logs to sit facing each other. I ask him the only thing on my mind. "Have your propellers struck any whales yet?"

He peers at me through bushy eyebrows, then responds in a hurt voice.

"The orcas are quite capable of staying away from our blades. They're just big dolphins riding our bow wave."

"They're not riding your bow wave," I answer sharply. "You're driving your boat up on their backs!"

The producer and I glare at each other for a few tense moments. I relent, encourage him to contact other filmmakers who cruised these same waters a month ago, a year ago, a decade ago. Instead of harassing the whales over and over again to get the same basic shots, filmmakers ought to share their outtakes. The producer grimaces, then informs me that every crew has to do it themselves if they ever hope to catch unique behavior.

"Are there really more than five or six different shots any filmmaker takes of these orcas?" I count on my fingers. "You got your rolls, you got breaches, spyhops. Double spyhops. Big splashes. Babies. You got smooth, slow-motion head-on shots of male dorsal fins. The backgrounds stay consistently majestic everywhere you look. The light is the one thing I grant you. Great light is priceless. Even so, the fifty-plus hours of footage you've shot this week is mostly indistinguishable from what the other five crews this summer have shot." I glare at him. "Would you be willing to share your outtakes with next year's crop of filmmakers so they don't have to harass whales?"

"Of course I would," he answers sullenly.

I don't believe him. In my experience, filmmakers treat their clichéd whale shots as if they were the Zapruder film of the JFK assassination. And this conversation is going nowhere. I sigh deeply and turn to stare at the snowcapped mountains on Vancouver Island directly across the strait, then tip my chin higher to enjoy a few minutes of hot sun peeking through the heavy clouds. When a cloud covers the sun again, the temperature drops ten degrees. I sigh again, and invite the producer and his crew to stay on for lunch. They end up lounging around our campfire for the rest of the day. We start out sipping cocoa, but eventually switch to the Cuervo Gold and limes that Lute's sound man pulls out of his day pack. By midafternoon we are joined by another visitor, who pulls his Zodiac hard against the beach in the departing tide, then walks over to join the party without bothering to set an anchor. It's JS, one of the best known of the local orca scientists, who's been studying whales on this coast for ten years.

I offer to help him secure his Zodiac. "It's not a Zodiac, it's an Avon." I smile, then answer that the name is generic; a "zodiac" is like a "bandaid" or a "kleenex." He shrugs his shoulders without responding, and wanders off to the kitchen to grab a cup of tea and introduce himself with a cavalier flourish to the people who gather around to question him about his research. I hear someone ask him how he identifies individual orcas. "By reading the ID book very carefully." JS's patter suggests that he places quotation marks around key words. He occasionally flutters his fingers as if writing the quotes directly in the air. "I'm from the good ol' boys' school of biology," he announces in response to a question about whether he senses anything telepathic around the orcas. "Every animal's a dumb animal. Why, I know more about these orcas than they know about themselves."

He doesn't mean it. Anyone who spends as much time around the whales as JS does is bound to witness behavior that annihilates anyone's conception of dumb animals. Every year for the past three, the whales of B-pod have driven a monster king salmon up onto the gravel beach directly fronting his tent site. One salmon each year. Last year it was a forty-pounder. This gifting always occurs at night. JS, asleep in his tent, is awakened by the mortar fire of orcas blowing close to shore. He pulls himself out of his sleeping bag, puts on his pants and boots, and exits the tent with a flashlight to encounter a salmon flopping so high on the gravel that one might wonder if an orca chipped it up the beach with a golf club. The first time it occurred, JS told me it was an accident. The orcas were corralling salmon, when one fish was inadvertently batted out of the water. And the second year it happened? "This good ol' boy still thinks it was an accident." And the third year? JS was still wide-eyed when he visited Orcananda three days later. "Why me?" He asked in an uncharacteristically subdued voice. "I'm the guy who harasses whales all day long."

These wistful moments of self-reflection demonstrate how deviously the orcas entangle JS in the subject/object paradox, a problem Steve Templor does not encounter studying the far less precocious humpbacks. If JS followed the straight and narrow of field biology, he would filter such experiences from his data as meticulously as he filters *Giardia* from his drinking water. It hasn't worked that way. When he's around strangers, other biologists, and wide-eyed orca lovers, he talks about the whales the way a champion skier relates to his skis, as beautiful, functional objects with which he has developed a codependent relationship. But among friends, he describes the same data as trinkets he barters with editors of obscure journals in trade for a university paycheck and one more contented summer spent living in a tent, plying the waters every day in his beloved inflatable, and watching the orcas.

JS acknowledges that his data and his experience do not always jibe. This discrepancy gets resolved as the stand-up comedy routine he spins about his life's work. He always has a funny joke to tell if you ask him what he feels about whale communication. By avoiding a straight answer, he defuses the uncomfortable position "good old boy" science cannot validate. He's a dreamer who's taught himself, perhaps too well, how to forget his dreams once he wakes.

When JS finishes fielding questions at the campfire, he picks up two cups of tea and journeys to the flat piece of driftwood where Lute and I sit, still trying to resolve our differences. JS hands me my cup and regales us with an account of a meeting between two of the local pods. "A5 started chasing A7 in circles. Wouldn't stop." He makes it sound like an interoffice softball game, which reduces the two of us to laughter. The sun pops from behind a cloud. The temperature rises ten degrees. The three of us stare across the strait at the clipped whitecaps that dot the waterway at two o'clock most every afternoon. The wind should die down again after five. JS rolls up the sleeves of his flannel shirt. I pull off a wool sweater and lift my face to the sun. Lute asks JS what he's studying.

JS takes a sip of tea and prefaces his remarks by declaring we won't find it interesting. "Whales spend only ten percent of their time on the surface, so any behavioral observation is necessarily sketchy. I've started cross-referencing the number of breaths an orca takes between dives with observed behavioral patterns on the surface. I hope it will eventually lead to a correlative table that better predicts underwater behavior from observed surface behavior." His eyes have started twinkling. "I'm sure you will be overjoyed to learn that, this week, each animal in my study group breathed an average of 179.7 times per hour."

"Why are you doing it?" I ask gently. JS pulls a half pint of brandy out of his day pack, unscrews the cap, and takes a nip. He holds the bottle out for us, but we both decline. JS pulls at his golden handlebar mustache, and then answers in a Mexican accent, "I am helping the whales, señor, by expanding the boundaries of our knowledge." I peer at the shore a moment to watch three little girls bending over a tide pool poking sticks into a hole. One of them wades into the water, bends down, turns over a rock, and lets out a squeal. "It's a red crab. Come see, come see, it's the fourth red crab I found." Another little girl sticks her hand in the water, tries to grab it, but keeps stepping backward and squealing every time the crab turns to defend itself. I sigh to recognize that the little girls have answered my question to JS. It is human nature to study and learn, and JS's curiosity to count orca breaths is cut from the same cloth as the inquisitiveness of these little girls to count crabs. "Remember," adds JS, shaking a finger as if my question makes me a naughty boy needing a reprimand. "Twenty years ago, biologists were killing whales to measure the length of their penises. Measuring breaths is a step up. Please, señor, it is the only way I can get the doctor's deee-gree."

Lute scowls, then clicks his tongue. He is tall, chubby, and pink, with long, delicate fingers. A Miami Dolphins cap adds a certain wry touch. An expensive knife with a bulky antler handle and an ornately carved sheath dangles from his belt. JS levels his glance at this appendage. "You know, you really need to get rid of that hood ornament. What you need is a Swiss army knife to cut line, open bottles, and fiddle with the carburetor of your outboard." A thick pause hangs in the air. Lute is clearly getting his comeuppance from both barrels. He turns to ask me about my future plans for playing music with orcas.

"I think this is the last year of the project."

"Why's that?"

"This place is too crowded."

"You've got to be kidding?" he replies, sweeping his hand at the wild expanse all around us.

JS shakes his head. "Hey man, look again. The island we're standing on is slated for clear-cutting within the next two years. Those explosions you hear every afternoon are logging roads getting cut into the *last* old growth watershed on the entire east coast of Vancouver Island. The silt runoff is sure to impact the pink salmon run on the river. The logging company, Mac-

Millan Bloedel, plans to leave nothing but a beauty strip of trees along the shore to keep the tourists on the whale-watching boats blissfully ignorant."

The acoustic nature of my work is severely compromised by noise pollution. Huge cargo ships pass up and down the strait all day long carrying fish and minerals south, heavy machinery and tomatoes north. Add to this the constant buzz of hundreds of commercial fishing boats, private fishing boats, whale-watching charters, the low throb of ocean liners, and the high-pitched whine of inflatables bearing researchers and filmmakers. Tugboats are the worst offenders. They are the heavy machinery of the inland waterway, hauling barges whose deck space is measured by the quarter acre, veritable islands loaded forty feet high with logs. They chug through the straits slowly and purposefully, usually at night, taking half an hour to pass by our camp. Listening to them through hydrophones, we hear the nagging bass resonance long before, and long after, we see them. As the throb fades, another one takes its place.

Human beings are visual creatures. Inspiration enters the heart and mind primarily through our eyes, which explains why the main activity of tourism is called *sight-seeing*. With the logging industry's beauty strip in place, the vista of wilderness *looks* intact. Tourists rhapsodize over a glimpse of the whales, mountains, or forest. Yet they remain oblivious to the uproar underwater. Boats are everywhere, but they appear as inconsequential toys lost in the vastness of the scenery. Whales perceive their environment primarily through sound.

Before the clamor began in the mid-1980s, the underwater environment was composed of three fundamentals. First was the percussive sound created by the various shrimp species who swim as a door hinge opening and closing. One stroke equals one crackle of the exoskeleton. A million shrimp sounds like radio static. Second was the pleasant low *whoosh* of current, a sound modulated primarily by kelp. Third was the strident soprano saxophone vocalization of the orcas themselves. If the current traveled toward us, we could hear whales two miles from a hydrophone. Orcas rarely vocalize in air, so few people get to experience the sound, although a kayaker traveling below a high cliff may hear the calls in air through a trick of resonance. The sound travels through the rock, emanating outward like a ghost whispering from every direction at once.

This kayaker's delight hardly ever happens now that whale-watching boats run their engines close behind the pods all day long. There were no whale-watching boats in this strait in 1980. Ten years later there were four companies with six boats between them. The government lays down rules of conduct ostensibly to regulate the industry and protect the whales. No boat may travel within one hundred feet of an orca. But since whales perceive their world acoustically, two kayakers paddling fifty feet from a pod generates far less noise pollution than a whale-watching charter running a loud diesel engine two hundred feet away. "Whale cops" are hired by the Canadian government and, in a conflict of interest, are subsidized by the whale-watching industry to issue warnings to private boats that venture too close to the orcas. When asked how a silent kayaker might possibly pose a danger to an orca, I once heard a cop retort that kayakers are too quiet. An orca could rise beneath one and bump its head.

The sheer number of motorboats following whales has spawned a constructive countermovement within the professional research community that restricts the observation of whales to shore-based facilities. The momentum of this *benign* research is whale-centered, motivated by genuine compassion to protect the increasingly vulnerable orca community from acoustic pollution.

It may be too little too late. This summer, listening to the low hiss of current and the high crackle of shrimp for a few brief hours late at night, I feel uneasy over the absence of the orca pods. They have been gone from the strait for nearly a week. No one has seen them, and many suspect that they are somewhere off the uninhabited northwest coast of Vancouver Island. Most members of the research community believe the orcas have fled because of lack of food. The commercial fishing industry has declared this year an exceptionally bad one for salmon. I worry that it is a false equation. Though there are fewer fish than normal, the orcas' disappearance cannot yet be laid on the sleek head of the salmon. *Only* ten million returning salmon, instead of the usual fifteen million, should not effect the orcas' ability to feed themselves. I worry that the acoustically sensitive whales have departed the strait in their own defense. There are thousands of miles of salmon-filled coastline in British Columbia where whales do not yet fall prey to the constant buzz and throb of the internal combustion engine.

Our own musical relationship with the orcas prospered between 1984 and 1987. Something worked. Interactions got more intense and lasted longer each passing summer. There were nights the orcas surrounded our boat for three or four hours. During the longest sessions, musicians sometimes stopped playing for lack of musical ideas. Or sheer exhaustion. In 1988, I first suspected that the process was reversing itself. The whales disappeared from the strait for a few days at a time. When they reappeared, they didn't seem to linger as long as before. In the summers that followed, the orcas vanished for up to two weeks at a time. When they were present, they vocalized far less than before. Whereas I produced twenty hours of interactive recordings in 1985, in 1990 I recorded only eight minutes. Nickola had died the previous winter. The next summer A6 lost interest in making music with us. The bond between species was broken. A group of us returned belatedly the next summer to hold a ceremony marking the conclusion of the Orca Project. It was then that the cougar appeared in our midst. Nature itself seemed to be saying the wilderness was gone. I have not returned since.

Before the Orcananda sound system was built, I relied on a waterphone to play music with the whales, and a dry suit to keep myself warm in the frigid water. It was 1975. A perusal of orca literature uncovered no occurrence of a person willingly swimming with wild orcas. Orcas were called killer whales and considered to be a danger to anyone unfortunate enough to fall into the water near them. To my unpracticed eyes, they appeared as they were: large dolphins. I swam with them several times over the next five years.

On one occasion, a photographer asked if he could shoot me in the water with the whales. I agreed, and we soon located a pod milling in the strait. I slipped into the sea a few hundred yards in front of the pod and rubbed the waterphone to produce a clear tone. A large bull with a wavy dorsal fin advanced on me underwater until I noticed his white eye patch directly in front of me, eight feet below the surface. The refractive effect of the surface made his features appear larger than life. When he rose horizontally to the surface, his six-foot dorsal fin took on the magnitude of the *2001* monolith. I rubbed the waterphone. From fifty yards away the photographer hollered, "Keep playing, this is incredible!"

The bull remained in view for ten seconds, then dove. A second bull passed directly beneath my feet, followed by two females and two juveniles who blew an arm's length to either side of me. When the entire pod had passed my position, they turned to face me. I kept playing. The camera's motor drive whirred in the background. The two juveniles suddenly charged me at a speed fast enough to leave a significant wake on either side of their bodies. Just before they plowed into me, they dove. My heart was in my throat. I stopped playing. The photographer cheered. "I'm getting some great shots! Keep playing!"

Looking down, I gazed at the broad snouts of two juveniles standing vertically in the water column mere inches beyond the soles of my own dangling feet. My breathing turned shallow; I started shaking all over. "Help!" I gasped at the photographer. Then louder, "Get me out of here!" As he started the engine, the juveniles dropped deeper, then vanished entirely. The photographer pulled me into the boat, jabbering that he needed a few more good shots. I lay in the bottom of the Zodiac as if in a dream, staring up at the overcast sky and wondering what on earth I was trying to prove.

The bull with the wavy fin rose directly beside the inflatable and blew a plume that pattered lightly on my face. I sat up to watch him roll onto his back, showing a white belly longer than our entire boat. My body relaxed; I stopped shaking. In the context of this charged moment at the charged border, I instantly comprehended the bull's gesture as a sign of conciliation. By displaying his vulnerable belly, he communicated a message as clearly as if he spoke the words in plain English. There was no danger here. I had been the victim of a harmless response by frisky teenagers. If I decided to get back in the water, the teenagers would behave themselves.

The bull slowly turned over until the huge triangular dorsal once again stood upright. Then he swam off to rejoin his family. I rested a moment, ate a sandwich, watched the whales laze on the surface a hundred feet away. I finally slipped into the water, began stroking the prongs of the waterphone with my hand. The whales moved slightly forward.

They listened without vocalizing for two minutes, then turned to make their way down the strait.

NOTES

1. THE BLACK DAISY

1. Yamamoto Tsunetomo, *Hagakure*, trans. William Scott Wilson (New York: Kodansha International, 1979), p. 17.
2. The *oki gondo iruka* are pseudorcas, or false killer whales, although literally translated from the Japanese as "big-headed dolphins" after the large "melon" that bulges from the species's forehead. The melon is an oil-filled organ used as an acoustic lens for focusing sound.
3. Bobby Lake Thom, *Spirits of the Earth* (New York: Plume, 1997), p. 97.
4. Personal correspondence with Laurie Levy of the Australian Stranding Network.
5. In a personal interview with the author, parts of which were eventually written up as a cover story, "What Dolphins Are Teaching Us About Communication," *NewAge Magazine*, March 1980, pp. 26–37.
6. Both quotes are from J. W. Porter, "Pseudorca Strandings," *Oceans Magazine* 10, no. 4 (1977).
7. Candace Savage, *Bird Brains* (San Francisco: Sierra Club Books, 1995), p. 79.
8. Pliny the Elder, "Naturalis Historica," quoted in Alberto Manguel and Gianni Guadalupi, *The Dictionary of Imaginary Places* (New York: Macmillan, 1980), p. 171.
9. Filmmaker Hardy Jones in a personal communication to the author.

10. Dave Phillips, *Earth Island Journal*, edited by Gar Smith.

11. From a speech on "The Cetacean's Message" by Kamala Hope-Campbell at the Brussels ICERC Conference, May 1996.

2. WHALE NATURE AND HUMAN NATURE

1. The International Whaling Commission opened its fiftieth annual meeting in Muscat, Oman, in May 1998, with the announcement that Japan and Norway continued to violate the whaling moratorium and are expected to kill 1,200 whales in 1998.

2. E. J. Slijper, *Whales* (Ithaca, N.Y.: Cornell University Press, 1979), p. 63.

3. Richard Ellis, *The Book of Whales* (New York: Alfred A. Knopf, 1980), p. 90.

4. Roger Payne, *Among Whales* (New York: Macmillan, 1993), p. 7.

5. Ellis, *Book of Whales*, 152.

6. Ibid., p. 100.

7. Frank Bullen, *The Cruise of the Cachalot* (New York: Dodd, Mead and Co., 1947), p. 111.

8. Ellis, *Book of Whales*, p. 109.

9. John Downer, *Supersense* (New York: Henry Holt and Co., 1988), p. 93.

10. Joan Ocean, brochure for a dolphin swim program addressed to dolphin friends, 1996.

11. Timothy Wyllie, *The DETA Factor* (Farmingdale, N.Y.: Coleman Publishing, 1984), p. 37.

12. Lana Miller, *Call of the Dolphins* (Portland, Ore.: Rainbow Bridge Publishing, 1989), p. 93.

13. Horace Dobbs, *Journey into Dolphin Dreamtime* (London: Jonathan Cape Publisher, 1992), p. 131.

3. THE LURE OF THE MEGAFAUNA

1. Edward O. Wilson, *Biophilia* (Cambridge, Mass.: Harvard University Press, 1984), p. 58.

2. Bruce Hampton, *The Great American Wolf* (New York: Henry Holt and Co., 1997), p. 13.

3. Roger Payne, *Among Whales* (New York: Macmillan, 1995).

4. George Johnson, *Fire in the Mind* (New York: Alfred A. Knopf, 1995), p. 54.

5. Rupert Sheldrake, *The Presence of the Past* (New York: Vintage Books, 1988), p. 140.

6. Paul Spong, in a personal communication to the author, 1992.

7. In conversation with the author, April 16, 1988.

8. Payne, *Among Whales*, p. 150.
9. Ivan Sanderson, *Follow the Whale* (Boston, Mass.: Little, Brown and Co., 1956).

4. ON THEIR OWN BEHALF

1. Elias Lönnrot, ed., *The Kalevala*, translated from the Finnish by Keith Bosley (New York: Oxford University Press, 1989), p. 27.
2. Ivan T. Sanderson, *A History of Whaling* (New York: Barnes and Noble Books, 1993), p. 141.
3. Ibid., p.120.
4. Ibid., p. 170.
5. Ibid., p. 210.
6. Karl-Erik Fichtelius and Sverre Sjölander, *Smarter Than Man: Intelligence in Whales, Dolphins, and Humans* (New York: Ballantine Books, 1972), p. 29.
7. Heathcote Williams, *Whale Nation* (London: Jonathan Cape Publisher, 1988), p. 314.
8. Roger Payne, *Among Whales* (New York: Macmillan, 1993), p. 314.
9. Peter Shenstone, "The Legend of the Golden Dolphin," a multimedia presentation of human/cetacean relations.
10. Jeff Poniewaz, *Dolphin Leaping in the Milky Way* (Milwaukee, Wisc.: Inland Ocean Books, 1986), p. 30.
11. Rick O'Barry, *Behind the Dolphin's Smile* (Chapel Hill, N.C.: Algonquin Books, 1988).
12. Tim Radford, "Secret Naval Sonar Experiments May Lure Whales," *The Guardian* (Manchester, England), 5 March 1998.
13. Jacques Cousteau, *Calypso Log* (Los Angeles: The Cousteau Society, 1989), p. 6.

5. WHEN NATURE IS LARGER THAN LIFE

1. John C. Wu, trans., *Tao Te Ching* (New York: St. John's University Press, 1961), p. 71.
2. Barbara Tuchman, *The March of Folly* (New York: Alfred A. Knopf, 1984), p. 26.
3. Farley Mowat, *Sea of Slaughter* (New York: Bantam Books, 1986), pp. 223–31.
4. Ibid.
5. From a public talk ("The Makah Whale Issue") by Albert Thompson at The Whale Museum, Friday Harbor, Washington, February 21, 1998.
6. Ibid.
7. Joseph Campbell, *The Way of the Animal Powers* (New York: Harper and Row, 1983), p. 9.
8. Editorial from *The Hartford Courant*, 29 October 1988. Quoted in Jim Nollman, *Spiritual Ecology* (New York: Bantam Books, 1990), p. 141.

9. James Kilpatrick, The Universal Press Syndicate, 1988.

10. All quotes from Jim Nollman, "What Dolphins Are Teaching Us About Communication," *NewAge Magazine*, March 1980, pp. 26–31.

11. Ibid.

6. THE DOLPHINS IN THE LAKE

1. Birgit Klein, translated from "Den Evige Livsspiral" ("The Eternal Spiral of Life"), reputed to be channeled by Johannes (Birgit's guide), Martinus, Adif, Henry Ytting, and other members of the White Brotherhood.

2. For the best discussion of this concept, read Joan Halifax, *Shaman: The Wounded Healer* (New York: Crossroads Press, 1982).

3. Jim Nollman, *Dolphin Dreamtime* (New York: Bantam Books, 1987), p. 39.

4. *Columbia Encyclopedia*, 1940 edition, s.v. "Osiris."

5. Quoted in Alberto Manguel and Gianni Guadalupi, *The Dictionary of Imaginary Places*, (New York: Macmillan, 1980) p. 171.

6. From a brochure announcing a workshop entitled "Into the Future with Joan Ocean."

7. Kathleen Dudzinski, in a personal written commentary about the events described in this chapter.

8. Michelle Hall and Howard Hall, *Secrets of the Ocean Realm* (Hillsboro, Ore.: Beyond Words Publishing, 1997), p. 99.

9. Dudzinski, written commentary.

10 Dudzinski, written commentary.

11 J. C. Lilly, "Critical Brain Size and Language," quoted from his autobiography, *The Scientist* (Berkeley, Calif.: Ronin Publishing, 1988), p. 133.

12. Ibid.

13. Named after the god of portals, its initials stood for Joint Analog Numerical Understanding System.

14. Douglas Adams, *The Hitchhiker's Guide to the Galaxy* (New York: Harmony Books, 1979).

15. The spiny anteater, an egg-laying marsupial related to the platypus, also has a neocortex relatively larger than a human's and at least as large as a dolphin's. Cetaceans and spiny anteaters are also the only two animals tested that do not possess REM sleep, which all other animals use to prioritize and erase memory connections through a process called "reverse learning." Reverse learning keeps unneeded memories from overloading the neural network. It has been postulated that large neocortex in cetaceans may function as a buffer to prevent overloading in a creature that must sleep guardedly to prevent drowning. This

explanation does not apply to the terrestrial-living spiny anteater. From Margaret Klinowska, "Brains, Behavior, and Intelligence in Cetaceans," in *Eleven Essays on Whales and Man* (1994).

16. Parts of this explanation are taken from an unpublished transcript of a dolphin channeling by Neville and Melanie Rowe, sent to the author by filmmaker Christopher Carson.

17. Personal communication to the author by Joan Ocean, now commonly used to explain the mystical bond with dolphins, 1990.

18. Mitchell Leister, "Inner Voices: Distinguishing Transcendent and Pathological Characteristics," *The Journal of Transpersonal Psychology* 28, no. 1 (1996).

19. From *Seeing Castaneda*, ed. Daniel Noel (New York: G. P. Putnam's Sons, 1976), quoting Morris Berman, *The Reenchantment of the World* (New York: Bantam, 1984), p. 85.

20. Peter Shenstone, "The Legend of the Golden Dolphin," a multimedia presentation of human/cetacean relations. Thanks to Scott Taylor for specific aspects mentioned here.

21. Douglas Baglin, *People of the Dreamtime* (New York: Walker/Weatherhill, 1970).

22. Nollman, *Dolphin Dreamtime*.

23. Ibid.

24. Personal communication with the author at the Sixth International ICERC cetacean conference held at Hervey Bay, Australia, August 1997.

25. This discussion of dolphins, the Aboriginal dreamtime, and the Imragen originally appeared in Nollman, *Dolphin Dreamtime*, p. 25.

7. SIX HONEST SERVING MEN OF LEARNING

1. Douglas Hand, *Gone Whaling* (New York: Simon and Schuster, 1994), p. 61.

2. A thermocline marks abrupt temperature changes in the ocean's water column. Because water gets denser as temperatures drop, the thermocline serves the whales as a reflective surface for echoing vocalizations.

3. Karl von Frisch, *The Dance Language and Orientation of Bees* (Cambridge, Mass.: Harvard University Press, 1967). The speculated fields of discipline placed within parentheses are entirely my own.

4. Stephen Hart, *The Language of Animals* (New York: Henry Holt and Co., 1996), p. 64.

5. Doug Starr, "Calls of the Wild," *Omni*, December 1986, p. 122.

6. "Getting Through to Others," *The New Yorker*, 24 April 1978, p. 57.

7. Rudyard Kipling, *Just So Stories* (London: Macmillan and Co., 1902).

8. "Conversations with a Gorilla," *National Geographic*, October 1978, p. 465.

9. Wyatt Townley, "Animals: Are They the Real Wise Guys?," *Cosmopolitan*, August 1990, p. 209.

10. Theodore Xenophon Barber, *The Human Nature of Birds* (New York: Penguin Books, 1993), p. 7.

11. Ibid. Also described in Jim Nollman, "Who Communicates," *Interspecies Newsletter*, winter 1995.

12. Brenda Peterson, *NewAge Magazine*, April 1993, p. 86.

13. Quoted in Reuters News Media, April 24, 1998. Patterson's quote was prompted by a journalist asking why Koko showed so little interest in participating in a much-hyped Internet chat group in which people typed in questions for Koko to answer.

14. Townley, op. cit.

15. In conversation with the author, June 1994, Ogasawara, Japan.

16. Gregory Bateson, *Steps to an Ecology of Mind* (New York: Ballantine Books, 1975).

17. Kathleen Dudzinski, in private communication to the author, 1998.

18. John Lilly, *Lilly on Dolphins* (Garden City, N.J.: Anchor Doubleday, 1975).

19. Gathered in conversation with a group of Cambridge University beluga researchers at Cunningham Inlet in the Canadian High Arctic, 1992.

20. Nollman, *Dolphin Dreamtime*.

21. *Webster's New World Dictionary*, College Edition, 1958, "intelligence."

22. Townley, op. cit., p. 211.

23. *Webster's New World Dictionary*, College Edition, 1958, "sentience."

24. Barber, *Human Nature of Birds*, p. 7.

25. An interview with Russell Targ entitled "The Interconnected Universe," from *Museletter*, no. 74, February 1998.

26. Joanne Lauck, *The Voice of the Infinite in the Small: Revisioning the Insect-Human Connection* (Mill Spring, N.C.: Swan Raven & Co., 1998).

8. GETTING INTO THE GROOVE

1. From Gary Lawless, *Poems for the Wild Earth* (Nobleboro, Maine: Blackberry Books, 1994).

2. Paraphrased from the Spanish ambassador to the U.N., whose actual statement was, "Diplomatic immunity is like virginity: you either have it or you don't."

3. George Will, *Men at Work* (New York: HarperPerennial, 1990), p. 211.

4. Told to the author by Victor Perera (later corroborated by a photo spread that appeared in a Spanish-language magazine).

5. From an alphanumeric system devised by local biologists to identify the two-hundred-odd orcas residing in the immediate area. This is the sixth whale identified as a member of the A-pod.

6. From a personal conversation with Jim O'Donnell, bolstered by his own log notes from that night.

7. Howard Garrett, a Puget Sound orca researcher. From a personal conversation with the author.

8. Bruce Hampton, *The Great American Wolf* (New York: Henry Holt and Co., 1997), p. 23.

9. Randall L. Eaton, *The Orca Project* (Enterprise, Ore.: Sacred Books), p. 84.

10. Ibid.

11. John Ford has done so for me by analyzing cassette tapes of my music with the wild pods of Johnstone Strait, British Columbia.

INDEX